ISBN 978-1-332-81708-5
PIBN 10466736

Diary of

Sir Michael Connal

1835 to 1893

Edited
With Biographical Sketch by
John C. Gibson

Glasgow
James MacLehose and Sons
Publishers to the University
1895

"Ille velut fidis arcana sodalibus olim
Credebat libris, neque, si male cesserat, usquam
Decurrens alio, neque si bene: quo fit ut omnis
Votiva pateat veluti descripta tabella
Vita senis."

PREFACE

SHORTLY after Sir Michael Connal's death, Lady Connal was frequently asked if he had left anything of an autobiographical nature which could be printed and circulated among his friends. It was suspected, perhaps known by a few, that Sir Michael had kept a Diary, but not even Lady Connal had any idea that for nearly sixty years he had kept an almost daily record of his life. There are in existence no less than seventeen volumes of closely written matter. These are continuous and written in the well-known firm hand which he retained to the last. To them he confided all his doings, feelings, and struggles; to their pages he committed both his discouragements and successes.

Lady Connal read the Diary herself and then gave it to me. After carefully reading it and considering the question of publication, I concluded that while the general tenor of the contents was strictly private, still copious extracts might be made from each year. The Diary throws so much light on the character and motives of Sir Michael that it will help to clear away much that has often caused his actions to be misinterpreted by those who did not understand or could not sympathize with him. The following entry shows that Sir Michael had contemplated an autobiography, but probably want of time kept him from carrying out his purpose:

"*August* 16, 1871.—There are some things to do. . . . The writing of an autobiography, so that all my MSS. may be utilized for whoever may care to preserve the

The living hand which could have given connection to the jottings and reminiscences of this Diary never even began the contemplated task, and no other hand can accomplish it successfully. The following brief notes have a purpose only in bringing into prominence a few of the leading ideas suggested by some degree of personal inter course with Sir Michael and by a careful perusal of the letters and memorials he has left.

As far as Sir Michael is personally concerned, the whole Diary might have been printed. His life will stand the keenest scrutiny, and his worst enemy would never subject him to such merciless criticism as he does himself. Had this Diary not been of such a private nature it would have been put into the hands of a more experienced editor, who could have given more time and undivided attention to it. Of this, however, the reader may rest assured, that, as far as I can be conscious, my judgment has been unbiased. In the extracts I have made, my object has been to select what will show Sir Michael on all sides of his character. Where it was necessary to make insertions for the sake of clearness I have used square brackets, but as a rule the exact text has been given, even at the cost of expression. If even a few are impressed by the revelation of this quietly heroic life, my labour will not have been in vain, and I shall have helped him who is no longer with us further to realize his cherished wish and his earnest prayer, "to be useful in his day and generation."

J. C. G.

October, 1895.

CONTENTS.

	Page
BIOGRAPHICAL SKETCH, ...	ix
EXTRACTS FROM DIARY, ...	1
APPENDICES, ...	357

ILLUSTRATIONS.

Portrait of Sir Michael Connal, Feb. 1876, aet. 60,	*frontispiece*	
Parkhall, Killearn, ...	*facing* p.	110
Portrait of Sir Michael Connal, aet. 50, . . .	,,	130
Facsimile of Sir Michael Connal's Handwriting,	,,	224

BIOGRAPHICAL SKETCH.

SIR MICHAEL CONNAL was the elder son of Michael Connal of Parkhall, Stirlingshire, and was born at 42 Miller Street, Glasgow, the house of his uncle William Connal, on 11th August 1817. His father was a "Son of the Rock," the third son of Michael Connal,[1] Provost of Stirling, by his wife Marion Glas, and was born at Stirling 1st August 1785. Sir Michael's father was for many years in the naval service of the Honourable East India Company, and was in India at the time of his elder son's birth. Sir Michael's mother was Eliza Wright, daughter of William Wright of Broom, Stirlingshire. His father retired from the East India Company's service in 1818 and acquired the estate of Parkhall, in the parish of Killearn, Stirlingshire, and we find the family living there in that year.

The estate of Parkhall is situated about two and a half miles from Killearn station, and is surrounded by most romantic scenery, comprising the Western Grampians, the Campsie and the Fintry hills. From the moor near the house can be seen the deep woods of Buchanan and Loch Lomond lying among the lonely hills. The district is full of history and legend. At Killearn is the obelisk which reminds us that George Buchanan, the celebrated Scottish historian and scholar, was born in the neighbourhood, and in the parish of Balfron are the estates of Ballindalloch and Edinbellie, the one the seat, probably the birthplace, of the "good" Earl of Glencairn, the other that of Napier of Merchiston, the famous inventor of

[1] See Appendix A.

Logarithms. Over the door of the old house of Parkhall was the date of 1745. Sir Michael's earliest days were spent in the midst of this romantic scenery with its enchanted associations, and they made a deep and lasting impression on him. To one so susceptible to the beauty of nature and the influence of history, it was an ideal home, and the entries in the Diary tell how passionately he loved the hills and streams and trees of the district.

His father had two other children—a son William who died at the age of six, and a daughter Frances Stevenson. He seems to have been very fond of his eldest child Michael, and endeavoured to create in him an interest in all his surroundings. There is an interesting entry referring to these days under date 30th November 1880.

But these bright days were not to last long. Mr. Connal had invested money in the business of two of his brothers whose adventures were unfortunate; everything was lost, and Parkhall had to be sold in 1828.

The whole countryside appears to have been sorry when the Connals left the district. Mr. Connal led a busy, useful life, and was greatly liked and respected by all ranks and classes of the community. The Duke of Montrose, in proposing him for a Justice of Peace in 1823, bore testimony to his high character; and on his leaving for India the inhabitants of the village of Balfron presented him with a richly chased silver snuff box[1] and an address which has a true heart-ring about it, and shows that his kindly interest in the people had drawn out their best feelings to him. He is spoken of as their friend and adviser, always easy of access, and his impartiality in his official duties is freely acknowledged. The *Glasgow Herald* devoted a column to the proceedings of the day in its issue of 11th August 1828.

Mr. Connal was a man of considerable natural ability,

[1] The following inscription was engraved on its lid: "Presented to Michael Connal, Esq., on the eve of his departure for India, 18th July, 1828, by the inhabitants of Balfron and neighbourhood, as a mark of the respect they have for his services amongst them as a public magistrate of the county, and of the esteem with which they remember his counsels as a friend."

and a Diary kept by him during 1809, on a voyage in the "Neptune" to Bombay, is most interesting, and probably contributed to the formation of the idea in his son's mind of beginning and continuing a similar record. Mr. Connal returned to India with his wife and only daughter in 1828 and became an indigo planter at Obia, but he died in the following year.

Sir Michael's education began at the Grammar School of Glasgow, but he only remained there from 1826 till 1827. In 1827 he was sent to the boarding school of the Rev. Archibald Browning at Tillicoultry. Mr. Browning used to tell how thoughtful he was, and how bravely he behaved when he heard of his father's death. His grief was very great, but his sympathy and affection for his mother made him try to curb the expression of his own sorrow.

Sir Michael's schooldays were very happy, and the following letter, which was kindly sent me by the daughter of the Rev. Archibald Browning, gives an interesting picture of these days :—

4th November, 1893.

DEAR SIR,—"'Tis sixty years since" and more, and the vision through such a vista must be dim; yet I remember Michael Connal at Tillicoultry as a boy of gentle, retiring manner, neat and tidy in dress, precise and methodical in all his movements. I cannot say anything of the position he took as a scholar or student. I had the pleasure of meeting Sir Michael for the first time since these early days, accidentally, not very long before his death. As a proof of very retentive memory on his part, he remarked, "You are like your mother," and then he inquired particularly for the different members of the family.

The year 1827 is rather memorable on one account. A number of the essays and translations of the pupils were printed, in pamphlet form, and circulated among friends. Among the contributors to that little brochure were :—Richard Mitchell, son of Dr. Mitchell of Wellington Street; James Barlas; Andrew Robertson and his brother James, late of Newington. About the same time or a little later, Donald M'Gregor, late member for Leith; John Millar, afterwards Lord Craighill; Burns Kidston; Peter M'Lagan, late member for West Lothian, and several others who attained prominent positions in life, were boarders at Tilly; very few, I fear, remain to this day. The house and school are still to be seen, though very different from what they were, being broken up and let to various families.

It was at Tillicoultry that he learned to love the Ochil

Diary of having overslept himself—even then rising about 6.30. He spent a very busy life in London, using every spare hour for self-culture of one kind or another. He was fond of pictures, sculpture, and music, and lost no opportunity of visiting collections and attending classical concerts and on occasion the opera. His religious sympathies, though decided, were wide and led him to give an attentive hearing to eminent preachers of all churches. His remarks on all these things show that it was not merely for curiosity that he went about so much, but in order to study the expression of man in every form. During these years we find methodical lists of books read and to be read, which testify to the ardour of a mind devoted to self-improvement. It must never be forgotten that he was largely thrown on himself in the choice and direction of his studies, in which he always aimed at a thorough mastery of principles, and was never content with an accumulation of facts or disjointed information. The philanthropical institutions of London interested him very much, and even at this period of his life the beginnings of what he afterwards accomplished in so great a degree showed themselves. He remained in London till 1838, when he returned to Glasgow. The Diary will explain his surroundings and circumstances, and show how he felt out of harmony with them. He had to take a stand for himself, a thing always difficult to do when those we would most like to please are not in sympathy with what is of paramount interest to us.

At this time Sir Michael was offered all the attractions of a gay luxurious life. His uncle, being a man of genial and courteous disposition, gathered troops of friends round him, and the hospitality of Garscadden was proverbial. Sir Michael had now to make a choice. On the one side there were offered to him all the delights of a bright and attractive social life, abundance of friends, ease and pleasure, often the temptations towards an exclusive development of self. On the other, a life of self-denial, contact with crime and sorrow, much weariness and disappointment, a dying to self. He chose the latter, and with his eyes wide open. No one had a greater capability for enjoyment, a keener relish for the good things of life, or a better knowledge of the use of power and position. But he looked upon the talents he possessed as a trust to be accounted for; and raising the veil of life boldly, he saw that to enjoy a life of luxury was only possible to those who chose to shut out the misery, the ignorance and the crime surrounding them, and that for him at least there was no other path open than the narrow one. Just as he was beginning this life his sister Fanny died and he was left alone with his mother. The year 1841 was a very sad one for him, relatives and friends being removed by death and alienation. Much seemed to come in the way of his working out his life on his own lines. His friends would fain have put in his way comforts which were no comforts. He felt more and more impelled towards a life of usefulness, a life by which he might help the will of God to prevail.

As early as 1838-39 he began working in the east end of Glasgow, taking a special interest in the district called the Spoutmouth, and here, on 10th June 1848, he founded the Spoutmouth Bible Institution.[1] The members of the Institute went by the name of "Spouts" or "Spoutonians."

In 1845 Sir Michael was admitted a partner in his uncle's business, and this brought more responsibility and involved a greater tax on his time and energies. In the

[1] "The name gives no idea of the quality of the Institute, which was made up of Bible plus Mechanics' Institute, plus Toynbee, plus Penny Savings' Bank, plus Fresh-Air Fortnight. The last was quite a feature of this Institute. Himself a lover of nature, Michael Connal first set the fashion of taking people out of the smoke into the fresh air, and giving the dwellers in our east-end streets a sight of the green fields and the trotting burns, and a whiff of the sea and the heather. The first summer after founding the Institute he took a band of young 'Spouts' to Garelochhead, walked them over the hills by Whistlefield to Coulport, and fetched them home in a tug. Out of this modest beginning grew his annual fair week's excursions to Arran, the Bass, Iona, etc., with scenery, botany, geology, archaeology, dooking, and delights untold. Some opposition came at first from the Sabbath School Union, who feared that these trips would lead to Sabbath desecration, but the very opposite has been the result."—Dr. J. O. Mitchell, "Auld Hoose of William Connal & Co."

midst of his busy and energetic life he still had time for feeling and sentiment. It was about this period that the idea seems to have entered his mind for the first time of repurchasing his father's little property of Parkhall, for which he had always cherished a longing and pious affection. He often thought and dreamt about it. In 1856 his uncle William Connal died. This made another great change in his life, bringing still more responsibility and a wider influence. With all the cares and demands of business, he incessantly worked for every good object he could. The amount of work he was going through at this time was enormous.

In 1858 he had the great satisfaction of buying back Parkhall and presenting it to his mother, thus carrying out his father's will.

In 1864 he married Miss Helen Catherine Leckie Ewing, daughter of his uncle's old friend, William Leckie Ewing of Arngomery, by his wife, Eleanora, daughter of John M'Farlan of Ballincleroch, Advocate, Edinburgh. His life was very bright and full at this time. With all his buoyancy, however, he was endowed with a highly susceptible nature which responded quickly to the varying pressure of outward things. It may be strange to those who in later life looked on him as the example of calm, almost severe common-sense, to know that he would weep in church, that the beauty of wild flowers also moved him in this way, and that mountain beauty and the sound of the sea stirred him more than the greatest eloquence. He had a strong love for children and animals, and a great delight in simple and natural pleasures.

In 1875 his mother died, and for a time his world seemed to have crumbled away. He had lived so long with her, and had his life so bound up in hers, that it seemed to change the whole hue of life for him. But time brought its softening influences, and with each new sorrow there seemed to come the stronger endeavour to give up every power to the service of God and man.

Education had an absorbing interest for him all through his life, and with the passing of the Education Bill in 1872 a new field for his energy was opened up. The acknowledgment of his services to the cause of education, when the Queen honoured him with knighthood, seemed to give general satisfaction. He was utterly devoid of fear of the opinion of man, and yet he had a tender yearning to be loved and liked. He admired generously genius or talent in others and where he felt he could, he encouraged it.

In his early years he had known the necessity of thrift and he could not bear to see waste of any kind. He often appeared to be stingy in small matters, but he could do a large and generous action well and handsomely. I have purposely left out from the Diary anything which might be misinterpreted as self-glorification, but the name of the kind deeds done by him is legion. I may give an instance of a quiet generous action. A relative of his lost her husband, and, considering that her house entailed too great expense, put it into the hands of her lawyers for sale. Sir Michael heard of this, and promptly telegraphed, saying that he wished to purchase it, and on his being advised that it was his, restored it to the former possessor for life.

His tastes and interests were very varied. His love of botany, of antiquity, of family history,[1] and his interest in the association of names and places were strong characteristics. He had what might seem a passion for buying back lands or houses which had once belonged to his family, but this had its root in a not unjustifiable pride in retaining associations connected with those whose memories were very dear to him. In 1882 he bought back the estate of Arngomery, which had been the property of his wife's ancestors, the Leckies, and subsequently to this, in 1886, he secured the house of his maternal grandfather, William Wright of Broom; and finally, as late as 1893, shortly before his death, he tried to acquire the lands of Broom, but in this he was disappointed. He was a staunch friend, as will be seen from many instances in the Diary. He took a wide interest in life, and was a keen observer of character. Nothing interested him more than to know how men in all ranks and professions lived and what their interests and amusements were. He felt the pathos of life very deeply, and his sympathy and pity were unbounded. One sin he felt to be unpardonable—the sin against one's highest light—the deterioration, the going backward, of a human soul.

His religious life was a very deep one. He lived in the spirit of the 139th Psalm—in the light of God. He believed utterly that God saw and weighed his every motive and action, and that these were not merely concerned with time, but with eternity. In these extracts much has of necessity been omitted from the copious outpourings of spirit which reveal the workings of the tenderness of his soul in its relation to the highest questions of duty and aspiration through his long life. These were continuous and progressive, and show a growth and advance towards the spiritual peace which marked that inner life more and more towards its close. Notwithstanding premonitions of failing health, and a sense of the growing weakness of his robust constitution, he continued unwearied in the pursuit of his public duties and attention to the growing interests of the cause of education in Glasgow. His attendance at fatiguing meetings of the School Board was punctual and regular to the last.

Sir Michael died at Parkhall, after a short illness, on 6th July 1893, and was buried beside his mother in the High Church burial ground, under the shadow of the old Cathedral.

The Diary reveals a character of great complexity, unfolding itself for more than sixty years. The preceding sketch may serve to show the outward results, the shapings which the spirit achieved, and the circumstances and surroundings that it had to work in and through. From the Diary we are enabled, so far, to judge of the motives and spiritual influences which urged and directed

tastes and dispositions totally different from his own. This again threw him very much in upon himself. His generous feelings had frequently to be curbed and his sympathies repressed. He seemed to be baffled when he tried to do good. Doubts sprang up, troubles surrounded him, and he became irritable and almost soured with his fellow-men. He never ceased, however, to yearn for some good object to work for; and it was about this time that the cry to God was so often on his lips, "Oh! to be useful in my day and generation!"

The year 1841 opened with very sad forebodings. The bright young life of his much-loved and only sister was cut off with appalling suddenness. The home was darkened, and, with a heart almost breaking, he had at least to appear brave, in order to keep his mother from endless sorrow. Like most thinking men he had a terrible spiritual tragedy to go through. He came out of the trial with his soul arrayed in its own proper jewels—moderation, justice and courage, nobleness and truth. From this time his life was one of complete consecration to the service of God and man. He had within himself much to battle with and subdue. His temper was naturally very quick, proud and haughty, and his external demeanour—when obstructed in the rapid fulfilment of any of his unselfish wishes or schemes—frequently most overbearing. But even when this was the outcome of loyalty to principle, he was always deeply grieved if he thought he had hurt the feelings of any one. Many a prayer is recorded in the Diary; many a cry of sorrow for want of self-control. He was a man of moods, and many have too hastily formed their opinion of him from some sharp rebuke or almost rude reception, but others would hardly believe these things if they were told of them. How otherwise can we account for the number of men of entirely different dispositions who looked up to him with so much reverence and love? As years passed on, those nearest him saw the mellowing and softening of the character, the great sympathy and the large hope. Throughout his life Sir Michael was an ambitious man, especially during his earlier years. He frankly acknowledged that he did not care to play "second fiddle" to any one.

But ambition in the form of desire for personal distinction gradually fell away, and it satisfied him to do quiet persistent work and let others come to the front. A simpler life could not well have been lived. He did not pretend to despise this world's good things. When they came he received them thankfully, and used them for what they were worth.

Sir Michael was largely influenced by the historic sentiment, which showed itself in that love of antiquity, that strong clannish feeling which was at the root of his life. He was a man of strong imagination, and it seems natural to such a disposition to venerate the past. This side of his character accounts for many of his apparent eccentricities. It often helped him—certainly before religion took the place in his life it afterwards did—in his chivalrous conception of duty. The key to his character is to be found in his absolute sincerity and singleness of purpose, brought about by an unswerving fidelity to the highest light that was in him. He was a man of deeds, not words. He had schooled himself to give up much that appeared glowing and generous in sentiment but difficult to accomplish, in order to give present help and begin a good work. Not that he did not sympathize with generous projects of reform which required time for their realization, but his principle was rather to find out what was possible to be done under existing conditions and to do it.

As a merchant he always held a lofty ideal before him, and whatever he did was characterized by the strictest integrity and love of fairness and justice. As a philanthropist his love and pity went out wherever there was an object. It is comparatively easy to give means; he gave his life. As time rolled on he seemed ever more eager to grasp every opportunity for usefulness, always judging himself an unprofitable servant.

EXTRACTS FROM
SIR MICHAEL CONNAL'S DIARY

1835—1838

EXTRACTS FROM
SIR MICHAEL CONNAL'S DIARY.

1835.

May 30.—Left Glasgow for London about 1 o'clock P.M.

July 23.—Saw the King and Queen, with many nobility, clergy, etc., go and return from Caenwood, the seat of the Earl of Mansfield. A fine arch of evergreens—fireworks.

November 9.—Lord-Mayor's Day. Got nearly squeezed to death among a set of the lowest of the low. So much for the gratification of curiosity. Since my arrival in the Metropolis, having no companion up to about this time, I am in some measure solitary. My evenings are spent in my garret, reading or writing. I have chalked out no plan of study yet. Often melancholy, I have wandered about the streets, gazing in at windows, or listening to a poor little boy playing on a stringed instrument. Lamps lighted—streets crowded—grand equipages—misery—destitution—vice.

1836.

January 3.—Arrived in London after three weeks' absence, having left on the morning of the 12th December, 1835. Travelled through Holland, Belgium, and France. Glad to get home; a feeling of comfortable satisfaction pervaded my first day at home.

February 17.—Saw Madame Vestris, haggard in the coun-

praised the poems in the class-rooms, and more useful in the sale of them.

August 11.—Visited Thomson's grave on reaching Richmond. He lies buried in the old church. A plain brass plate at the corner of a private pew marks the spot where the poet of *The Seasons* lies. The Thames wound its silent but broad waters through the park beneath till the intervening woods concealed it. The view is confined, and the hope of passing an hour's reverie, when contemplating it, is baffled by the crowds that promenade the spot from which it is seen. The very idea of a promenade being the seat of contemplation destroys all poetical feeling. That spirit can only muse when far from the gaze of others, let the spot be the top of a mountain or a crevice in a rock. The sweetness, the placidity of the whole scene beneath you, cannot fail to soften and calm the mind, notwithstanding the hum of a crowd; perhaps such luxurious scenery is the only kind that can be dwelt on when the mind is distracted by the presence of others.

August 23.—Saw Wren, the architect's, tomb, and Rennie's, the engineer. Saw Dr. Donne's statue in a shroud, as well as several other figures that had escaped destruction in the fire that burnt the old cathedral [St. Paul's]; Nelson's body, in a sarcophagus that Cardinal Wolsey had prepared for his own corpse at Hampton Court, immediately in the centre of the building; the library floor curiously made of wood without nails; geometrical staircase; model of St. Paul's, the original of Wren; trophies used at Nelson's funeral.

October 19.—I have, ever since my arrival in London, been endeavouring to pursue a plan of study; but I have found that a regular system cannot be followed out, without exhausting the mind, after a day of the routine of a counting-house. I am convinced of my own want of perseverance calmly to grapple with difficulties, to be diligent in the mastery of them I own myself unable. A fickleness of mind, perhaps rather an overflow of animal spirits, has tended to make me long to be finished with every study I undertake at the expense of a thorough understanding of it. I am ever looking out beyond the matter before me. Not only my own peace, but that of the nearest and the dearest of my relations is bound up in my steadiness and industry. Try and think more and speak less. The ornaments of language can easily be applied where there is little strength of statement or truth; when a man speaks without thinking he is the machine of habit, and his advice will always be undervalued, if not despised. To improve your style in writing, though it ought not to open up any ambition foreign to your profession, is always a useful object; and to promote purity and elegance of composition read the more elegant essays of Addison and endeavour to put them in your own words. . . . Finished reading a course of lectures by Watt on the *Pilgrim's Progress*. They open up much Christian experience which Bunyan has shrouded in allegory not very intelligible.

October 24.—Entered Mr. James Thompson's counting-house to acquire a knowledge of tea. . . . I have felt confused for some time past about that prayer in the English Liturgy, "Vouchsafe to keep us this day without sin." This cannot be looked for in a man unregenerate. How can he, whose every thought is sin, far more every word and action, utter, in the hope of its being answered, such a prayer.

November 3.—Stood looking, with Joe Hooker [Sir Joseph Hooker] for an hour and a half at a fire in the City Road. It is a strange propensity that a rabble have in looking at the progress of the devouring element. Can there be in their interest any real sympathy with the unfortunates, any real desire to see *it* (fire) extinguished? Timber after timber is destroyed, wall after wall falls in, building after building adds to the devastation, and proportionally does the satisfaction of the thoughtless onlookers increase.

November 5.—Saw a van full of convicts pass London Bridge. What must they have thought, shut up in their confinement, of the noise and rattle and bustle without them; for, though the bells of a steeple close to me were ringing, their sound was drowned in the noise of passing vehicles. If there was a penitent man amongst them, how must he have envied the freedom and cheerfulness of the crowd that were hurrying past him to their respective duties.

December 5.—Received, in answer to request to visit Scotland, full liberty to do so from my very dear Uncle [William Connal]. A gush of feeling is apt to come over me, so as to drown the very exquisiteness of the pleasure. It can only be a season of satisfaction if it has been well earned and if it is well employed.

December 7.—Went to Stoke Newington to see a play performed by the boys of Green's school. May not such an amusement infuse a taste for the theatre, perhaps a passion for the profession of an actor? Became interested in a little foreigner, a Spaniard. There is so much apparent sweetness in many boys, an amiableness that endears, and a liveliness that fascinates, that the heart in the momentary fondness would fain claim the object of interest as its own; but we are apt to forget that perfection is a stranger here, and the experience of the characters corroborates the truth of it; and when we look away into futurity, there is a sadness, the offspring of doubts and fears, that the beauty and the innocence of the boy may give place to the guilt-stained and deep-designing man.

December 9.—Had Gibbard, M'Kean, Harrison, and Wm. Thompson to supper. In convivial society it is difficult to restrain the natural impulses of the heart to evil. A subject improving as well as interesting ought always to be kept in view, and leave no room for vain and impure jests.

December 17.—Arrived [Glasgow]—all well and happy to see me.

December 18.—Heard Robert Montgomery, the author of *Satan*, and other poems, preach—wordy, and too much of the poetical spouter, and too little of the deep and inquiring theologian.

December 27.—Visited Stirling for two days.

During the past years I have read regularly *Chambers's Journal*, a weekly publication. My time was much interrupted by college exercises, and the reading necessary to compose them. About the months of April and May, 1835, filled with a very great desire to leave home for a year or so. Thought the retirement of a lodging would give me more time for study. Framed schemes far too extensive, and indulged in too sanguine hopes of my successfully following them out. Looked upon my going to London as a crisis, I fondly trusted, for the better; but the experience of sixteen months (October 15, 1836) bitterly reproaches me with indolence and want of steadiness.

1837.

January 2.—Wrote Mr. Henderson,[1] the minister, on L.'s prospects.

January 3.—Left again for London with a heavy heart, but with the hope that I may, in God's good providence, return in health and strength to enter upon the duties to which I may be called, and for which I pray I may be capable in a year at the most.

January 29.—Had a conversation with Mr. Dunoon about the middle of this month, and he gave much ease to my mind on the subject of a profession. Many enter on one profession, find it not to answer their hopes, and enter on another, and thus become unsettled for life.

February 28.—About the beginning of February, from a few wholesome observations accidentally made by William Thompson, my eyes were opened to the necessity of struggling hard at the duties I have entered on, and I can only account for the blindness and indifference, and the consequent inactivity and indolence that have so long been with me, as the result of some fanciful ideas as to another profession. If I do not work for what is before me, shame and disappointment must be my lot, as others will step in to take away my advantages, and the world will laugh at my folly.

March 24.—Being Good Friday, I spent the day in the house, and began the second part of my continental journal. A distaste, increasing as each day brought a return of the same dry and mechanical duties in a profession that neither seemed to be suited to my mind nor temper, drew to a head about the beginning of April, and the mania that took possession of my mind was a strong wish to have some government clerkship or some attaché appointment. To render myself useful to the

[1] Rev. Robert Henderson, Stirling.

influential, to have leisure and opportunity to become more and more so, by meditation and a course of study, and with the hope to rise through thus recommending myself to their notice, seemed to be the course I was born to follow. The mercantile profession presents fair opportunities to me, and my own folly, indolence, want of purpose, will lose me all unless I now bestir myself. A vain, conceited aggrandizing spirit is at the bottom of all. The philanthropist and the patriot in me would be at heart the popularity hunter and self-seeker. Nature in endowing one too liberally often curses, for it is forgotten in the spontaneous harvest that springs up, that a far more wholesome and abundant crop would be the result of a little labour.

April 13.—Mr. E. B. Haly took me to the opera house; the music in some parts beautiful, but the plot and circumstance of the play wretched.

April 26.—Finished the second part of my journal, a third to succeed it. Also Sir Walter Scott's *Paul's Letters to his Kinsfolk.* The same ambitious aspirings have again taken hold of me. They are not defined—they have no specific object in view. If the enthusiasm that may be natural thus carries me into extravagant ideas, I am warring with my constitution of mind and body, and if it were to be of any service to me, I only wish the time were come for its exercise.

May .—The principle of duty to those around you and dependent on you and self, may take the place of love to man.

May 2.—Went to Newgate; crowds in the street opposite the gaol, some close to the walls; windows opposite open, with placards stuck up, "Seats here"; smoking, drinking, laughing vagabonds waiting the public execution of James Greenacre the murderer.

May 4.—Went to the exhibition of paintings in the National Gallery. Mountains, lakes, forests, the whole of the wildness and the beauty of nature brought before us at a glance—the scenes of by-gone days—the tournament, the battle, the defeat; and those of the present—the harvest home, the deer hunt, the gipsy encampment—

are all gathered into a focus by the pencil of art, and what an art, that can thus recall the past or so vividly copy the present.

Went to Exeter Hall to hear Dr. Duff; eloquent as last year; Sir Andrew Agnew in the chair; Scotch Mission.

May 5.—Went to Percy Chapel to hear E. Bickersteth preach on behalf of the Reformation Society—clear and very sound, but no orator.

May 9.—Heard Edwin Sydney preach for the Newfoundland Society.

May 12.—To a constitution such as mine disappointment is the more keen, that the hope or rather the illusion was the brighter. To give to the rank and honours, the wealth, the intellectual power of this world, a magnitude of importance which they do not possess, is to cheat the soul—to conjure up delights, earthly, however refined and bewitching, and to give to them the hue of my excited imagination, is only to mock my heart in the result of them. The devil sits in the heart thus occupied with the world, to hurry it at once to destruction; he has an enthusiasm, a heated spirit to deal with, and where so much of headstrong impulse is, he looks forward to the easy conquest. But the grace of God is all powerful—we are taught that "lying vanities" in letters of burning bitterness is written on all things here below. The love of Him, and within the last week I have felt but a ray of that love, can alone dispel illusion, can alone ennoble above the world, can alone save.

May 17.—Went to Greenwich fair for about an hour; the hill, though at 8.30 P.M., covered with wanderers; the town crowded in the extreme; cabs, omnibuses, and coaches pushing along at a furious rate; the booth brilliantly lighted up; the Algiers Booth hung with festoons of party-coloured lamps and filled with the dissipated of all ranks.

June 1.—Went with Miss Forman to the anniversary meeting of the charity children "within the Bills of Mortality in and around London" at St. Paul's. The sermon was preached by the Lord Bishop of Chichester. The chanting of the Psalms in the choir was most beautiful, distance mellowed the voices into the most heavenly music.

June 4.—Went with William Thompson to Lincoln's Inn Fields Chapel—the most beautiful Gothic building I have ever been in.

June 10.—Went to the Horticultural Society's garden.

June 11.—Went to Clapham Parish Church, heard part of a sermon, and then bounded over the common in the ecstasy of a soul emancipated from the drudgery and poisonous atmosphere of the Metropolis. The broom displayed golden luxuriance of blossom, while the hawthorn sent forth a ravishing fragrance; the chestnut hung laden with its rich blossoms, and the laburnum drooped with its graceful pendants. The eye, the ear—for the cuckoo and the blackbird were heard—and smell were all gratified; yet, whether it is that I have too sanguine a mind, too imaginative, I know not, but I felt the chain of mortality binding me down.

June 12.—Went to see the prizes distributed at the Hanover Square rooms of the Society for the Encouragement of Art, Manufactures, and Commerce. Duke of Sutherland gave them away—chiefly medals. Went afterwards to the Pantheon, Oxford Street.

June 14.—Esther T.'s birthday—nineteen; gave her a copy of *Daily Thoughts* as a gift, and inserted at the beginning of the book these lines composed on the same day:

The Regal Emblem may be wrought
  With every lustrous, costly gem;
But here's a circlet of pure thought,
  A far more precious diadem.

Fair Esther bowed a conscious head
  Beneath the crown the King had given,
But "peace" in eye, on brow is shed
  By this the brilliant gift of heaven.

The gold shall mix with parent earth,
  The rubies all be colourless,
This coronet of nobler birth
  Shall sparkle aye in rays of bliss.

And as each day that passes by,
  Laden with mercies from above,
Makes up the year, oh, kindly try
  To bind these "Thoughts" in Christian love.

MICHAEL CONNAL.

June 18 (Sunday).—Christie breakfasted. Went into St. Saviour's and saw the altar piece; went into the Temple Church and then struck up to Lincoln's Inn Fields Church; worshipped at St. Bride's "Since the transgression of the law"; remarked the splendour, extent, wonders of London as we passed along; went into St. James' Palace, and passing through antechambers lined with the Beef-eaters, yeoman guard with halberts, and servants in court dresses in waiting, reached a fine chamber where the bulletin of His Majesty's health was displayed; wrote our names down as visitors; and went out by a chamber with portraits full size of the monarchs Henry VIII., William and Mary—Noll Cromwell in bad taste left out. Went into Tattersall's—many fine horses.

June 20.—Had a bathe in the Peerless Pool. King dead. Bulletin with a border of black of an inch; bell of St. Paul's tolled at 12 o'clock. Then took Harry Thompson to St. James' Palace, passed on to Westminster Abbey; Henry VII. Chapel, like lace or network,—the seats of the monks [sloped] to keep them from sleeping. Signed the Catholic Repeal bill; walked through Westminster Hall; went through part of the buildings of Westminster School.

June 21.—Longest day; Queen A. V. 1st proclaimed; saw the last part of the procession going past the Mansion House. The contrast from yesterday striking—shops shut and bells tolling; to-day bells ringing and crowds hurrying in all directions to see the proclamation.

June 24.—Started with Harry Thompson on a tour to the Isle of Wight and returned in a fortnight.

July 16.—Heard Rev. Derwent Coleridge preach in Dr. Croly's church. While tempted to suppose that my tastes are indisposed for the mercantile profession, still the strong duties that I have to perform in it as to my uncle and mother, and the prospects that I have in it in comparison to any other that I can think of, have determined me to lay my mind down in close attention to the details of it, however disagreeable, and to trust for daily strength to act aright.

July 31.—Had D. Christie, J. Waring, W. Little, Wm. Thompson, and my cousin to tea; passed pleasant evening, some excellent imitations of the Codger's Hall speaker by D. Christie.

August 4.—Went to the British Museum with William Little—the Elgin Saloon. The only feeling that pervades one at first is that of robbery; but when we think of the opportunities of patient investigation of their contents, the consciousness of their comparative security from destruction reconciles us to the noble thief; amidst the multitude of these ruins in Greece they must have been forgotten, at least comparatively. Was much struck with the advanced stage of the art of sculpture; there is, comparatively speaking, no advance now.

August 9.—Stood by a grave and heard the church service read in the burial ground of Aldgate Church.

August 11.—Reached my twentieth year; dined at R. B. F.'s. It should be a most powerful stimulus to duty when I consider that my years are running on.

August 17.—Read Abercrombie's inaugural address on "The Culture of the Mind," and read Robert Hall on "Infidelity," and on "The Freedom of the Press." During illness read, and heard read, by William Little, Shakespeare's *Midsummer Night's Dream* and *Twelfth Night;* Byron's *Mystery of Cain;* Sir Walter Scott's *History of Scotland*, 1st series; *Paradise Lost*, with Addison's remarks on it in the *Spectator*.

August 23.—Read *Tristram Shandy* by Sterne.

August 26.—Went with Little to Covent Garden market before six o'clock on Saturday morning. Fruits and vegetables of all kinds,—a busy scene.

September 19.—Went to Regent's Park and visited the Zoological Gardens.

September 25.—Fairly entered upon business, after a visit at Highbury grove.

October 10.—L.'s birthday—twenty-six years old.

October 11.—He left for Cambridge University.

October 22.—Went to Foundling Hospital. Divine service conducted with great interest; professional singing. After sermon walked through the different rooms, saw "The March to Finchley" by Hogarth, "The Murder of the Innocents" by Raphael, and several portraits and scriptural pieces; Captain Coram's portrait and miniature statue. The boys at dinner and the girls—a fine sight. My uncle John [1] leaving for Madeira with his family, for his health.

November 8.—Have had a recurrence of my doubt about my eligibility for a profession that is discordant with all that is most congenial to my feelings. Taste is nothing; sentiment is nothing; refinement is set at nought except where coarse interests find themselves compelled to bend to it. Imagination and all the more acute and ingenious powers of the mind are useless; eloquence is dangerous in such a profession, and the generous sentiments of the soul are extinguished by caution and jealousy; but I shall still persevere in it till a more decided dislike, or rather distrust, gives my mind no other course to pursue than to quit it. I have many motives to persevere and these perhaps stronger than can be always furnished, but I have a distrust of my success that makes me wish the opposite side.

November 26.— ——'s affairs give me much distress; the mind feels in its poverty a greater acuteness in not being able to assist or relieve; the most earnest desire is smothered by the inability to be useful.

December 4.—Fog very dense; the individuals who passed shot away into the gloom, and after a gradually increasing faintness of outline, wholly disappeared at about ten yards distance. A good simile for futurity, as there was only clearness immediately around; so there is in this life sufficient light to guide, and strength to support us is given for the moment, none for to-morrow.

December 8.—Went to the House of Lords; heard Brougham attack Lord Glenelg on the tardiness of government in furnishing him with certain papers relative to the Slave Emancipation Act; saw Lord Lyndhurst, the Duke of Wellington, and Lord Melbourne. Stood in the lobby of the House of Commons and saw Sir F. Burdett, Joseph Hume, Sir Robert Peel, Lord Stanley, Spring Rice, and Poulett Thompson, Lords Hawick and Morpeth. The two doorkeepers—one a tall, the other a little man—characters, white hair and red faces.

[1] John Wright of Broom.

December 12.—Went to the House of Commons; heard Harvey on the Glasgow Weavers' petition, the Lord Advocate in reply; Joseph Hume; General Evans in reply to Peter Borthwick about Portugal; Sir Robert Peel, Spring Rice, Lord John Russell, Lord Palmerston, Colonel Sibthorpe on a grant of £8000 to the Duchess of Kent's private incomes; saw and heard big Daniel O'Connell, without exception the coarsest man I have seen occupy such a station. House adjourned at a quarter-past twelve P.M.

December 17.—Went to St. Giles', Cripplegate, and saw Milton's monument. His father and he were buried in the same church, as also Fox the martyrologist; felt a veneration as I left the church for the memory of so glorious a man and now in dust—alas for fame and earthly greatness. Brougham's mind, vast as to extensive information, a meteor genius, more fitted to dazzle than to guide.

December 22.—Went with E., M. T., and S. H. to the synagogue, Duke Street—hats on. Dr. Solomon Hirschell blessed the children. The priests who sang, attired as our own, but with three-cornered hats on; the music most splendid.

December 23.—Went to Formans and stayed till Monday 25th.

December 25.—Thought more seriously on my duties and the object of my existence from reading part of the *Martyr's Journal*; felt a greater wish to live to God's glory; felt conscious of the necessity for vigorous application, though the desire to know and understand should not be used as a means to gain worldly emolument. More and more alive to the fact that the more I know soundly, the happier I shall be, and less prone to a trifling vanity of spirit. Vanity must not distract me, nor indolence overcome me, in carrying out a steady course of acquirement. Determined to understand everything, and rather lose time with repetition than hurry off to something else. In this world a man is only valued according to the solidity of his judgment and the extent, as well as the depth, of his researches. Brougham, though every one acknowledges his genius, few grant him the homage that is paid to far inferior talent, but greater consistency.

Purpose to be an early riser in Glasgow and to read hard, to be very little out, and to seek might and main to master my business; but, above all, may God's Holy Spirit lead me to believe to the saving of my soul, and in the daily glorification of God to live up to the true dignity of my nature. This world is not our home; not a day passes but something awakens evil thought or evil passion; not a day passes but we find our purest wills thwarted, or, when gratified, far short in the fruition.

December 29.—Went with the Thompsons to Exeter Hall to hear Handel's oratorio of the *Messiah*; hall crowded; 500 performers; Braham sang "Comfort ye." The choruses splendid, but almost thrillingly painful.

1838.

January 17.—Dined at Walkinshaw's with a son of Allan Cunningham.

January 20.—Went to Sir Francis Chantrey's studio; saw the process of casting statues in bronze—Sir Thomas Munro (equestrian). Saw the whole process of marble statuary. Busts of a countless variety of men of talent and greatness. To represent nature without any embellishment of poetry; to depict it faithfully, yet to chisel the marble exquisitely, perhaps to depict the most striking position, is his genius. There is no attempt at fiction, the statesman or the warrior stands forth as he did when alive, and perhaps while he (Chantrey) is thus only a mere copyist of nature, he got a more simple, dignified, or simply beautiful impression, than if nature had gifted him with the power to combine as the poet. Met, when there, and had the pleasure of speaking (but a few words, however) to Allan Cunningham, the poet.

February 3.—Received a letter from Uncle, prolonging my stay till about the end of April.

February 13.—I have felt for the last month a growing sense of the object of my being created—God's glory. When it is reflected that we cannot live happier than by operating with the Great Author of our being, according to our several capacities, it is the most dignified, as well as the most rational employment of our powers; wealth is looked on only as a means to do good; honour as a means to be more extensively useful; learning as a means to open and enlarge the mind, at the same time to extend the general sum of information, and thus to promote civilization. Whenever vain desires after rank or influence or wealth, or any earthly satisfactions, take possession of our minds, peace, humility, order are banished. If the desire to do good be really in the heart it will show itself in situations comparatively humble, as well as in the lofty position of the man of fortune, rank, or great scientific or literary fame, and God's blessing follows on him who gives a cup of cold water in His name, being all that he has to give, as abundantly as on those who enjoy every capacity and every opportunity.

March 1.—Read Aikin's letters on English poetry.

March 4.—Saw the monument of John Selden in the Temple. I see that much of my indifference to the love of truth, to sound and valuable information, arose from vanity; to hurry over information from a vainly excited spirit was only to gnaw my heart still more with ambitions, for I could not feel any delight in reading except as an end to it. I gathered images and collected trains of thought but for display; I never enjoyed them except when they ministered to vanity. But a better spirit has visited me. God has given me to see my vanity; to be content with the disposal of me in His providence; to pursue to His glory my labours, whether mental, professional, or social; to be patient under every provocation or distress.

March 7.—Must read history, biography, literature, science, to cultivate the intellect, and read with a humble, patient spirit; read not to gratify vanity, but to store the mind with more comprehensive, more accurate, more interesting views of God in creation, providence, and grace. Understand as you go along, for, independent of giving a good habit to the mind, it yields more inward satisfaction in the perception and mastery of truth. Nothing should restrain from seeking information. . . . To be the promoter of great projects, and to live for generations as the philanthropist, the poet, the philosopher, the great, is too much my ambition, and I fear that I could not silently, obscurely sit down to work as an instrument, knowing that God worketh in me. To teach men to live happily is the true aim of love of the brethren; and every act which can promote that, by word or by conduct, is so much gained by the community; and by daily endeavour in God's strength to make God's creatures more happy is the only way to substantial happiness in ourselves. Gratify self, and how poor the gratification; make others happy and you are an humble worker in God's vineyard, nay, a co-operator!

March 28.—Went to Cambridge, and returned on 30th.

April 4.—Sat in Dr. Johnson's chair from Mrs. Piozzi's villa.

April 5.—Went with Mr. Wiltshire to see the drawing-room assemble. Peel, and Lady Peel; Lord John Russell; Archbishops of Canterbury and York and Bishop of London. Fine liveries; beautiful carriages; a great deal of parade: feathers, red coats, lace, diamonds; but many a careworn spirit, many a haggard countenance. Mused as I returned home on rank and its influence as well as its evils—on the luxury displayed as tending to diffuse wealth among the community and to encourage arts and manufactures; passed an illustrated copy of Gray's *Elegy*, and never did those elegant stanzas appear so true, "The boast of heraldry," etc., etc. What does it matter whether we die great and victorious, or unknown and without anything to make that hour interesting to any? A life spent to God's glory in loving Him and our brother is worth it all, and whether I be poor or rich and great, may that be my only aim.

April 12.—Went to see H. T. and M. T. confirmed in Bow Church by the Archbishop of Canterbury—a very imposing sight.

April 13.—Went to the Temple and heard Smith on the sacrament. Went to St. Lawrence Jewry in the evening to hear Mr. Pratt speak in behalf of the Spitalfields Charitable Society; the great destitution and poverty of these districts shown by the visitors; St. Lawrence a most beautiful church; organ very fine, and the seat of the Lord Mayor. Saw Archbishop Tillotson's monument.

April 22.—Evil a negative, not a positive; God never created evil.

May 1.—Had a most interesting evening with Christie. I detailed to him my plan of study—approved it. Advises me to lay aside any study when I have a greater desire for something else, and then I shall pursue with more pleasure what I intended doing before. Delighted with some views of the application of natural philosophy to life and its pleasures. Philosophy the handmaid of religion. We talked of the geysers of Iceland and of the equality of condition in man—society gradually approaching that state; monopoly of wealth useful at present, but it will be ultimately injurious to society if it continues to exist. Dr. Combe, in his physiology as applied to health and education, speaks of the habit of pursuing certain studies at stated hours; for at that time there is a greater facility for entering on them than after a long vacation from them. Irregular pursuit, therefore, more laborious in the end.

May 3.—Went with Barlas to the National Gallery. He advised me to study mathematics before I fully started natural philosophy, *i.e.* after a general view of it (Phil.). Talked of language—the use of learning the technicalities of a tongue when so much lay before me. He argued that language gives far more interest to the author, and that in reading you have more analysis of his ideas.

May 5.—Went down to Headley by a coach passing at four o'clock through Epsom. A delightful ride; reached Headly by seven o'clock in the evening; ran with Wm. Thompson along the heath in the neighbourhood; tired myself with capering, and bawled so loud as to lose my voice.

May 16.—Left London; spent the afternoon at Hampstead; went on board the "Monarch" steamer a few minutes after ten P.M.

May 17.—Spent a melancholy night—leaving friends is a sad thing; we may never meet again. Heaven has no partings. The Thompsons have been so kind—what a happy family. How has my prayer uttered on the top of

Dumyat (Ochils) been answered? Lord, Thou art merciful to me, giving me so many blessings in London; grant Thy grace, that I may serve Thee in humility and love in the new situation in which I am about to be placed. Mr. Tennant on board—talked to him. Dr. Chalmers sat opposite me at breakfast.

May 22.—Fixed on a house in Dixon Street with my mother.

June 11.—After much delay and annoyance, at last fairly fixed in our house. Spent in it a very agreeable Sunday—went to Dr. Muir's in the morning and heard him on Revelation iii., and in the afternoon heard him in the latter part of the second chapter. Very animated and very original; may I now have grace given me to realize my desires as to a useful life in study, in business, in good works.

June 24.—This morning, after a sleepless night, I have felt more at home in our new abode—the calm and blessedness of the Sabbath always restores me to clearness and peace of mind. I am determined now to commence to do all that I can (by God's grace working in me) for God's glory—in my own house, in business, and in my social connection with others, in thought, words, and works. I am too prone to aspire to a loftier eminence than I ought to expect reasonably to fall to my share here in this world, in the course of Providence; yet, while I would pray for an humble mind, I would most earnestly covet all excellence in knowledge and wisdom, knowing that if I be contented with a moderate amount of information, I shall never reach any height of attainment; may God's blessing be upon me in thus pursuing a course of useful acquirement, that in all I have or all I am, I may be devoted to His glory. Amen.

June 28.—In the retirement of my little room, hung round with the curiosities of my father, surrounded by my papers and books (while my mother and sister are away to see the review, and the bells of the city are pealing merrily above the crowded streets—while the most solemn vows are passing between our youthful sovereign and her people in the Abbey of Westminster), I would calmly consult with myself as to my duty in this life, that in the world to come I may attain the glory, honour, and immortality promised to those who have patiently endured and continued in well-doing. I am determined, by God's grace working in me, from this time henceforth to set a guard upon my lips that I sin not with my tongue; to cultivate charity; to improve my time more and more, knowing that the present only is mine, that an account must be rendered of the way in which I have spent it; to pray daily for a heart to love God and my fellowmen, and strength to resist every imagination that would exalt itself above God, that I may serve Him in body and soul with all my strength and might.

"Money is not the only thing that is not our own; time and thought and knowledge, and power, moral influence, and spiritual advantage,—all must be answered for, for all are God's."—*Fry*.

Early rising good for body and mind.

July 14.—Read *Coleridge's Aids to Reflection*, which, from the laboured style of the author and the subtlety of his argument, I must read again.

July 25.—I am too prone to think myself likely to be *some one* yet, which, from there being no grounds to lead me to such an expectation, is romantic or visionary; that the love of fame and rank and talent is the only grand motive to diligence and strenuous labour, or that there must be a great devotion of purpose, some all-exciting cause for good or evil. Now the first proceeds from discontent with your situation in life, forgetting that God's wisdom has ordained all ranks and degrees of men, and that each man in his own station, to fulfil the purpose of his being here, must glorify God in all his powers and faculties; and the second proceeds from the corrupted heart that can only be aroused from indolence and sensuality at the call of the world and its applause. Can I not by God's grace contentedly, yet earnestly, and diligently pursue my path in life?

August 27.—I have felt for some time past an indolent scepticism as to the objects of life. I looked on all the affairs of life, the business and the toil and care of the

pursuits. They tend in God's providence to prepare the way for higher and yet higher efforts, and though all their productions be as vanity in the eyes of the Eternal, yet God's providence is working out the great design of the raising of man, even here, to primeval blessedness and dignity. Therefore, though a man apparently is working for his bread or gratifying covetousness or ambition (though guilty motives), he is an instrument for God's glory though he seeks it not; and the Christian in all the duties and opportunities of the situation in which he may be placed is bound to have God's glory constantly in view by the consideration that the part allotted him is God's, and that in it, however dark it be as to its ultimate end for God, he is bound to exercise all diligence and all his faculties and to cultivate all knowledge and refinement, adorning with the graces of the Christian every duty he is engaged in. Mental exertion as such is as much a duty then as providing for your own household, without which a man is worse than an infidel. Act the part well God has given you to act, and however poor or humble, if acted well, you have as effectually promoted His glory as if it had been the loftiest in this world; the part is not yours but God's.

September 8.—I see more and more plainly that to think of mastering everything is ambitious and not from a real love of knowledge. The great end of study is to open and enlarge the mind, to discipline and enrich it, and one or two studies may effect what the whole range of science undigested cannot do.

September 15.—Read *Goldsmith's Works.*

September 17.—A beautiful morning—bright, clear, mild yet refreshing. How well we feel in fine weather, how lively, imaginative, serene. The aspect under which some places present themselves in fine weather is never effaced; they glow and cheer us in our recollections of them for many years after.

October 20.—Read *Edmund Burke's Works*, eight volumes 8vo. Read articles in the *Edinburgh Review* and *Tait's Magazine* on the works of Charles Dickens, author of *Boz*; the *Wellington Dispatches*, and *Nichol's Astronomical Works.*

November 6.—Visited two poor women, as a member of the Stirlingshire Charitable Society; one a Mrs. Buchanan, a poor object, five children just out of scarlet fever, three stairs up in a back land in the High Street; dreadful poverty, suffocating smell, rags, filth; these sights should make me more and more active in doing good. I feel more and more satisfied with my position in providence; may I improve it aright, devoting mind and body to the pursuit so far as is consistent with Christian light and love. May I be blessed in my mental pursuits as enlarging and strengthening my mind.

November 16.—Attended the funeral of Dr. Dymock[1] in procession to the Necropolis.

November 23.—Fanny's birthday, born 1821. Attending Wilson's class on Natural Philosophy between eight and nine o'clock morning—very interesting. Saw the engines of the "British Queen"—a most stupendous erection that makes one feel the power of man over nature. I have felt within the last few days an oppressive sense of mental weakness; it seemed to me as if I wanted power to think and to act, and yet I have experienced such lofty feelings and have thought myself capable of so much that these sensations are humbling. I trust I may, by patient perseverance in well-doing and a constant desire to fulfil to the best of my power whatever I am engaged in, be enabled to overcome these moments of depression.

December 31.—Felt rather unwell; a very stormy night; sitting alone. A solemn moment as the clock of St. Enoch's told of the departure of another year. The distribution of our time into days and months and years should remind us more and more of the shortness of our span. These periods mark out distinctly how swiftly and how surely we pass away to the brink of eternity; may God grant that it be an eternity of blessedness.

[1] Classical Master of the Grammar School, appointed 1808.

1839—1842

January .—Received news of John Connal's[1] (mate of "Mary Sharp") death on the night of the 5th, before the very great storm.

January 12.—Have finished for L. a poem on "Bannockburn." Read Campbell's "Pleasures of Hope" and Scott's "Lord of the Isles."

January 18.—Have finished for L. a poem on "Elephanta and Salsette."[2] Read for it several works: Maurice's *Indian Antiquities* and Maria Graham's *Journal on India*, Brewster's *Encyclopedia*, and Byron's *Childe Harold* to get the verse. Determined never to do anything of the kind again.

[1] Washed overboard when giving orders quite near land. Was on his way home to take command of a ship.

[2] As the sad spirit often wears a smile
  To hide the thoughts from which it cannot flee:
So rises Elephanta's mountain isle,
  Looming luxurious 'mid the dark blue sea;
Yet solemn in its very mystery,
  Yet no tradition lingers to reveal,
When, as a temple of idolatry,
  Its rocks were hollowed by the artist's steel,
  Who deemed his patient toil secured eternal weal.

With varied shapes, the darkened soul's creation,
  With genii gods, the sculptured walls are rife;
Some sit absorbed in lofty meditation,
  Some wildly mingle in the battle's strife.
Siva stands forth with sacrificial knife
  And grasps a victim in his vengeful ire;
The fiendish Doorga seems to start to life,
  With dangling corses as her fell attire,
  Among the countless powers of ocean, earth, air, fire.

April 18.—Finished the prose works of Abraham Cowley and as much of Shenstone as I intend reading, comprising all his essays and many of his poems. I have felt again oppressed with a desire for worldly honours from reading slight sketches of Franklin and Sir William Jones. I would seek direction and guidance in all that I put my hand unto, for Christ's sake, and for His sake may I have grace to live wholly to Him.

May 5.—First held a Sabbath school; very much gratified by the presence of many of Mr. Graham's scholars.

May 9.—In the course of my visits in the Spoutmouth came in contact with a family in very great poverty; man a shoemaker; wife lying on the floor; dirt, nakedness, disease, and famine. No table, chair, or bed; one stool

And far within, in awful grandeur wrought,
  Colossal towers the triune power divine—
God, the creator, wrapt in pregnant thought;
  God, the preserver, bending all benign;
God, the avenger, with His frown malign—
  Amid the host the Deity supreme;
But now no pilgrim worships at His shrine.
  The sacred cells with hissing serpents teem,
  Where once the Brahman mused and revelled in his dream.

Invested in the like mysterious gloom,
  The deep oblivion of three thousand years,
And shrouding, like the dateless mossy tomb,
  Forgotten joys and hopes and jealous fears,
The rival powers of Canara appears
  With all its cavern chambers, where alone,
In silent desolation Buddha rears
  His form gigantic on his rocky throne,
  His blessing unbesought, his pompous rites unknown.

There science marked the planets' ceaseless roll,
  There superstition gloried to disclose
The transmigrations of the guilty soul
  Ere it should blend, redeemed from all its woes,
In Deity in ever blest repose;
  While through the vault with glittering lustres hung,
In mystic dance the idol's praise arose;
  Yet once the almost Gothic temple rung
  With God Jehovah's name by Christian exiles sung.

and a few tools of the craft. What a picture! Boy taken by Mr. Thompson into his Sabbath school. Came in contact with a very worthy couple of the name of Lyon; they have a son, their second, who frequently runs away from them and often decamps with money. Often lies on stairs all night, and seldom comes home (when he does) before one or two in the morning.

May 14.—Led to consider happiness as consisting not so much in outward condition, but in the state of mind.

May 27.—Had a delightful walk into the country with my mother and sister.

June 8.—Had a most beautiful walk through the country with mother and sister, John Fisher, and Tom Campbell. A most delightful view of the vale of Clyde.

June 11.—I have read through the entire Bible, having begun in June 11th, 1838. Oh! that His word may not return unto Him void in my case.

July 13.—Went with my mother and sister to Dunoon. Went on the Monday to Lochgoilhead, by crossing over to Gourock. A most beautiful sail; fine villas, rocks, clusters of mountains, brushwood, trees, dells, and ravines, all inspiring with a love of the wildness and the sublimity of nature.

August 11.—I have now completed my twenty-second year of this life. My uncle having left on the 29th July for a month, I have been left to a good deal of responsibility, and a consequent interest has been created in my profession, and my energies have been more exercised.

September 24.—Had a very good day at Loch Goil with Little.

September 25.—Visited Lanark, Fall of Stonebyers, the Mills, Lady Mary Ross's grounds, Cora Linn—white, thundering in masses, within a large amphitheatre of precipitous rock. Bonnington Linn more picturesque—small island in the middle of the fall—Wallace's Cave. Cartland Crags bridge light and the highest bridge in Scotland; very steep crags; variously wooded.

September 30.—I have felt very unhappy for a long time. To seek constant and intense employment as a means of happiness is wrong. On 20th inst. (Friday evening) Henry Thompson and John Waring called on us.

Went with them through various parts of the city on Saturday.

November 6.—Set out for Tillicoultry—the variegated woods of Airthrey Castle most interesting. Mr. Browning [Rev. Archibald Browning] disputed on the advancement of the millennium season.

November 21.—I have finished the lecture by Channing on self-culture, and as a production for style, as to terseness and pungency, it is excellent.

1840.

June 10.—Finished, for the second time, the annual perusal of the whole Bible.

June 27.—I have had a most delightful walk, in a retired part of the road between two plantations. The birds sang so sweetly, while the setting sun spread a beautifully subdued light all over the sky to the north-west, that I could not but thank the Father for so many expressions of His goodness.

July 6.—I thought the world was indeed vanity, and that to serve God in my day and generation in it was all my duty. How soon I might be called to lay me down in the dust, and then what matters it what I had enjoyed of the world?

August 31.—I spent Friday, the 21st, in an excursion on board the "Conqueror." The day was very fine and I was much struck with the beauty of the entrance to the river Clyde. The Firth opens out into the sea, so majestically surrounded by the mountains of Argyleshire and the softly-swelling heights of the southern shore. The lofty peaks of Arran under the ever-changing sunshine were very grand; and when, on going round the Island of Bute, a mist enveloped all to the south and west, yet the dark, frowning heights of Arran rose out of the sea most majestically and even more imposing than under the sunshine.

September 10.—I may say, in a word, that my religion consists in a desire to have the desire to love God, and make Him my chief joy. Scepticism, hardness of heart, and indolence beset me. Some are drawn by God to delight in Him by the cords of love. I know nothing of this, and those whom I bear on my heart frequently before God, what is to become of them ? May God, in His mercy, lead me and them to Christ.

September 22.—The British Association is holding its tenth meeting here. After one speaker had sat down Dr. Chalmers rose, and from twelve o'clock till a quarter to four he occupied the attention of his audience in a most lucid statement on the resources within—or *ab intra*—every parish to support its own poor without any assistance *ab extra*, or from civil authorities or public charity. He showed that there was a sympathy among the poorer classes which had only to be cultivated to supply the deserving with the means of sustenance, and that when the parish interfered it should be only to assist and not support the paupers—in short, to help the poor to help themselves. That to afford relief without any regard to the resources the poor might possess among relatives or neighbours, or their opportunities of and capacity for employment, was to relax the desire to labour, and thus render them lower in the scale of civilization. Dr. Chalmers is a man of vast capacity. I felt painfully convinced how little I was putting forth of that which was within me. Though it be by little and little, yet I must put forth all my mind and soul and strength to glorify God. The Lord give me wisdom and grace—grace to seek to live to it; wisdom how to live to it. Amen.

September 26.—Yesterday attended a dinner to the Marquis of Breadalbane, for his standing up for the Church of Scotland in the House of Peers. The Moderator, Dr. M'Kellar, gave a most nervous speech, . . . concluding with the hope that the enthusiasm evinced was the pledge that every man felt, "If I forget thee, O Jerusalem, let my right hand forget her cunning."

October 1.—A meeting for prayer on behalf of the Jews was held. I felt all the scornful indifference of an atheist, but yet a kind of alarm at the very thoughts of my heart. I know my temper is not that of God's children.

October 2.—No peace, no satisfaction. My heart impenitent, proud; yet with all the deceitfulness and desperate wickedness of it, I cannot but say that I would it were otherwise—that God would visit me with the knowledge and love of Himself. I feel much repugnance to self-denial. I would here again record my prayers for my near and dear relations—my mother, uncle, and sister, my uncles and their families, and all whom I am coming in contact with as relations and friends.

Fast Day Evening, October 22.—Careless of even man's opinion, and restrained alone by the grace of God from becoming a terror to myself and others.

November 11.—I have experienced much change; my soul seemed to take a delight in God's service. Peaceful in my daily occupations, I, however, find no true rest of soul.

November 24.—On Sabbath I heard Dr. Muir all day, and was much interested.

November 29.—I have some idea that I must realize conceptions of God's moral glory before I can say that I am changed, which may God in His mercy grant may be, however to the humbling and crossing of a vile, proud heart.

1841.

January 6.—I have begun this year in the same state of mind in which I closed the last—enduring life in a manner, rather than being happy. . I seldom see any man of talent—as I had the opportunity in the trial at the court-house, where were all the first men of the Scottish Bar—without thinking of another state of existence. Intensity shown in any pursuit makes me think of its end, its governing principle. I see just now as if life must soon merge into eternity, and if eternity is not a state of acceptance and favour with God it must be unutterable woe. . . . I have been led to think that Christians are too chary of their intercourse with others. There may be a concealed desire to get into their company which yet is not expressed, and a little more winningness may be given to the Christian character. Assuredly it is better to win sinners over to Christ by uncompromising, yet, at the same time, gentle conduct, than to look on those who may not profess so much as being swine and as if every spiritual truth introduced were a pearl thrown away.

I have heard Dr. Bryce of Belfast lecture on "The Art and Science of Education." His first lecture was on three great principles in the human mind: Assimilation (Imitation), Association, and Curiosity, and that these principles have been overlooked in education. His lecture of to-day was "How to Form the Habit of Attention," and he described it as voluntary and involuntary. . . . I felt painfully alive to the conviction that my intellectual cultivation had been much impeded by injudicious overloading of the mind before distinct conceptions had been formed, and by being driven to learning by fear, and not by curiosity or a thirst for knowledge; and that when left to my own exertions, without any motive at all, I sank back into a state of intellectual torpidity. My great defect has been in being too ready to form preconceptions, and thus enter on a study with erroneous views. Study should have been made a pleasant exercise to me and not a remote advantage, of which I could not perceive the value when my habits were in their formation. In treating of "Language" Dr. Bryce highly eulogized the classics as a gymnasium for the mind, in *the formation of these languages being inflected*, and in the Greek particularly there was a power of expressing minute shades of thought not in any other language. He therefore disapproved of the present movement for the study of the modern languages to the exclusion of the ancient. He recommended a similar course of study for young ladies as for young men, inasmuch as they possessed a powerful influence over the minds of children, and the more highly educated the mother, the more naturally would result a well-trained child. . He recommended the highest education that could be afforded to every member of a family. . . . Dr. Bryce's manner as a lecturer was most excellent; very clear and distinct, and evidencing a very searching and comprehensive mind.

January 18.—Dr. Burns called to consult with Dr. Rainy on the state of my sister now lying ill of fever. Poor Fanny . . . I would now heartily commend her spirit to the care of God.

of my grief. To see worldly people with whom the dear one had associated could only give pain. . . . Religion must have appeared most morose in the eyes of such in my solemn and gloomy countenance, as well as in my impatient constraint in such society. I did not recommend the gospel of Christ either in bursting out of the room to attend my meeting, which no doubt further increased the sneers against me. I should not have been asked at all, or, at least, have been permitted to refuse.

April 10.—Poor, dear Fanny said more than once during her illness, on being questioned, "I am quite well." Little did she know that the fever that was to lay her in the tomb was upon her. So I am no good judge of my own state. I feel I am not right with God, and yet this may be the result of desiring Him truly and honestly. I am going forward to a Communion table. I fasted on Thursday, having therefore taken nothing for twenty-two hours or so. I did this with a view to enter into the services of a day of humiliation with more sensible prostration.

April 26.—A matter has hung heavy on my mind, and that is, that I have been acting unrighteously towards my uncle in not letting him know the extent of my assistance to Mr. L——. I have had frequent intentions of opening my mind to him, . . . but have feared adding to his distress. Still, it is my intention to tell him, as much, however, from necessity as a desire to open my mind to him. The object is gained for which I have for three years laboured, and I hope, on consideration of the whole matter, as well also that I have learned much experience by the difficulty, he may receive my communications with patience and forgive me. I have a fear that I have been injuring my spiritual state in keeping this matter secret from him.

May 17.—L—— recommended to me *Rutherford's Letters* as a book which his mother had placed on the mantelpiece in the room where he sat, purposely that he might look into it, and he bids me ask it from his mother in a quiet way without giving her any hint about his having read it. . . . On Friday afternoon, after much torment in my mind as to the concealment of the assistance I had rendered to Mr. L——, I opened my mind to my uncle, and, while he heartily disapproved of my giving so much of my substance to this object, he gave me liberty to do as I liked; and accordingly I trust that I may yet have the satisfaction of seeing him in the church. . . . On the 8th of this month I returned from Kinross with my mother, where I spent several days in the quiet repose of the country; and there was so much of beauty in everything I saw, so much testimony to the wisdom and grace of God, that I looked up to God very frequently as the Maker of them all, and thanked and praised Him.

May 22.—My mother being at Garscadden, where I left her, I went over this evening to see Mr. F——. We talked about the beautiful sunset—the sun just then sinking behind masses of clouds, which reflected the light in the most gorgeous colours . . . On coming home I found a horse had broken its leg in dragging a canal boat. It was a painful sight. The patience of the docile animal, and the painful heavings and moanings after it fell over, with its ineffectual struggles to rise, impressed me.

July 13.—I have felt my own folly in not diligently and faithfully occupying my leisure hours. I determined to be more faithful in filling up my time. I find my temper—doubtless rendered irritable by the present difficulties that Mr. L——'s matters have brought me into—very unsocial . . . I often think of dear Fanny. We soon forget to number our days and apply our hearts unto wisdom.

August 2.—I spent Saturday afternoon with Mr. James Thomson walking along the river to Dalmarnock Bridge.

August 5.—I have felt all day great irritability of temper . . . a terror to myself as well as to others . . . My friend William Thompson and his young [illegible] with me this night . . .

trouble of a worldly kind. I have had Mr. L——'s matter, the depressing state of business, the painful bereavement of my dear sister, much depression of a spiritual kind, great darkness about my state before God, and often convictions of the enmity of my state to God and to my fellowmen. I think that I have the glory of God as the end of my being more before my eyes than some years ago. The water-colour drawings of my dear Fanny have been sent home to-day with frames to them. They cannot supply her place, but they are a very interesting memorial of her; but I would give far more to find some Diary.

August 15.—The first Sabbath day of my twenty-fifth year is now about to close on me. Visited poor E—— C——. He is a dying man, and very near his end.

August 29.—The Kirk of Scotland often in my prayers. I think that I could, through grace, contend for the principle which she struggles for to the extent of many sacrifices—should it ever come to it, to death. The Lord quicken and strengthen for trial in this cause, should it come. She occupies, amidst all her distresses, a position that extorts admiration from her enemies, and may draw to her communion and aid many of those who have hitherto persecuted her as an endowed church.

October 6.—In walking to the North Bridge, Edinburgh, was much pleased with the kindly embrace of a poor little boy by one of the street porters. There was so much of kindly tenderness in it. Montgomery, the poet, in Glasgow.

October 12.—The Lord break my heart with godly sorrow for sin, and quicken me in the way everlasting . . . . I had no love to God and did not seem to care much about it either.

October 26.—My dear mother in tears this morning when I went into her room. The Lord sanctify that solemn bereavement to her soul; and I would record my thanks to Him that there is an interest in Divine things that promises a work begun, which, if begun, shall be perfected in glory.

November 6.—Dr. Rainy called on Saturday, and I

May 9.—It is now nearly three weeks since my mother and I came to this house, 46 Albert Place, Hill Street. The former house was one where every apartment awakened melancholy associations; and yet I could have lived there, surrounded by the memorials of my dear Fanny, because I feel no desire to shut out the thought that I am a dying creature. . . . Determined to read the Greek Testament, and to fill up my time more fully with useful reading. . . . Went with mother to the Botanic Gardens (the new), open to the public, for the first and only time. I feel how the power of an indolent and apathetic spirit is pressing me down from all useful and vigorous employment.

May 30.—On Monday, the 23rd, I went into Edinburgh by the coach, having still some scruples to go by the railway. Witnessed the proceedings of the General Assembly. Fell in with a Mr. Lindsay of St. James's Church on my way on the top of the coach. Went with him to the Assembly, at present meeting in St. Andrew's Church. The throne was not filled by the Commissioner. Principal Dewar was speaking on the scripture argument against patronage. It was about half-past 9 P.M. Dr. Leishman rose and detailed the views of Sir George Sinclair's men. Heard Dr. Bryce, Mr. James Moncrieff, Dr. Candlish, and Mr. Cunningham. Candlish was electrical in his effect on the house, though then nearly two o'clock on Tuesday morning. Cunningham made his opponents a laughing-stock. A majority of 69 in favour of abolition of patronage.

It was deeply interesting to witness the proceedings of a court that had been in existence so long, and was so interwoven with the history of the country, and now more so that it is the supreme judicatory of a Church of Christ struggling for its privileges and blood-bought rights. What is to be the issue of the struggle none can tell. Lindsay and I slept in the same room; and it proves how closely Christian people—if, indeed, I be a Christian—can draw together at once, the more so when members of the same church, that I read a chapter and he prayed, with our eyes turned to Arthur's Seat, in the grey light of the morning. On

Tuesday morning, after as little sleep as I could well take, I went with W—— to the Assembly at half-past nine. At eleven the Commissioner, the Marquis of Bute, came in state. He had his pages, his purse-bearer, ushers, and chaplain. His servants in gorgeous yellow livery. He was dressed in a uniform with silver epaulettes. The Moderator, Dr. Welsh, also in a court dress, rose up with the Assembly to greet him. He bowed to him, then to either side, and sat down, and the business then commenced with the religious exercises. It was truly interesting to see a free court of the Church of Christ holding its deliberations under the sanction and eye of royalty, yet preserving its integrity and independence.

After some business on the Indian Mission, Dr. Chalmers rose to speak of the Claim of Right put forth by the evangelical portion of the Church. His speech was an earnest appeal to the justice and generosity of the English Parliament, and full of warning to it should it deny the just privilege of the Church of Scotland. It was truly heart-stirring to hear that saintly old man appeal with all the fire of his youth. It was like a steam-engine of vast power under high pressure. Dr. Gordon, a highly-intellectual looking man, and with all the dignity of an apostle, seconded Dr. Chalmers's motion. Dr. Cook, Dr. Bryce, Principal Haldane, looked as if they were cowed. In the evening heard Mr. Dunlop state the case for the Church. Heard Robertson of Ellon[1] and some other members of the House; but, being exhausted, returned to Glasgow.

June 1.—Determined to read the Greek Testament with L——. The very best discipline that I can submit to in the way of study.

July 20.—A long interval has elapsed since I wrote anything in this book. Have been reading pretty regularly, twice a week, the Greek Testament with L——, and find it useful in many ways. It is a study, at any rate, which can never be finished. It will be ever new, the more the Holy Spirit shines into my soul, giving me to see the light in His light. I visited, in prison, the boy who stole Mr. Elias Gibb's handkerchief. . . . Went to Edinburgh

[1] James Robertson, M.A., Moderator General Assembly, 1856.

on morning of the 12th instant. Met with John Millar [afterwards Lord Craighill], and went up with him to Arthur's Seat and had a magnificent view. Truly, it is a "city of palaces." The Forth spread far out, a sheet of deep blue water, and the distant peaks to the westward were glowing with light. . . . I cannot agree with him, however, on what is near my heart. In literature there may be some sympathy, but in religion there is none. . . .

Walked out this beautiful night to the Royal Lunatic Asylum. Sad, sad, amidst so much beauty of a natural kind, to find the need should be for such an hospital. The sun tinged the western horizon with a deep fiery red, and the moon, full-orbed, rose over the city. Oh, to know peace with God! I find the world can give no peace, and it is a weary pilgrimage indeed if He withhold the light of His countenance. There are pleasures at His right hand for evermore. There shall be no sighing, nor sorrow, nor any more pain, for the former things have passed away. Lord, keep me from being a talking Christian. Make me an honest, diligent, faithful servant.

July 21.—I begin to see how difficult it is to be a Christian. . . . Determined to be more careful of

July 29.—Walked out to-night. Again a beautiful night. Isaac went forth to meditate at even-tide. I thought to-night, as I stood by the Kelvin, with no one near me, of dear Fanny's death.

August 6.—Felt to-night lonely. Better to be alone than to be in the company of the vain and

August 15.—On Thursday last, the 11th, I entered on my 26th year. A sense of weariness oppressed me all day. During the past year I have gone on much [the same] as the preceding. I have read far too little. I am too fond of ease.

September 3.—If I carried my principles out to their full extent, I must needs go out of the world or otherwise snare my conscience at every step. During the last week away to Edinburgh to see the Queen. The whole city full of excitement. Banners flying, processions, carriages flying up and down, Calton Hill crowded with people, commanding a fine view of the Firth, with the distant shores of Fife. A glorious day. No arrival of the Queen till next day. Drove down to Granton pier: a magnificent structure. At night bonfires blazing from the heights of the hills round the country for many miles; the one on Arthur's Seat very brilliant. On Thursday drove with my uncle, aunt, mother, and other friends into town. The Queen had arrived, passed through, and away on to Dalkeith. Vexation and disappointment in almost every countenance. Returned to Glasgow that evening. Went back on Thursday morning, 3rd instant, with L—— Saw the Queen and Prince Albert, Sir Robert Peel, and other distinguished personages, as they passed by Holyrood House into the city. An interesting sight to see the Queen of this vast empire. . Ran to the High Street; found it living with human heads. Ran to Princes Street, and from it beheld the Queen and her suite standing beside "Mons Meg" on the battlements of the Castle, and responding to the congratulations of her subjects below by waving her handkerchief.

September 6.—Came home to-night, looking up at the stars, wondering at their magnificence and number. Thought of God in His immensity, yet love and mercy to man in his utter unworthiness.

October 25.—The good Lord keep me from frothiness, from pride, from self-confidence, from indolence, from unbelief, from despondency. May I be stirred up to walk before God with more cheerfulness, more faithfulness, more humility.

October 29.—Before giving my uncle a definite answer, I thought over the matter [a partnership] for a night, and, so far as I know my own heart, did commend the matter to God, seeking wisdom and direction. . . . The Queen's College opened formally in the Assembly Rooms on Friday last, and everything as yet augurs well for its success. Sir James Campbell in the chair—Dr. Hill, Dr. Symington, Dr. King, and John Leadbetter; place crowded. . . . Heard Moffat on Thursday last, the great missionary from South Africa. A man of great energy of character, abundant in labour for the truth.

November .—After carefully considering with myself as to the propriety of attending the Logic class in the morning with the view of acquiring the habit of closer thought and of being stirred up to economize time more, I entered with Professor Buchanan the private Logic class to-day.

November 15.—Heard yesterday that Edward Gawne was dead—my cousin's husband.

1843—1846

1843.

January 3.—In the adorable providence of God I am now in a fair way to recovery from an attack of typhus fever. The close of this week will complete the seventh week of my illness. I would record His mercy that I am spared, with thankfulness. I have had, during this illness, the most lively sympathy from friends and acquaintances—from many whom I could not have imagined at all interested in me or mine.

January 17.—On my considering L——'s ingratitude to me, and the useless anxiety and annoyance he has given me, almost tempted to have nothing more to do with him. But the gospel of Jesus Christ teaches me to forgive and be kind to the unthankful and to relieve the distressed.

January 24.—I went down yesterday earlier than usual to the counting-house to return to the business of life after my illness—on the very day that my poor sister two years before left this world. Everyone who meets me and extends towards me his sympathy in my recovery speaks as if he never expected to see me again. One said that he thought, with others, they had lost me.

January 30.—On Thursday, the 26th, I went with my mother to visit Dr. and Mrs. Beveridge at Hamilton. It is a beautiful part of the country. On Friday walked down the splendid avenue to the palace. The vistas of trees, stretching out to a great distance, opened out into a luxuriant prospect of hill and valley. The Duke a cipher in the world, . . . a man with such wealth, such power, and living as a recluse—living only to himself—

incurs a fearful responsibility. I thought how little all this could make me happy.

February 14.—I am inclined to think my besetting sin is indolence of spirit. I have been often distressed by the way in which L—— has acted towards me. He has never called since I was able to see anyone during my late illness. I know not what is to become of him. On the 31st ultimo I went with my mother to Greenock to visit my uncle, and stayed there till Friday, 3rd February. The mountains, the foam-crested waves of the sea, the constant variety of steamboats and vessels passing and re-passing, and the sudden bursts of the tempest, which every now and then shrouded everything in mist, and, passing away, disclosed the fair, blue sky and the distant landscape—all these were full of interest to me, and I tried to lift my heart to God by the sight of His works. . . .

We went to Stirling on Saturday, the 4th instant, and came home on the 10th. Monday, the 6th, was a most beautiful day, the sun being very powerful, though the ice was bearing. Went to the curling with my uncle. The country very interesting; the rich Carse bounded by the bold Ochils and the more distant mountains towards the west; the heights of Craigforth and the Abbey Craig giving interest to it, with the proud castle crowning another bold promontory, and the links of the Forth—all deeply interesting. Saw the sun rise two or three mornings with much interest. What a variety of natural beauty I saw! . . . I looked with much interest on that height of the Ochils just above Logie where I knelt down and prayed before I went to London in the year 1835, that God would bless me in going there; and surely He has followed me with mercy all through my stay there and since. It was doubtless a prayer offered up in much darkness and much pride. I heard Mr. Henderson in the Episcopal Church on

February 16.—I have been in great darkness, confusion, and distress of mind these two days past, but this night

encing. In the year 1742, in the twenty-sixth year of his age, he got relief in believing in Christ. My distress arose from a sense of my deadness in God's service. . . .

I intend going to London on Tuesday, 21st, to see my friends there. Mrs. Thompson and William have most kindly invited me.

March —On the 21st February sailed with my mother on board the "Princess Royal" for Liverpool; arrived on 22nd; on 23rd started for London; found our kind friends in Brunswick Square—glad to see us. On the 10th went to the Temple, rendered a gaudy show by painting and other decorations, quite different from the solemn appearance it had when I was last in London. On 13th took farewell of my friends; took a walk with my mother through the parks down to Westminster Abbey. Saw several members arriving at the Houses of Parliament—Lord Cottenham, Sir Richard Phillipps, Forbes of Callendar—and on leaving the place, disappointed at not seeing the Duke of Wellington—met him while he was walking to the House—a firm, erect, gentlemanly old man.

March 28.—I long looked forward to this visit. I had formed many friendships in London, and I longed to renew them personally. I was exhilarated with the change of scene. Everything I saw came home to me full of old recollections. There was the charm of association in my walks and intercourse with others. The constant society, the little time for retirement, the tone of conversation, the world revealed in its most attractive and bewitching appearance, together with my own corrupt and deceitful heart, made me careless about spiritual things and induced a vanity of mind. Yet I count it a matter of deep thankfulness that I was spared to see these friends once

March 30.—To-night a great meeting in the City Hall. Fox Maule, Dr. Candlish, Dr. Buchanan, Dr. Macfarlane, Greenock, to speak. A crisis is now hanging over the church, but it is as imminent with regard to the country at large. Should there be no pure church established there will be every effort made to overthrow the Erastian Establishment. There may be much interference on the

revolution which may end in the spre
England and Scotland. All is in the h

April 10.—Heard Dr. Candlish in St
xiv. 13. A very powerful sermon, bu
being speculative in his views about the
It was more original than improving.

April 11.—I am away down into t
fight with corruption within and withou
it may be with trials of no ordinary char
really to fight the good fight of faith?
but "Thy grace is sufficient for me."

May 2.—I think I see my way more
a part with those coming out.

May 4.—Surely if ever there was an
it is mine; if ever a distempered spirit,
a load of debt on me—debt, too, cor
friend; debt, too, contracted from tho
now willingly repay at almost any sa
payment of which I must incur my
by letting him know the extent of it,
to those who owe me no good wish a s
a laughing-stock. But at least I am
fully towards my uncle in not concea
temper brought on by this. . . .
spirit? what proud thoughts sometimes
becoming independent in some other li
leaving one where I have only the pr
sources of annoyance and trial. This is
God knows everything in my situation th
and truly I have seen somewhat of its
until His providence lead the way otherw
take His will as my will.

May 18.—Went into Edinburgh this
eight o'clock train to witness the sol
disruption of the National Establishme
city of many historical associations of th
Went to the High Church to hear
streets lined with the military. The

Marquis of Bute, came in great state, attended by the magistrates and several military and naval officers.

On the Commissioner taking his seat under the canopy on the throne, the Moderator, Dr. Welsh, bowed to him, and the devotional exercises were commenced by singing the second Scriptural Paraphrase. He then prayed in appropriate and impressive language, and preached from Romans xiv. 5—"Let every man be fully persuaded in his own mind." Very abstruse and rapidly delivered. I didn't wait till the conclusion, but hurried over to gain admittance to the General Assembly in St. Andrew's Church. Could not gain admittance till an event took place which will make men inquire into the principles of it throughout Europe. I heard a cheer, and immediately after, the doors of the Assembly were opened to the seceding ministers, who in a body walked down to the place of meeting at Canonmills. The Moderator, as I understood, after tabling a protest declaring the Assembly not a free Assembly, walked out, followed by ministers and elders.

After this I found access to the General Assembly. Principal Haldane was called to the chair, and after prayer, in which he alluded to the circumstances in which the Church was now placed, the roll was called; and when the Strathbogie men were called Mr. Moncrieff objected to that, and, after some discussion, this grave matter was postponed. Principal Macfarlane was then elected Moderator, and the Commissioner's commission was read (a large document in Latin, with a very large seal appended to it). Then the Queen's letter was read, embodying the declaration that she would willingly give her sanction to a bill giving every latitude of objection on the part of the people, with the exclusive jurisdiction of the Church. Nothing could sound more like a settlement of the question than this, yet Mr. Dickson, a man of considerable influence, who had always given great annoyance to the Convocationists, rose and left the Assembly for the other. The Commissioner's address was nothing else but an assurance that Her Majesty, according to her solemn pledge, would preserve inviolate the Presbyterian Establishment in all its rights and privileges. I hastened down to the Assembly at Canonmills, but could gain no admittance. Dr. Chalmers in the chair, and 408 ministers present. What a solemn event has taken place! It will require some time to realize it.

July 17.—I attended Dr. Muir's Church for one Sabbath after the Disruption, but he was so violent and unfeeling in his attack on his out-going brethren that I found I could derive no benefit from his ministry.

July 19.—Heard this morning, after coming in from Garscadden, where I had gone out to breakfast, of the death of William L. Graham, in the island of St. Thomas, after an illness of only six days. He was of a most sober judgment, of a most tender conscience, of a walk and conversation blameless, of high spirituality of mind, of lofty character. His reserve of manner wore off as I knew him; but the characteristic of his piety was not so much that of open warm-heartedness as of solidity and discretion. I went with Mr. Moody on Tuesday afternoon to Bothwell. His sister very quiet. A sweet placidity in Mr. Moody's countenance. Walked with him and his sister through the beautiful walks at Auchinraith, Mr. Alston's place. . . . My uncle, John Wright, far from well. His family at Tunbridge Wells, whither he has gone for some time.

July 21.—Went down to the Spoutmouth this evening. The people there all apparently much interested in the death of Mr. Graham. (The memory of the just is blessed.) Heard to-day that there was little hope of Hugh Matheson, one whom I would have liked to have known better. With a highly cultivated mind he was at the same time serious. What lessons I am getting! I am continually reminded of the painful circumstances ——— has placed me in. Truly I am reaping the bitter fruits of my own folly!

July 25.—I have been all day in much distress of mind and difficulty as to my state about ———. Irritability of temper is the natural fruit of a mind ill at ease. I am not at all frank, because I know I have not acted rightly towards my uncle. He sees that. Evil may be put into his head. He is far from being pleasant in his intercourse with me at times, and all this suffering on my part of now nearly six years to forward ———'s views at College—most imprudently—may be terminated by a worse suffering—the loss of my uncle's confidence. I cannot speak to him on these subjects; they embitter my life, while the mention of them will give him pain. I have determined on sending him this letter: "My Dear Uncle,—However painful this communication may be to you, with the import of which you are already acquainted, it is a relief to my own mind to make it, and I now think it high time to confess, with much sorrow, my imprudent and unjustifiable conduct in rendering assistance without your sanction to ———. I have reaped the fruits of my own folly in continual fretfulness of mind, much self-reproach on my own account as well as that of others, and I now fear to add the loss of your confidence. I have had six years of suffering, prolonged in the vain hope that a successful issue might await ———'s career. I have been miserably disappointed. But my own peace of mind demands that I should now put this matter to rest. I have often intended for years back opening my mind to you. Now I have done it. I regret my folly, and, while I hope you will make this a matter of confidence, I beg your forgiveness."

August 1.—After keeping this letter for some days beside me I sent it out to my uncle at Garscadden. On the Monday he spoke about the painful matter with much calmness and said he was both disposed to forgive and forget it. The manner in which the whole of the matter has been arranged is gratifying to me. My mind is quite lightened by the payment of Mr. T—— and others. I have now a weight off my mind which I trust I may never again have imposed. I hope and trust that I am now delivered from much that irritated my temper and made me look morose and sullen in the eyes of others. What a down-draught on my spiritual course has this matter been. I hope I shall be more dutiful to everyone

August 4.—I regret that from a haughty carriage in receiving ——— after his return from the coast when we met . . . I have hurt that good man. I think he feels it to this moment, though I have endeavoured to remove that cold indifference at the time by subsequent attention.

September 22.—I have this evening visited the Spout-mouth. Some families in great distress. My uncle is stopping with me, being a juryman in the Circuit Court. Saw there two schoolfellows, John Millar and R. Kerr, in gowns and wigs. What a change a few years make! Yesterday signed the call to David Brown in presence of the presbytery. On the 14th went down with Michael Connal to Dunoon; bathed in the sea—quite a luxury. One of the finest days I ever beheld. The outline of every mountain peak was clearly seen in the pure atmosphere, the sweet-lying watering places were basking in the sun. Before dining with Mrs. D. Campbell visited "Malcolm's Glen," another "Shanklin Chine," as in the Isle of Wight. Very romantic. On the 8th I took a "breathing" for the sea, and went off by the 4.30 train to Ardrossan. . . . Went out next morning and bathed, and after breakfast went out with my cousin Helen and my mother in a boat to fish. Came home that night. The broad expanse of the ocean has great attractions for me.

October 30.—What is hell, but the principles of earth allowed full sway. . . . On Monday night Mr. Fleming kindly gave me the opportunity of dining with Mr. Wilson from Bombay, a man of intelligence and refinement.

December 25.—On Wednesday last, the 20th, I was chosen by the congregation, along with other twelve, to act as deacon. What am I that I should be an office-bearer in the Christian Church? What an awful thing to have a place in the visible Church and yet have no interest in her Living Head. I have been getting up every morning for the last two months at half-past six.

I have attended Dr. Reid's lectures on Civil History. I can thus, without interfering with the business of life, make some progress in my education.

1844.

April 8.—On Sabbath morning Mr. Brown preached from Canticles iii. 11. His discourse was very affecting. I was affected sometimes to tears.

May 6.—I began to attend Dr. Balfour's lectures on Botany. Deeply interested.

May 11.—Returned from a walk with my mother this evening. I have of late been out seeing poor N—— T—— in deep affliction. My cousin Helen dying. Do I fully realize this? I fear not. It is most painful to see the Spring in all its freshness, and the place where she is lying, full of beauty, and her life fading away.

May 15.—Went to-night to the Spoutmouth and gave, as a little encouragement to my Sabbath school scholars, presents of books.

June 12.—I have been so hurried and pressed in so many ways I have scarcely meditated on the Bible at all, morning or evening. The business of the Free Church of St. James's has been pressing and exhausting. My attendance on the Botanical Class has also been very pressing on my spare time.

September 7.—On Monday, 29th July, I was elected a member of the Botanical Society. Breakfasted with Dr. Balfour, Professor Babington of Cambridge, and Gourlay, after their return from Islay. Learned some songs at Garscadden. I am now looking forward to the winter, and I trust I may be able to work hard and fill up my time well. I have it in my heart to thoroughly educate myself. Why should I not, especially with the advantages I possess in a city like this?

September 10.—Yesterday evening, at six o'clock, the foundation stone was laid of Free St. James's Church. The office-bearers walked in procession to the site, and after a most solemn prayer by the minister, Mr. Peter

Ewing laid the stone, which now lies on the left hand of the entrance to the church.

October 12.—Dr. Nichol's lectures on Astronomy finished on Thursday evening. I have been very irregular of late as to rising and going to bed seasonably.

October 28.—On Monday evening called round upon various families in my district. I was interested in one family especially. How much real elegance and politeness and decorum there is in a family under the influence of religion, however poor.

November 16.—Attended Dr. Fleming's introductory lecture on Tuesday afternoon—Political Economy class.

1845.

January —On Friday, 27th December, attended a conversazione to Dr. Balfour. A very good and instructive meeting. I have got my cousin, Francis Wright Connal, to reside with me.

March 8.—On Monday last, circulars were issued formally announcing my connection with my uncle in business, along with Mr. Cochrane and my cousin William. Attending, every Wednesday, a meeting at Mr. Barr's to learn singing. I would have attended to-day, even though under great press of business, the examination of Dr. Fleming's class of Political Economy, but I thought I should not interfere with those to whom the honours that might be adjudged might be more useful academically.

March 12.—How various my employments often in the evening. Visited a Roman Catholic dying of consumption. Attempted to speak, but was put off with many excuses. Took up a missal and read a few verses of the 51st Psalm.

April 8.—Signed the petition against the grant to the College of Maynooth of £30,000.

May 23.—Had a long walk with my cousin Frank, which, I think, has done me good.

June 6.—I have some longings about being useful—some stirrings within me to great and arduous enterprise. I must not now be diverted from my business by anything else. . . . Walked in from Hamilton on the evening of the 2nd June, having seen Mrs. Beveridge at Captain Vaughan's. Walked through the Duke's grounds on our way home. A lovely evening. Went to the City Hall on Wednesday evening to hear the foreigners' addresses about the state of religion on the Continent. Dr. Buchanan, always a gentlemanly speaker, surpassed himself in introducing the Rev. Napoleon Roussell of Villefavard. D'Aubigné, a tall, powerful-looking man, with a full forehead and a deep voice, commanded the intense interest of the meeting.

June 10.—At home by myself; my mother and cousin at Garscadden. How I sometimes long for a friend—some affectionate, kindred spirit. I would seek to take God's will as my will. I feel now and then strong movings within me to be useful, to be more studious, to learn more, to fill up time better; but how much of self in this. Heard Dr. Chalmers on Sabbath. His allusion to the changes that had come over the congregation of St. John's since he had left was very touching.

June 24.—My mother, uncle, and aunt home from the Isle of Man, bringing Marion Gawne and her two pets with her. Have come home to-night from the botanical lecture—Dr. Balfour in his own rooms at the College—conversed afterwards freely with some medical students, and I feel how little my whole energies are directed to make a good use of time. I feel ashamed of my own want of knowledge. Their advance in various departments of science, their minds enlarged, their dignity as intellectual beings affected me, who have but few ideas, few noble thoughts. I have felt, more particularly in glancing over some of the letters of Dr. Arnold of Rugby, some [illegible] to be useful.

June 30.—Found J—— T——'s teacher to be a poor lad, struggling away, making a livelihood by teaching. Has passed through one winter at college, and is now preparing himself for another by reading Horace and Herodotus, and preparing for Logic. Up at three in the morning. What intense energy! Would that I could steadily and ardently thus devote myself! Offered him

me; but I feel that music, however sweet, cannot give peace to the soul.

November 4.—Miss M—— asked me to become a trustee over the £1000 sent home by her brother for female education purposes. Surely God has some work for me to do that I should thus early in life have such confidence placed in me. May I be kept humble.

November 25.—Went with my mother and Mrs. James Campbell to an amateur concert. The music very sweet. Many of the performers known to me. A glee by Calcott taken from a passage in Ossian, "Green Thorn of the Hill of Ghosts." Instrumental with John Millar, etc., in getting up a testimonial for Dr. Balfour on his leaving this for Edinburgh.

1846.

January 13.—I have been so busy that I have scarcely had time to write anything in this book. Heard Lord John Russell yesterday in the City Hall deliver an address in reply to the presentation of the freedom of the city. On New Year's Day went to call in the Spoutmouth on the woman Mackay; found that she had died that morning. Got a lesson not to speak harshly to those whom I visited. Was much pleased with the affection of the Roman Catholic woman, with whom she lived, for the deceased.

January 28.—Went to-night to the conversational meeting in Griffin's Chemical Museum. Much pleased with the new stereotype process, the electro-type casts from the daguerrotype plates, etc. . . . Felt the dignity of high purpose kindling within me; wished for some field of labour where I might work with all my energy. In coming home in the mornings from Fleming's class I have often interesting conversations with Guthrie. I have frequently of late had it in contemplation to set to work in getting up a good school and a regular system of visitation amongst the poor in that quarter of the Gallowgate lying between East Nile Street and Great

February 3.—Went into Edinburgh to attend the funeral of Miss A. Forman. Spent a few hours with that kind-hearted soul, Mr. R. B. Forman, at 2 Warristone Crescent. What a change comes over our friends in the lapse of a few short years.

February 4.—Learned to-day, with mingled surprise and satisfaction, that the congregation of Free St. James's had chosen me to the office of elder. I am younger than any of the rest.

February 28.—Had my uncle and aunt and other friends to dinner on the 26th—on the 27th a good many friends connected with the church. A very pleasant evening. To-night I have been obliged to spend the whole evening at my uncle's. The recommendation to spend the evenings very much alone has not been followed out in my case. I have before me the solemn prospect of being to-morrow ordained to the highest office which a layman can hold in the Christian Church. What must be expected from me? What consistency, what blamelessness, what faithfulness? How often have I marred my character by what is uncharitable?

March 1.—There are two views of religion which connect our holy Christianity with Christ Himself—objective and subjective.

May 2.—I have endeavoured this night to give myself to God. How prone am I to be "at ease in Zion." I live in a kind of dull daylight; there is no cheerfulness in me.

June 12.—Nothing of interest has occurred for some time past so far as regards myself, except a visit to Ireland. Went on Monday night at half-past nine on board the "Thetis." Called on various people in Belfast; went out to stay with Mr. Boyd—a pretty place. Dined next day with Mr. M'Clure, and with him and Mr. Lake visited the Botanic Gardens. Belfast a clean and interesting town.

July 4.—Walked out to-night with my mother's little dog "Trim." He gambolled on the road while I conversed with myself. How suitable a place for meditation is the road leading by the banks of the Kelvin from the mill to the public road. The shadowy trees, the low walls that line the road and yet shut one in that the mind may have freer scope, and the rush of the river over the embankment that crosses it, all lead the soul to meditate, and on such a night—calm, mild, the moon three-quarters full. I have just been endeavouring to get my soul into a right state. Time to meditate is very sweet when snatched from the manifold cares and annoyances of life. What a struggle life is! jealousy, deceit, pride, vanity, covetousness, censoriousness, impatience of spirit, idolatry of self in one form or another. How I have been depressed by the crosses which I am called on to bear. This depression of mind is natural to me. I am extremely sensitive, of a very subjective cast of mind, and of an indolent habit of mind. The want of sympathy with my habits, my views of things, distances me from others at once. I cannot trifle, and yet I see that human intercourse is not made up of earnestness. Passing shadows of worldly ambition flit across me. I should be content and humble. I am called to fill a certain station. I must abide till Providence opens up some other way for me. Reminded to-day by —— bitterly complaining of a paragraph inserted by me on business, that the world is not to be trifled with as to its interests, and that it is for me to study to be harmless with a good conscience.

July 5.—A thunderstorm breaking over my head; all the more fearful that little rain was falling at the time. How solemn and awe-inspiring the thunder, breaking out now and then until the heavens shook. The lightning very vivid. What is that lightning to His searching purity and justice? Dreamt in church about re-visiting Parkhall.

July 18.—On Thursday afternoon went to Stirling. Had some very pleasant intercourse with my cousins and uncle. Found my poor little bird dead in its cage that same morning before leaving for Stirling. A pet for more than seven years, hopping and chirruping. It was a silent cage now, and I sent it away. I was affected by the circumstance. Its dear little mistress was taken away more than five years ago. I have a sensitive and yet proud spirit. I cannot bear to play second fiddle to anyone. . . . Am I to return evil for evil? A meek and quiet spirit, what an ornament it is!

August 9.—After a quiet walk to-night my blood boils at the disappointments and vexations the state of things at present has occasioned me. I find that the kindest and most generous of dispositions naturally, has already become soured by the manifold petty annoyances which I have been experiencing.

September 4.—I seem almost as if I had exhausted all for which men ordinarily deem life worth having. Introduced to Dr. Chalmers; had some conversation with him. Shook hands with him at Castlecary and bade him good-bye.

September 8.—Found my cousins Flo. and William disposed to go to Aberdeen; sailed at four o'clock down the Forth. The castle and town seen again and again as if we had never left them.

September —Visit to Stirling; holiday thoroughly enjoyed. Paragraph in *The Guardian* referring to the appointment of Dr. James Thomson's son to the position of Professor of Natural Philosophy, Glasgow, in which by high authority he is represented as the first man of science of the rising generation in the country. That his writings, especially on electricity, had all attracted much attention in Paris, and that they were thought very valuable contributions to science. The struggle for the highest honours, political or scientific, is a cheat if the victory or the mastery of either is to be the ultimate good.

September 28.—How full of idols my heart is!—The world, domestic comfort, human sympathy, influence, vanity, —self in one form or another. What motive can actuate me to be diligent, active, hopeful, enterprising, availing myself of every advantage to self-improvement or advancement? Can the world supply it? I see how the way to all that is desirable in this world is beset with thorns.

1847—1849

February 13.—After an interval too long to recall all that has impressed me, I have to commence with what is mournful. The death of that hopeful youth, John Thomson, son of the Professor of Mathematics, is a solemn and affecting thing; full of hopes and ardent in the pursuit of truth. Lately I had the opportunity of meeting with his brother, the great mathematician—modest in his appearance. A very great throng of business has left me but little time to myself for several months. My mind left little opportunity of expanding at home on subjects congenial to my tastes. I took a good deal of interest in the City Hall Exhibition; I sent my Chinese pictures there and some other things.

April 10.—How easily could I be made, from what I often experience—if the curtain that covers the past were suddenly withdrawn—to possess the iniquities of my youth—indolence, vanity, malice, pride, and the works of the flesh of every kind.

June 7.—Attended church in the morning. In mourning for Dr. Chalmers—pulpit hung with black cloth. It is striking how general the regret is for his removal. He was raised up evidently for a great purpose. The most touching thing at his funeral must have been the poor little boys from the West Port with the tears in their eyes as the coffin passed them. His sudden death, however, created no other feeling in me than that his time was come like a shock of corn fully ripe.

June 19.—Felt a longing to go to see Parkhall some fine summer evening soon. I know that it will be full of melancholy associations, yet I cherish such. I am more of that temperament than of the bold, dashing cast. I have felt what care is of late. What a weary, heavy, trying thing it is to earn one's bread in the world! The state of France as to religion presents a wide contrast to our own present political state. Popery disgusts and alienates many of its adherents in that country.

June 29.—It is good to go to the houses of the poor and see how they struggle through with their difficulties. It puts to flight every shadow that may hang upon one's spirits. Visited an Irishman—a very specious fellow; I shall keep my eye on him.

July 5.—I put into execution my long-coveted intention of visiting Parkhall. I went out to Milngavie by the four o'clock coach and then took a gig to Balfron. Took a man of the name of Smith with me. Found that his father had been the individual who presented my father with the snuff-box, which I still have, on his leaving that part of the country, 18th July, 1828,—nineteen years ago. It was a pleasant drive. The evening was fine; my spirits were those of high and intense interest. Passed the enclosure where the deer were—a moor hemmed in by a stone wall—as if I had seen the place yesterday. Felt interested in the wild plants that grew along the hedges. I felt the value of knowledge as imparting an additional interest to a locality. These thoroughly country roads! Then when Killearn appeared in view, Buchanan monument towering above the village in the distance, I felt a strange, stifling sense of interest. Passed that, and then came a sight that I could almost have wished to return home than see, after going so far to see it. It was a painful sense of interest that wrung my heart. Oh, what changes have come over me since then—over mine! Twenty years ago I was there in all the buoyancy of youth, living only for the day. The same aspect the place bore at a distance, it had when I was there a happy child. I drove down past it. I almost feared to have another look of it. I met old Magnus Gunn. The old man did not at first know me. I drove up the road leading to that place that was once my father's. I found it changed in many respects. I walked into the drawing-room—the same apartment. Walked round the garden past the offices; drove up the road leading to the high road; bade good-bye to the place hallowed in my remembrance,—I did not dare to say for ever. I cannot tell what may be in the future. Twenty years have not made any changes of such consequence as to put my memory at fault. The road, the trees, the bridges, the running streamlets, are as fresh as if I had never been absent from them.

Drove on to the road over the water of Endrick; on to Balfron. One man very politely bowed to me as I entered the village. Called on a number of friends. The hills to the east cast a shadow, as it were, over the strath. The setting sun gave them a dark, deep, blue colour. . . . I had no idea that the country was so hilly and mountainous. Took up a poor umbrella-maker, who was glad to get a ride so far into the city. Got a good deal of information from him as to many things connected with the district. I came home to thank God that I had been permitted to see this place once more, to renew the dreams of youth, to recall long-buried associations, to learn a fresh lesson of the mysterious providence of God in sweeping a family away from a country-side altogether.

July 21.—I write at Garscadden. After considerable hesitation I made up my mind to go with Dr. Balfour to Arran. Left with Keddie by the three o'clock train for Greenock on Thursday the 15th, and met the Doctor and his party in the steamer. Arrived at Arran about eight o'clock. Found that the Grand Duke Constantine and his suite occupied the accommodation to be had at the inn, and after deliberation and some management the whole party, amounting to thirty, were provided for. A loft filled with hay was at first seriously spoken of as the only accommodation which one-half of the party could get. The party consisted of Dr. Balfour, Dr. Greville, Dr. Ransford, Alexander, Keddie, Ivory, Balfour, and a good many others. Had most intercourse throughout with Duncan (Yankee), Balfour (Colinton), Keddie, Alexander, Douglas (Prince Charles). Got a place cleared for us (the old court-house of the Island). After supper, or rather dinner, went out and sang and danced with Keddie, Yankee, and others. Oh, the flow of spirits! The calm evening, it must have been ten or eleven o'clock, the calm sea, the sky, the repose of the place, the quiet inn, with its solemn shades of trees, would have led under any other circumstances to a deeply meditative walk, but the excitement of the change of scene and circumstances and the presence of others rendered this out of the question. The Grand Duke's suite were moving in and out, and a certain air of mysterious interest was around the old inn.

After many jokes we turned in. It was not to sleep. The Yankee and the Blackie in one bed, but not without some misgivings, as Yankee afterwards assured us. I rose at three, never having closed my eyes in sleep. I bathed with Yankee. Went to bed again, but the sound of voices and the general stir soon roused me up, and I was on the hill with the rest at half-past seven. Had a most fatiguing pull up Goatfell. Found the Grand Duke and his party on ponies on their way up. Some of our party reached the top before them. The Grand Duke carved his name, partly with Keddie's geological hammer, on the rock, "КОНСТАНТІНЪ." Talked with a young man, who appeared to be one of the foreign nobles accompanying the Duke, about the plants, etc. Gave Ramsay's *Account of Arran* to Col. Gray to glance at. The Grand Duke, a young man of about twenty-five years of age, had tartan dress on; bracelet of torquoise on left wrist. He bade our party courteously, good-bye.

July 17.—Rose at six; bathed; started about eight along the shore. Met Balfour; sailed at four for Glasgow.

September 10.—I have lost my little dog "Trim." Poor little companion! He died under my mother's chair

matter of talk among those whose assembly I shun. O Lord, give me wisdom and grace to live every such report down! . . Trying times. But I am here, not to get some measure of light and comfort and then to go away, but to glorify God. I am not to be taken out of the world, but to be kept from the evil. I am to serve God as I am enabled through grace in my day and generation, until I fall on sleep. A calm feeling to-night. I feel as if I would turn over a new leaf and shine in my walk and profession brighter than before; but I can do this only through grace.

November 7.—How dark is the prospect over the nation, and over my own individual career. Moderate expectations of prosperity in this world blighted; means of usefulness abridged, cut down, as it were, to the water's edge. The vanity, the self-sufficiency, the cupidity of others having much to do with the trial. I feel sick at heart.

November 27.—I have been reading Miller's *Impressions of England and the English.* I have never read such eloquent remarks on geological phenomena.

December 1.—I have finished the perusal of that interesting volume by Hugh Miller. Truly, he is a remarkable man, for the force and liveliness of his illustrations and the purity and excellence of his language.

December 4.—Oh what a strange temper I have—reserved, keenly sensitive, proud, so proud that I would rather suffer than condescend to ask sympathy; how changed from the once full-hearted, happy boy! How much has of late years marred my peace of mind, and rendered me extremely irritable. I am sure that my mind must have suffered severely.

December 16.—Surely it is early to learn such trying lessons. My youth is drunk up. The world—I cannot accept happiness from it; it appears to be splendid misery. I think I may say that rather than run the risk of such trials again I would, shall I say go out of the world?—live by the daily wages of the mechanic. Farewell to those friends who could call me friend only in the hour of prosperity. Shall I ever be able to smile, and feel happy in a position agreeable to my mind? It may be so. But for that hope I would rather go out of the world. It is hell to think otherwise!

December 25.—Called during the last week to act as juryman at the criminal trials before the Lord Justice Clerk and Lord Wood. Sat for the first time on Tuesday last. I was struck with the responsibility of the position. . . . How many happy meetings to-night. A Merry Christmas! It closes in upon me with subdued and melancholy feelings. It becomes me to be useful in my day and generation, through good report and bad report, in season and out of season.

1848.

January 6.—My grand-uncle, William Glas, dead. I have read over the pages of this memorandum book since the beginning of the year 1847. "Vanity—all is vanity!"

February 11.—I have come home from a meeting at George Lyon's. Saw mosses and *lepaticæ*: most delicate creations. Talked with Dr. Arnott on the way home about Freemasonry. It would appear to retain many remnants of heathen mysteries.

February 15.—Heard Ralph Waldo Emerson last night in the City Hall on "New England: the Characteristics of its People." Very interesting; every word full of meaning; the very quintessence of thought; the style faultless.

March 11.—Many things to note down since I last wrote in this book. The young men forming themselves into companies and being drilled. I have been enrolled in the 8th Division. The riots on Monday and Tuesday very serious. On Tuesday at one o'clock it assumed a very threatening aspect. The French Revolution has given an example to the disaffected throughout the country. The aspect of things is ominous throughout Europe. . . . The strange aspect of things at the Cross—the flaring gas lamps, the soldiers, the crowds as they passed along, the body of special constables—struck me very much.

March 22.—Down at Greenock and Port-Glasgow to-day on business. A weary world! The fearful losses in every description of property, the ruinous rates for produce, the dissatisfaction and depression in the pursuit of my calling, make me often heavy at heart.

April 5.—Went through my district; found the people glad to see me.

April 23.—I am anxious to be useful to the young men in the congregation: O Lord, direct me.

May 6.—Took a walk on Tuesday with Keddie to Garscadden. A beautiful day. How susceptible I am! it is part of my nature.

May 23.—I have read Borrow's *Bible in Spain*. A want of interest as a whole about it. A narrative of adventure, with some vivid description, and a great deal of egotism. A man of considerable talent and energy;—there is a certain graphic power about his narratives that is very fascinating. On Saturday walked with William Kidston to Kilmardinny. A very fine evening, and a good deal of pleasant intercourse.

May 26.—At home, having been in Edinburgh on Wednesday evening. Went by five o'clock train. A glorious evening; rich fields; summer in all its glory. One short month has made a great change. Interested in the railway to Stirling. How panoramic the view approaching Falkirk. Went down to the Free Assembly. . . . Lay on a sofa in North Bridge Street. Did not sleep; a continual rumbling of carts all night. Got up at half-past five; went down to the Botanic Gardens. What a quiet morning; what a paradise to gratify the senses. The sweet song of birds, the gardens full of melody, the perfume, the rich luxuriance of the shrubs regaled me. Heaven is not so much a locality as a state of mind. I feel this most strongly. Without these walls how many anxieties, sorrows, cares, struggles; and yet within them a heart how deceitful. Saw Balfour; glad to see him. He took me through the various hot-houses, the palm-house,—the "skrewpine." Happy Balfour!—so enthusiastic in his profession; 180 students. Looked through his collection of things; very complete. Visited the Courts of Law and the Royal Academy. Went to the *Witness* Office to try to get a sight of Hugh Miller. He had just left when I got there. Came home by the one o'clock train in an hour and a quarter.

May 29.—Progressing with my scheme in the Spoutmouth.

June 25 (*Sabbath evening*).—O Lord, make me to be useful in my day and generation.

July 1.—Another week at a close. Went to-night to the room in my district. Newspapers in abundance for all that have as yet availed themselves of the privilege of reading them. Hung up a map of Paris, showing the locality of the massacre. Had Dr. Anderson lecturing on the "Eye" on Friday night. About thirty or so present, all much interested.

July 9.—A lovely night. How still! the western and northern horizon without a cloud; a subdued yellow twilight. These sunsets lead my thoughts out of the world. At Archibald Colquhoun's yesterday at dinner—three miles east of Glasgow. Much affected with a sight of the Bush people on Wednesday last with my uncle Wright. . Enable me, O Lord, to run in the way of Thy commandments, and as I have freely received to freely give, accounting talent, time, strength, means, friends, everything Thine. Oh, keep me humble; prepare me for trial.

July 17.—Out at Garscadden on Thursday last, the 13th; went into Edinburgh with Keddie. Found Dr. Balfour waiting for us at his new house; pleasant intercourse. Went to Botanical meeting: Dr. Fleming, naturalist, in the chair. Met Ivory, Wright, etc., and found in the whole aspect of the meeting and the elevating character of the intercourse, deep interest. Was witness to a most beautiful aspect of Edinburgh under the rays of the setting sun: the whole mass of buildings bathed in a deep red light.

August 14.—The world has to be chastened in its pursuit of gain. I can, I think, submit to that; but to doubt one's honour in the long run, to be exposed to the trial of the world's frown, to be unfortunate, and to leave the scoffer a triumph against the truth in one's own person that is very hard to bear.

September 30.—I feel happy to be at home to-night to get rid of the world for twenty-four hours at any rate. I have had many things to try my temper and spirit of late in the depressing state of matters, in the enmity of others, in the jostling, vulgar struggle for business, in the many trials of business, and otherwise—yet how full of mercy my cup is. The Spoutmouth concern getting on slowly. Dr. Robert D. Thomson, Keddie, James A. Campbell, there last night.

October 11.—Last week, one friend after another at our house to hear Jenny Lind. Monday, the 2nd, Uncle John Wright; Wednesday, 4th, Hamilton; Friday, 6th, Miss Burn, Keddie, and my mother went. I went to my district. On Saturday went with Miss Burn and my mother to the Museum, College, Library, etc. Got Dr. Couper to-day to give me some specimens of coral for the illustrations of Mr. Landsborough's lecture on Friday.

October 19.—Much to try me from the spirit of others, even in the attempt to do good. It is a time of heavy trial. How much need to walk softly, to forgive, to be patient, to be self-denying. Mr. Landsborough's lecture on Friday night on "The Formation of Coral Islands." A considerable number of friends at dinner with us to meet him. Breakfasted next morning at Gourlie's.

November 10.—Life with me just now is little better than endurance. What right have I to busy myself with things of one kind or another when so much trial and trouble is at the door. Found out "piassava" to be opaline. Dr. Arnott came over to-day to show it me in his book, after having spent an hour last night in the endeavour to find it out. Heard Keddie's introductory lecture on Friday last to a course of botany with interest. The Spoutmouth turned out well. . . . The anxious tenderness of my poor little cat for her kitten sometimes amuses me, and teaches me a lesson to be kind and affectionate.

October 29.—How much more precious is character than

December 16.—Often think that if I were out of my present position, I would be happier, and I have made no secret of that feeling. . . I am sure that I must often appear very unamiable to many people just from the irritation my temper undergoes in business. To be admitted a member of the Philosophical Society on Wednesday, 27th instant. Received kind letters from Sir W. Hooker, J. G. Fleet, Dr. Greville, enclosing reports of the Brighton Institution. .

December 23.—Talked with D—— C—— about principle in business, not only as to the mode of conducting it, but as to the business itself. A long, kind letter from Sir William Hooker about the museum at Kew.

1849.

January 8.—Dr. James Thomson, mathematical professor, died of cholera.

January 22.—Came home late and tired after being an hour and a half in the Spoutmouth. How many cases of extreme necessity and hardship! On Wednesday, at the Philosophical; had the electric light exhibited; very interesting. On 15th, made a member of committee of the Stirlingshire Charitable Society.

February 8.—Attended the funeral of poor ——— to-day. Buried not far from the most precious dust to me in this world. . . . Surely there is in some characters a great want of generosity that so recommends Christian character. O Lord, give me a spirit of self-denying generosity.

February 17.—Feel stunned to-day by the want of kindness and good feeling of ——. I shall endeavour, if it be possible, to be peaceable with all men—to wait upon God until He makes darkness light before me. Oh, it is more difficult to wait, I think, than to serve.

February 20.—Am I to give up what is good from temper, because others have so little sympathy with me in it? I feel cut to the quick at the insinuations of ——, and yet I see that nothing will please him but a surrender of all that either dignifies or refines the mind.

February 23.—What a hell upon earth misunderstandings cause. Seriously thought of going to the bar, but want of means and a thousand other considerations hedge up my path.

April 7.—Went with Keddie to Mr. T——'s, and saw a good many objects of interest from the Holy Land. Drank of the waters of the Jordan.

May 5.—How precious is character! Lord, keep me from whatever wears even the appearance of evil.

May 22.—On Friday evening, at the annual meeting of the Spout Institution; some interesting reports read. Rev. D. Brown, Bailie Playfair, James A. Campbell, and others present. A very gratifying meeting. On Tuesday, 15th, met a deputation of teachers, who addressed us about the education fund. On Saturday, 12th, visited the Cathedral with about thirty young men. Several splendid sacred tunes under the roof of the nave.

June 8.—On Saturday morning last, 2nd instant, started by 7 o'clock train for Edinburgh. Went to Roslin by half-past 10 train. Visited the chapel and castle, and walked to Dalkeith. Walked through the Duke's grounds. Magnificent trees; an aspect of undefined magnificence about the woods behind the gardens. . . I have been reading the lives of Alexander Peden and Robert Gillespie, martyrs of the Bass. May I have grace to honour and serve God faithfully in my day and generation.

August 11.—At Julien's concert to-night. The fine burst of music was very thrilling and the softer parts exquisitely beautiful. After all, I did not experience a great deal of pleasure. I cannot live upon sweet sounds. I must have something that bears upon the future to influence me; yet the taste for music should be cultivated as an instrument for good. Great preparations making for the Queen's visit; my uncle one of a deputation of Justices. This is my birthday; I am now entering upon my thirty-third year. Every year narrows my expectations as to the future. I may not seek great things for myself.

August 12.—I have read with great interest *Sir Thomas Fowell Buxton's Life*. The characteristics of this great man—power and love and a sound mind. How impulsive, weak, irresolute I am! how little disposed for exertion.

August 27.—The Queen and Prince Albert visited Glasgow on Tuesday, 14th instant. With my mother at the grand stand, West Street. My uncle presented to the Queen. Five hundred thousand people agog and not an accident, not a riot. It is surely an answer to prayer. Visited Bothwell Castle through Lord Douglas's kindness; a party of forty-three. Walked home with about thirty.

September 24.—On Friday morning, 14th, went to Stirling. Went that forenoon to Drummond Castle Gardens with my cousins; railway to Greenloaning; drosky to the gardens. Crieff, Comrie, Grampians, mist, beauty, and sublimity; gardens, statues, terraces, old battlements, long avenue of trees. What fun and joking, punning, etc. Home in time for dinner; music. Saturday—Tillicoultry; the Glen; a little botany; A. Browning's family; drive home. Sabbath—Mr. Beith on Romans viii. 19-22; a Boanerges. On Monday, 17th instant, was on the Castle Hill at eight o'clock; lovely morning. Took a view from every point of the compass of the rich valley laden with plenty—a glorious sight! Passed through a garden and paced up and down a retired terrace. The sound of the sergeants drilling the men, the awakening town, the placid Forth, the peaceful landscape, the silent mountains—all interesting. In the train for Glasgow by 10.30 A.M. Went out to the Observatory with W. Ramsay, brother to the geologist, and saw, through Dr. Nichol's courtesy, Saturn with his rings.

1850—1852

April 1.—Fairly set the Spoutmouth Library agoing. Appointed secretary of the proposed re-union of the pupils of the Rev. A. Browning, Tillicoultry; to meet on the 17th ultimo. I have been turning over in my mind the idea of going up to London to see the Exhibition of 1851, and taking some of the Spoutmouth lads with me, each of them to save in the meantime a sum equal to the expense of the passage up and down.

April 26.—I have just come home from giving the lads in the "Spout" an opportunity of seeing the "Destruction of Jerusalem by Titus"—a very magnificent picture. On Thursday, 18th inst., the Tillicoultry dinner passed off very well. Twenty-one present, inclusive of James Browning; a very pleasant evening. Dr. Eadie in the chair, with James Morrison croupier. A list made of all old pupils as far as could be ascertained.

May 27.—Fished up two lads that had hitherto escaped me, and I think it probable they may be induced to join the class. One, a gardener, seems to be an intelligent lad. Lent him a book on trees. I am more and more convinced that good will come out of the Spoutmouth Institution. The annual meeting on Friday, the 17th, was interesting. Got John Thomson despatched to the botanical lectures at the College through Dr. Arnott's kindness.

May 31.—Went to Edinburgh. At the Assembly; heard the whole proceedings with much interest. Mr. Anderson's (Madras) speech very good; Dr. Duff's courageous, but diffuse. Some most interesting views about caste

June 19.—The heart-distressing news of the loss of the "Orion" steamer on her passage from Liverpool, and within a hundred yards of the shore of Portpatrick, on a fine summer night, or rather morning. About a hundred persons supposed to have perished. The news stunning; the Exchange crowded and anxious both yesterday and to-day. Old Dr. John Burns amongst those drowned.

July 10.—The death of Sir Robert Peel a solemn lesson.

July 17.—Went down to Ayr on Friday evening with Dr. Blair, etc., and about fifteen lads from the "Spout." Visited Burns's Cottage; entered the names of a few of the party there. Walked on the Blairstone Mains; a lovely evening. Slept in the barn; arose after a night of indifferent rest, about three o'clock. Walked through the parish of Auchendrain—a very lovely spot; fine trees, a most exquisite fragrance from the fields of wild flowers; bathed not far from Mount Greenan Castle. . . The commercial Exchange with its widespread ruinous embarrassments a fearful example of men falling into the lust of money and gain.

July 27.—The Rev. P. Rajah Gopaul in the house with me to-night. The conversation of a most interesting character. On Monday last went to Loch Lomond with "Spout" lads. Arrived at the head of the loch about eight o'clock. Dr. Arnott, Dr. Scoular, etc., with me. Ascended next morning to the top of Ben Voirlich. A Swiss gentleman gathering insects; discovered that he held infidel views. He confessed that he would be sorry that anyone held the same views; they were so sad. A fine night; went out with James Stevenson, Jun., to a waterfall about 80 feet high. Sang, "Come, come, come," and other things; roared and talked till I was exhausted. The silent hills in their majesty. What an ocean of mountains presented themselves before us from the top of Ben Voirlich, with the mist driving along their summits. I would try to carry away the majesty of that view. Much invigorated—the bleating sheep on the hills, the quiet loch, and the passing shadow on the hillsides. Started next morning for Inversnaid; visited Rob Roy's cave. The damp grass and the rain soaking through the trees completely drenched me. Reached it and got no further than the entrance; a very hazardous experiment altogether. Walked over to Loch Katrine and washed my hands in the loch; six miles across; almost constant rain. Much the better of the change of air and the exercise. Learned a lesson to-day about meddling with boys on the street. Shook a little fellow for thrashing a girl and inadvertently kicked him. Got no thanks, but was likely to get into words with rude, low people. I hope to try to do good, cautiously avoiding notice. How the world lays hold of anyone who may be dragged into notoriety. To do good quietly, without much being said about it, is the object I ought to aim at.

August 2.—How time passes silently but sternly. It cannot be recalled or caused to slacken its pace. Yesterday at the Cattle Show in the Green and in the evening at the dinner. The noblemen, etc., generally young, untried men—Duke of Roxburgh, Duke of Argyle, Marquis of Douglas, Lord Blantyre, Sir M. S. Stewart—men whose claim to consideration in a great measure lies in their great possessions and hereditary honours. Pleased with the Duke of Argyle's speech. The Duke of Montrose spoke well. A considerable number of other noblemen and gentlemen there. As a means of stimulating agricultural improvements, good. Found Rajah Gopaul there. He expressed himself interested in seeing so many men of whom he had heard, whether as to themselves personally or their ancestors. Preferred the quiet walk with —— on the preceding evening. Walked to the old Roman Bridge; very lovely evening; a star above it. Rowed on the Clyde to Bothwell Bridge.

August 3.—Last night at Garscadden. Reflected on the true dignity and happiness of life: not in the possession of honours or wealth, but in the honest out-putting of whatever talent, influence, energy I have, in what commends itself to my conscience as right. The vanity of my mind makes me too often anxious to live for display. Let me consider that I am here to carry on my business for

Christ; yes, for Him. How kindly, how honourably, yet scrupulously honest, how disinterested should I be—a business carried on for Him in a dark world, where there are jealousies and heartburnings, and ingratitude and hatred, and censoriousness and heartless rivalry—and to be carried on to recommend His cause. How often have I shown a pitiful spirit. O Lord, give me grace to walk so as to please Thee.

August 17.—The poor lads of the Spoutmouth at Garscadden on the 10th August. They sang very well, and walked home in good spirits. My birthday on the 11th inst.; did not sleep much that night.

August 20.—I have been tempted to despise the meanness and ingratitude of men. What is man? How has God borne with me! How, it may be, are fellowmen bearing with me! A high motive always present to my mind is the sure preservative of a peaceful serenity of spirit. . . . The Spoutmouth engages much of my time and thought.

September 3.—At dinner to-night at William Ferguson's; met Mr. Charlesworth. Strange that after being in his company for about two hours I began to think that I had seen him in the Thompsons', which proved to be the case.
Went by steamer to Lamlash—Major Martin, Dr. Landsborough, etc. Rather rough; the sensation anything but pleasant to me. Brodick in all its grandeur. Met Dr. Balfour out in a boat near Lamlash Bay. Dredged with him from twelve till four. A sail up now and then, and rather unpleasant from the boat leaning to one side. Found nothing very remarkable. Returned to Ardrossan by four—very rough and unpleasant.

September 21.—Managed to get thirty tickets for Dr. Scoular's lecture on Saturday, the 28th, from William Kidston—a battle to get them.

October 10.—My uncle chosen Dean of Guild on the 8th October—an honourable office, to which he has been elected unanimously. . Newspapers full of the bold and insolent attack on the Protestantism of England by the Pope in the creation of Dr. Wiseman, Cardinal Archbishop of Westminster. I have no confidence that the policy of Rome will be defeated by this hasty step; it may end in the more thorough separation of the Romanising party and the Orthodox party in the Church, and eventually in the destruction of the Establishment. Popular opinion, unless under the influence of the truth, is a sandbank. I have been pressed in spirit to purchase the Dovehill Church. I think that schools could be opened there to advantage. I do think that it is my duty to turn to the next great means of the elevation of that district of the city in the institution of a school. I know that it will cost me labour and trouble, but I have undertaken the adventure knowing that I have many opportunities to accomplish successfully *now* what I may not have at a future time. I pity the cold selfishness of some so-called Christians. Nothing but earnestness will do. Devotedness of purpose is the characteristic of Rome; why not of Protestants?

December 3.—I purpose to go to London to see friends whom I have not seen for eight years; to examine for myself some of the growing philanthropic schemes of London. I think I may employ ten days very profitably there.

December 19.—I have seen much in London that shocks me out of the usual habit of thought and feeling. In the overwhelming masses of that great Modern Babylon, with their ten thousand thousand different interests, a stranger is thrown back upon his own unimportance. There is a loneliness amongst the crowds that swarm through the streets, and a friend is more attractive where nearly every face is that of a stranger. O God, they are Thy creatures, made for Thy glory; nothing else almost makes me feel kin to them. I felt an elation of spirit in seeing old faces and visiting places full of old associations that was cheering to my mind and body. My mind had become more mature, my knowledge of the world and of the purposes of life had been strengthened by the reading and intercourse of eight years since I last saw London, and there were yet friends to whom I could unbosom myself, who could remember me as a dreamer and a youth of ardent mind, just entering on manhood. I think that there is one lesson I must try to learn: if others be rude and inconsiderate why should I?

I left home on the 6th December, at nine P.M. Struck on my way up with the wonderful change railways have wrought. Saw several young gentlemen at Rugby ready for hunting; everyone looked as if he had come out of a bandbox,—it struck me they were effeminate looking. Arrived in London about two o'clock; a strange fluttering at my heart. Drove to the "Tavistock." Struck with the crowd and overwhelming masses of human beings and vehicles—everyone driving on. It was a picture of the world. And yet this mighty mass could be agitated as in a storm by some great question of public interest. Saw the Rev. William Faithful, and when I stepped out of the omnibus struck with my umbrella over the back my very old friend, R. B. F., who was surprised to see me. Saw my cousin Michael [eldest son of Patrick Connal]. Dined at the Conservative Club—very handsome lobby. Went that evening to hear a concert at the Opera House. Went next morning to St. Paul's; much impressed with the service. Went to Westminster Abbey; venerable pile; heard service, but was not pleased with it as compared with that of St. Paul's. Went to Ragged School Union and gathered information as to the localities of schools. Visited the Ragged Dormitory, St. Ann's Street, Westminster; (thirty-one burglars); much pleased. Passed the new Houses of Parliament. Not much struck with the general style of the building, but when the great tower is up the effect may be very different. Next morning to Brighton. How full of exhilaration of spirits to see old friends [Thompsons]. How new, how pleasant, how gratifying these sensations of welcome. Drove with William and Esther to the cliff, and walked for a short time on the beach. . . . On Friday went to Kew: saw Sir W. Hooker, the Palm House, etc. Expected to have been accompanied by Sir Richard Brown, whom I accidentally met on Sunday, but he was unwell. Went by myself in the evening to the Field Lane Ragged Schools. Taught a class there for half-an-hour. The place full of thieves. Lord Ashley came in and I had the privilege of talking with him for some time about such institutions. Ventured to speak of the Spoutmouth. Struck with the desperate-looking characters there; some as old as twenty to thirty; the greater proportion being younger persons of both sexes. Came home delighted.

1851.

January 6.—I have returned from a short run to Stirling. . . . Life is not to be spent in that which is frivolous; it has a purpose for which we must answer to God. I would pray to spend and be spent in His service.

January 25.—Very tired and exhausted, yet find a Saturday night at home very soothing. Received a letter from Mr. T—— about a Bible Institute which he has started in imitation of the "Spout"; very gratifying. The meeting of the "Spout" on the 17th very interesting. Upwards of fifty young men present. Some of the remarks of the young lads were very much to the point and fitted to do good.

May 14.—Engaged in winding up the affairs of the Glasgow Gaelic and English Schools Society. It is a singular coincidence that the Youths' Auxiliary Society was instituted in September, 1817, and that I should now be engaged in burying it. It is to a month as old as I am.

May 24.—The annual meeting of the "Spout" passed off well. I have been tempted to think, why weary myself with it? Yet I should think, when anxious for my own improvement, of those who, but for that humble institution, would be without many sources and opportunities of improvement, and that I am responsible for the many blessings I enjoy.

June 8.—At Garscadden on Friday night. Took a walk with my uncle in [the] wood that lies to the north of Garscadden; full of wild flowers—red, purple, pink, white. A calm evening, and the sight of the country did me good.

June 15.—I am sensitively alive to the injury, real or supposed, of others towards me. Too feminine in my cast of mind; not of that rough, rugged cast of mind of others; of a retiring, yet proud, haughty spirit.

June 29.—A Sabbath day of excessive heat. Went with Dr. Andrew Anderson to the Eye Infirmary in Charlotte Street; saw about thirty patients. Much impressed with a sense of the value of sight. Thought of the Saviour's commission to open the eyes of the blind. Have I sight? What a privilege! what a responsibility!

July 9.—Went to Kinross [to funeral of Mrs. Stedman]; found my mother there. Sad the whole way; sadder still when those with me had no sympathy with the bereaved. My cousin, William Wright, chief mourner. Followed the hearse to the romantic burying-ground on the banks of the loch immediately opposite the castle. The Stedmans appear to have been resident in Kinross about three hundred years. It was strange to notice the many circumstances that identified Mrs. Stedman with the district, and with a past as well as a present generation. She has died at the age of eighty-five, having lived sixty-one years under the same roof, respected and esteemed by all. She was an old, old friend of my mother's. The medical man, Dr. Gray, thirty-seven years going about the house, the trustees thirty years, and the man of business upwards of thirty years connected with the family. What a break-up! what a change! Yet how soon will it all be forgotten, and a life spent thus tranquilly and unobtrusively as Mrs. Stedman's will be remembered by but a few who valued her as a friend, or who shared her little bounties. Called in at Mr. Browning's for a few minutes. He was looking old, but seemed to be much of the same spirit as ever—an independent thinking man.

July 18.—Obliged to destroy our poor little dog "Gipsy" from fear of hydrophobia. I feel as if I had lost a companion.

August 21.—I have spent the evening at Dr. Walter Arnott's in company with Dr. Joseph Hooker, Gourlie, and Keddie. Very glad to see Hooker, and we had some very pleasant reminiscences. Heard Father Gavazzi on Monday, the 18th, in the City Hall. On the 16th at Garscadden with the ladies—a wet, soaking night.

September 13.—Made a member, on Friday night, the 5th, of the Natural History Society of Glasgow. Became also, about ten days ago or so, a member of the Glasgow Benevolent Society.

September 24.—I cannot tell; it becomes me to be very humble, but I think that God has some work for me yet. . . . What is business but a complicated web of hazard and vexation.

November 27.—I have come home this afternoon from the wedding at Ormidale.[1] Went with the bridegroom and the friends on Tuesday morning at 11 o'clock by steamer; a lovely day. The Kyles of Bute lovely, and the drive to Ormidale enchanting. The marriage ceremony over, the tenants and party, with the piper, took a short cut to meet the carriage with the pair, and afresh cheered them. Guns fired, reverberating through the valley. Dancing in front of the house; Highland hospitality and gaiety. Glendaruel and his children, etc. . Much struck with an old woman of eighty-seven at the wedding.

December 5.—How difficult for a young man to influence men of mature years and reputed great experience in pursuing the safest and most expedient course.

1852.

February 25.—The whole commercial interests of the country are undergoing a sifting, and at the same time a levelling, process. Men are becoming poorer because adventures are unremunerative. Is this to be traced to Free Trade?—to a government that has thrust upon the country an ill-adjusted measure, and taken no pains to adjust difficulties? At a meeting in Dr. R. D. Thomson's to-night. These scientific re-unions are very pleasant, but they suit a cast of mind that is very dissimilar to that required in large and comprehensive undertakings. Saw the circulation in the foot of a frog; very beautiful.

[1] William Connal, of Solsgirth, married Emelia, second daughter of Colonel Campbell of Ormidale.

April 8.—Life cannot be to me full of much that can make me wish it to be prolonged if things go on as they have been going. Happiness dragged at the wheels of other people's temper and wishes and objects;—yet I may live in hope.

May 26.—On 24th June the anniversary of the Battle of Bannockburn is to be celebrated by the Stirlingshire Charitable Society, by walking to the field in procession. I have had some thoughts of revising, for publication, my poem on the battle. I fear, however, that I must let it alone. The fascination of adapting pleasant pictures to verse is apt to lead my mind away from close attention to the details of business.

June 24.—Accompanied the Glasgow Stirlingshire Charitable Society to the field of Bannockburn, which I visited with much interest, and witnessed the games afterwards in the old romantic green close to Cowan's Hospital. I published, after some misgivings, my poem on Bannockburn, and find that, like all poems, it gives no encouragement to repeat the dose.

August 9.—I have read to the young men, who have formed themselves into a society for the prosecution of the study of entomology, a letter from Miss Beavor, Ambleside, which is encouraging, enclosing a letter from the artizan who was, at the time she formed her acquaintanceship with him, pursuing the study of moths and butterflies in the midst of many difficulties. The poor fellow in earnest. The previous evening at Greenfield. On the Monday following away out by myself to Tollcross to look for the leguminous plant—the *ornithopus*; I found it, to my great delight.

September 15.—I had an excursion to Craigenglen, Campsie, on Saturday, 28th August, with W. Kidston. Met John Young and another young man out there, and was very much interested in what they pointed out of the

Lord Belfast read the address. Present—Mr. Whiteside (who, I understood, was counsel for O'Connell), Solicitor-General, and a great many great folks. Went in the evening to the meeting of the Association for the Advancement of Science. Thursday found my name unexpectedly included in the committee of Section D, — I daresay at Dr. Arnott's suggestion. Attended at the committee and had Prince Buonaparte pointed out to me. Saw the flower show at the Botanic Gardens. On Friday, 3rd September, said a few words on the paper by Dr. Royle on the "Tea Plant." Dined at the *table d'hôte*, and had some amusement with Sir John Ross, who, from extreme deafness, returned thanks for the "Army and Navy" to the toast of the "British Association." Was introduced to Dr. Curdie, who turned out to have been one of Dr. William Cowper's geological class in 1833 or so. Said he remembered the voice. A river in Australia called after him. Early next morning went to Ballymena, Round Tower of Antrim, Lough Neagh in the distance. Mail coach to Coleraine. Recognized plants as we went along; Dr. Balfour and Keddie with me. Hired a car for the Giant's Causeway. Pleased on the whole with the aspect of the country, yet a great want of farming. Beset by boatmen and guides at the Causeway. Hired a boat and went into one of the caves. The sea smooth as glass. A glorious day. The Causeway did not strike me with wonder; the whole coast of the same character. On Wednesday went to Cave Hill to gather some plants and fossils. Drove on to "Giant's Ring" (with a wild fellow of an Irishman for a driver), an interesting relic of Pagan times. The whole of my visit to Ireland full of pleasant associations. Struck with the thriving aspect of Belfast, and with the richness of the country. I had the opportunity of seeing Archbishop Whately, Sir W. R. Hamilton (astr.), the Rev. Dr. Robinson, Prof. Phillips, and the Rev. Dr. Hincks.

November 18.—I had the great pleasure of hearing Hugh Miller last night—a man of genius; and to-night Isaac Taylor on "Hebrew Poetry"—a profound thinker and nervous writer; some of the ideas he elaborated very

1853—1861

1853.

January 6.—I this day received intimation that I have been elected a director of the Chamber of Commerce and Manufactures in Glasgow.

January 18.—Dined yesterday with the Stirlingshire Society. My uncle[1] more than usually disposed to speak.

January 23.—Mrs. John Scott, Hyde Park, London, dead. I wrote Mr. Scott, a friend, since 1835, whom I shall ever gratefully remember.

January 31.—Sir Richard Brown in town just now, and trying to get people interested in his peat scheme.

February 22.—My mind taking a more decidedly practical character.

April 16.—I have been elected a Commissioner to the General Assembly by the Presbytery of Glasgow. The election took place about three weeks ago. I consider it a high honour, and I hope that any influence which I may thereby acquire may be exercised for the cause of God. . . . I cannot condescend to what is mean, and I hate all coarseness and indelicacy of mind. Mrs. Beecher-Stowe, the authoress of *Uncle Tom's Cabin*, in town. I have not as yet seen her. I hope that nothing may be done to or by her to injure the cause of the slave, or to protract the emancipation of that unhappy and degraded race. Much interested in a picture by De la Roche of "The Condemnation of Marie Antoinette." Through the kindness of Mr. M'Clure, the print-seller, intend to show it to the "Spout." A noble specimen of art.

April 26.—On Saturday last went with Keddie to the

[1] William Connal.

Botanic Gardens in the evening. Searched and found the *Draba verna*, on a dyke leading up to the Observatory, by moonlight.

April 28.—At a great Protestant meeting in the City Hall; struck with the fine earnest countenances of young mechanics. On Friday at School of Design with the [Spoutmouth] lads.

May 23.—Went into Edinburgh to fulfil my duties as member of Assembly. Met Dr. Fowlis and talked with him about refreshment rooms for the working classes. Tuesday being the Queen's birthday I went with Keddie, etc., to John Knox's house, and saw a good many interesting things in it. I saw from the stair the procession of the Commissioner pass. I then strolled up part of Arthur's Seat and behind Holyrood House, and dined at the "Rainbow." Talked with Keddie till past four A.M., and then went to bed. Introduced to Hugh Miller on our way down to the House—a man coarsely dressed, on his way down to see the fire (Adelphi Theatre burned). Breakfasted with the Moderator on Thursday morning. A kind of *levée* before the breakfast.

July 10.—The walks I take with the young men of the "Spout" very pleasant to me. My botanical attempts give me hope and pleasure;—the young men seem interested.

July 19.—Left on Friday evening by steamer with thirty-nine of a party. In the morning at six o'clock or so on Dumbarton rock; handled Wallace's sword. Left by train and steamer for Inverarnon; the curling mists along the hills very beautiful; the frequent heavy showers swelled the mountain torrents into cataracts. Arrived about five o'clock or so—wet to the skin. Soon in bed in the straw of the barn; twenty-one in the barn. An old yew tree in the place said to have sheltered King Robert the Bruce. . . . An expedition in which all were delighted. Tone of my mind fresher and my general health better in consequence. The stupendous mountains, the calm, deep lake, the majestic rolling curtains of mist, spoke of God.

August 20.—I have seen to-day the corner shop at Watt Street—a whisky shop—the very place I wanted as a coffee shop. There seems some strange trial in this. Very heavy at heart. I know that I need to be kept humble, but I would fain have my own way.

September 3.—The cast of my mind is very susceptible of what is fitted to cast down. My aim should be to serve God in my day and generation. I must soon fall asleep, but let me rather wear out than rust out. I hear of the success of others, of their taking a position in the public eye. I don't want to lay myself out for that, for I think there is much that is contemptible about the tendency of mind that loves to fill that position. Yet public spirit is a noble thing. I feel my mental weakness: I want grasp and go-ahead energy. I think sometimes that an opening may occur to give full scope to my energy of mind and character, if I have any. Again the restraint, the depression, the want of aim and purpose that I find often with me make me think that the particular business I am in at present is not to be the one I am to follow. There are three things that I feel called upon to pursue without a pause—the Spoutmouth Bible Institution, the Bell Street School, Calton, and the Chinese Society.

September 17.—I left Glasgow on the 9th. When once fairly past the Kyles of Bute I felt relieved. I was getting quit of all associations. A beautiful day. Walked along the banks of the Crinan Canal. The sight carried me back to old times—say 1826 or so. On board the steamer on Saturday, 10th September, at seven A.M. The Sound of Mull, Dunolly Castle, etc., beautiful scenery. Dr. M'Leod of Morven; Staffa in the distance; a haze that gave all the more interest to the view. I wish that I had been there (Staffa) alone. A mixed feeling of solemn awe, and a desire that others may share in the feeling. Picked up a few plants as a memorial. About two o'clock drew near Iona. I think I felt somewhat of the sentiment of Dr. Johnson—I felt a solemn sense of my own unfitness, and yet of veneration for the piety and devotedness which had been embalmed on that spot—the nurse of the truth in the darkest gloom of the Middle Ages. I have not got over that feeling yet, and

height of seventy feet or so (the rainbow reflected in the spray)—a sight well worth the hazard of the descent to it and of a visit to this part of the island. Bade farewell to interesting Iona, carrying a few plants and a few stones as a remembrance. Sailed at eleven o'clock P.M. The magnificent steamer rocked a little, but swept on her way. Jura, Islay; the moon obscured; the silent stars; I was alone as a passenger on deck at two o'clock A.M. Got up early to see the Mull; Machrihanish Bay; red streaks in the east; swell heavy; fresh breeze; the extreme point of the Mull Lighthouse; very heavy sea between it and Arran; glad to get into quiet water.

October 1.—I feel honoured in being the secretary of a society which now commands some share of public attention (Chinese Society). Heard Lord Palmerston on Tuesday last deliver a speech. I was not struck with it, but it was interesting to see a hard-worked minister of the Crown—a man so well known throughout Europe for his decision, liberality of mind, and high courage.

October 29.—The Chinese Society inviting me to fresh labours. The "Spout" becoming more important and onerous.

November 4.—The young men of the Spoutmouth Bible Institution presented me with a very handsome copy of Blackie's edition of the Bible—a useful and handsome gift. I attempted to give some idea of what I would be at in the further progress of the institution. I said that, valuable as it (the Bible) was as the token of their regard, it would be ten-fold more so as the pledge that they would help me to carry out the purposes of the institution, and help me to elaborate the idea which is aimed at by it.

December 14.—Went to-night with Mr. Thomas M'Clure,[1] of Belfast, to the exhibition of pictures in Dixon Street. Pleased with the sight of the "Rarotonga Chief"—a fine young man. On the 30th November at the public dinner of the West of Scotland Guarantee Association. Asked by Sir James Campbell to give the toast, "City of Glasgow and Trade of Clyde," which I could not refuse, though most

[1] M.P. for Belfast 1868-1874; created a Baronet 1874.

reluctant. Attempted to make a display. I am more and more anxious to be quietly useful than to attract notice. The applause of men very hollow.

1854.

January 24.—I have made repeated attempts to sit down and write what has interested me, but fatigue or engagements of one kind or another have prevented me. Renewed my former happy associations in a visit from Mr. R. B. Forman and his amiable wife. . I hope the correspondence opened up with William Thompson [London] as to the vacancy in the governorship of an establishment for juvenile delinquents may lead to something for W—— R——.

February 25.—Followed my uncle (Patrick Connal) to the grave on Tuesday, 14th inst. Glanced with my uncle John[1] at one or two gravestones immediately after the last offices were over. Heard to-day of the Government grant of £400 to the Bell Street School. I have some difficulties in connection with the Education Bill now before the country, introduced by Lord Advocate Moncrieff on Thursday last.

March 4.—Heard of Dr. James Thomson's death—a truly good man; one who urged me to become the secretary of the Chinese Society. The approach of war —the collision is not far distant—fills me with a solemn view of the future. Dr. Balfour kindly remembers me with a present of his new work on Botany.

March 15.—I have had an unexpected visit to London. On Monday rather alarmed to find my uncle [W. Connal] unable to go to Liverpool from illness. In the train that night strange mixture of thoughts in the prospect of seeing friends whom I had not seen for some years. I left Liverpool on Wednesday for London. Welsh scenery very interesting. Oxford; was much struck on waking up to find two gownsmen at the train. Arrived in London at 10.15 and drove to Wood's Hotel. Sallied out next morning with strange old associations revived. Went to William Thompson's trig place at Wimbledon Common. On

[1] John Wright.

Saturday went to Houses of Parliament. Very gorgeous, and interesting as concentrating the legislative wisdom of the country. Saw Mr. Chester at the Privy Council Office, at Downing Street, about Bell Street School. At 1.30 P.M. on my way in the train to Redhill. Visited the Philanthropic Farm. Much interested; but apparently expensively conducted. Spent a quiet, pleasant evening at Betchworth. On Sabbath went to Brockam Church, built by Mr. Goulburn under most interesting circumstances. His deceased son's dying request was that he should build it. The young man's college companions assisted. How sweet an English village! In coming home, passing through the lovely grounds of Mr. Kirkpatrick, crossed the Mole—"the sullen Mole." (Monday) —Bade adieu to the lovely neighbourhood of Betchworth, its swelling downs, its rich old trees and landscape. After an anxious busy day amidst much that oppresses from its vastness and wonderful variety of human condition, in the train for Glasgow at a quarter to nine P.M. Found how much alone I would be without friends in London when passing from London Bridge to Hungerford Bridge by water; not a face known to me. Regent Street, with its rolling chariots, depressed me. How much show; it may be how little happiness.

May 4.—Heard on the 1st inst. of the sudden death of poor little Alice Gawne[1] at Villa Marina. Found dead in bed. My uncle left on the 2nd for Moffat; I hope that he may get better: he is breaking down.

June 19.—Set out for Kinross with my mother, to be present at Mrs. Lennox's marriage with Mr. Williamson at Kinross. Met my Uncle John, etc., at Stirling. Walked along the shore to Loch Leven. Stood for some time within a mile of the castle on the north-east shore. My uncle apparently in the best of spirits. On Saturday took the lads of the Spoutmouth to Linlithgow. Strange that during the same week I should have been in places so widely apart associated with the name of Queen Mary.

[1] Daughter of Edward Gawne of Ballagawne, Isle of Man, and Marion

July 7.—Kossuth in town. I did not go to hear him, though doubtless an eloquent man and a patriot; but his visit ill-timed.

August 14.—Yesterday St. James's Free Church opened by Sir H. W. Moncrieff, Bart. The alterations, painting, and decorations beautiful. In the afternoon at the Ragged Schools, and found the exertion of trying to fix the attention of 130 boys too much for me. Struck to-day by seeing the death of Lord Jocelyn in Lord Palmerston's house, from cholera, after an illness of a few hours.

September 3.—Received a copy of the new edition of Gutzlaff's New Testament about ten days ago. Strange that I should have to do in any measure with sending the New Testament to the Chinese when my father brought home the first copy (Dr. Morrison's[1] translation) to this country more than thirty years ago as a present to a friend of Dr. Morrison's.

September 22.—Eliza Connal married at Garscadden to Dr. Gibson on Tuesday, the 19th inst. I hope that it may be a happy union. Read of the death of Mr. Pike, the author of *Persuasives to Early Piety*, the book which I read in 1835. He appears to have departed within the last ten days, at his study table, the pen in his hand and his spectacles on his face undisturbed, while his head rested on the desk.

October 14.—On the morning of Thursday last went to Stirling to Miss Burd's funeral.[2] This death, which is taken notice of in the *Stirling Observer* of 12th October. is a striking one—a link with the remote past broken. Ninety-four years of age. I think my mother will miss her more than any of the rest. She was a favourite of hers [Miss Burd's] and her brother's when a little girl. Captain Stevenson married Miss Oliver from Devonshire, who had an only daughter, Frances Stevenson. She married William Wright of Broom, whose family con-

[1] Robert Morrison, the first Protestant missionary to China. Sent out by London Missionary Society, but he acted as the servant of the East India Company. In 1813 he completed the translation of the New Testament.

[2] Niece of Captain Stevenson.

sisted of my Uncle John, the present Wright of Broom, my Aunt Frances, and my mother, Eliza.

November 11.—How much do I feel the value of having a constitution for the Spoutmouth Bible Institution; it will outlive me and my individual teaching.

December 2.—The fearful struggle in the Crimea absorbing public interest. O God, may the cause of truth prevail. There is a moral force in the attitude of Great Britain in this struggle that is sublime. There must be overturnings, overturnings till a highway is made for the Prince of Peace. I have thought that there is a close connection between the religious training and associations of home and the firm, independent position of our troops. They know the keen, universal interest of the Christian community in them and the issue of the struggle, and the strong sympathy with them in it. The 93rd Highlanders have done well. I am not called to engage in such a struggle, but I believe I have an important work at home. O God, strengthen me for it. . . . I begin to think how humble I should be in my knowledge of character. How readily I have mistaken character and capacity where my friendships were intimate. I should also distrust my own capacity. I am disposed to think too highly of myself. Luxurious ease not suited to me. I must be doing something that has a bearing on what is for the good of others, or for my own personal improvement.

December 9.—Solicited an interview on Friday morning with Mr. F. D. Maurice. Had half-an-hour's conversation with him on the subject of his Working-Men's College.

December 16.—Spent an hour with Maurice on Wednesday. Heard him on Thursday evening. Nebulous in his views; he has much yet to do to resolve them into bright, clear points.

1855.

January 20.—On the first January tried to visit the "Powerful" (84 guns) at Greenock. Tom Gawne[1] with us. On the eighth, at the Panorama of Hindostan—for one penny—a successful experiment. At the House of

[1] Son of Edward Gawne of Ballagawne, Isle of Man.

Refuge annual meeting. The post-boy's verses read by the Sheriff; the manly statement of Deacon-Convener Craig. On the fourth went with John Henderson of Park to Penny or Half-penny Theatre to see about the eligibility of the place for a higher class of amusement. On the fifteenth met a number of Free Church elders about the unhappy dispute about Dr. Cunningham and Dr. Buchanan. Stood alone in giving an opinion.

January 27.—Went to the Architectural Institute, expecting to hear Sheriff Bell and Mr. Smith, Jordanhill. Much pleased with the collection of things and the general character of the exhibition . . . My dear uncle far from well, yet going about.

March 3.—The news of the Czar Nicholas' death received last night. Heard it after having left Gourlie's, where I met Dr. Allen Thomson, etc., and a medical student, who goes out to Africa in search of objects of natural history. Went to ——'s to get him to sign his will. Agreed to do my best in seeing his young family, in the event of his death, brought up on the means left.

April 7.—The unscrupulous cupidity of some is foreign to my habit of mind. I could not condescend to it. Had a large party of friends on Thursday week to meet Mr. and Mrs. J. D. Bryce.

May 5.—I have had a week's service at the Circuit Court as juryman. Felt strongly how crime hinges on drink, yet I feel that I cannot be a total abstainer. Heard part of the evidence and saw Lord Cowan condemn the murderer, Colin Stewart, to death—a most solemn proceeding. The solemnity of the court while the sentence of death was being written out was affecting. The judge apparently much moved. . . . Lord Advocate's Education Bill a doubtful measure as to the hold over the religious character of the teacher.

May 22.—At the M'Lellan Rooms to-night with my mother and Marion Connal. The pictures very fine, but too many of one class. Had a meeting to-day to sign the agreement as to the Free Church College; £14,000 now in Constantinople. It is interesting to see men from all quarters of the world alive to one great mission.

May 28.—Went with the lads to Cathcart and Linn Houses on Saturday last. A lovely night after a storm of thunder and rain. The old castle seen by moonlight, and the Cart seen amidst trees with the moon reflected in it.

June 22.—Bad news from the Crimea to-day. O Lord, grant that the struggle may issue in a victory for the truth.——

August 4.—My uncle's future comfort very dear to me, and that of my mother.

September 19.—A long week of the British Association. . . . I have had the opportunity of seeing several men of eminence—Dr. Whewell, Sir Charles Lyell, Hugh Miller, Professor Sedgwick, Sir David Brewster, Prince Buonaparte, Dr. Carpenter, and others. It is very interesting to see men whose names will live, and I have felt a kind of fresh pull up. What am I doing?

November 9—I delivered, in the Dovehill Mission House, on Monday evening, a lecture on "The Antiquities of the Dovehill." I believe it was listened to with interest. I have just been called out of the room to see Robert Reid, a smith, who has brought me a present of game for my attention to his mother and sisters, on leaving for Texas. Poor fellow! What encouragement to me to be kind and useful.

December 1.—Called during the week on several applicants of the Stirlingshire Charitable Society. Some cases of humble poverty yet independence—very touching. My uncle at a meeting of Justices on an important case on Thursday last—kept till nine o'clock. I could not have believed he had the strength or spirit for it. Took my seat as a director of the Merchants' House on Tuesday last.

1856.

February 9.—I have a vague idea that I may yet be extensively useful, if it please God to make use of me for any of His holy and wise purposes. Have dreamed (day-dream) of recovering Parkhall.

March 1.—Began on the 25th a tracing of Barry's map of Glasgow, 1782.

March 17.—Much affected by reading the *Life of Hedley Vicars.* I [appear] ashamed of the Gospel of Christ compared with such a man.

April 12.—Printing Laurence Hill's letter on the Sub-Dean Mill, and getting the old deed of 1446 photographed by W. Church.

April 26.— . . . The very thought of being the means, however unwittingly, of loss to another painful. I am far too sensitive for tear and wear. Walked out with C—— B—— to call for Gourlie at Pollokshields on Saturday, 10th inst. A lovely day. Poor fellow, he had been sunning himself at the door some short time before. The blooming flowers specially reminded me of him.

June 4.—My uncle came home [from his tour on the Continent] on Saturday night. I was very glad to see him again. He had been away for nearly three months. I hope he may be spared to be useful yet, and find an industrious and honourable career followed by quietness and retirement. I have been elected a director of Stirling's Library within the last week.

June 14.—Elected a member of Committee of Stirling's Library.

July 11.—Had a long talk with Dr. M'Cosh on Wednesday. Endeavoured to overcome his scruples about the Chair of Apologetics in the new Theological College here.

July 22.—On Monday evening was privileged to meet Sir William Hooker at Dr. Arnott's. Had some very pleasant conversation with him. On Saturday started with thirty-three of a party for Loch Lomond. Had some interesting recollections by Mr. Graham, the boatman, as to my visit there as a child with my father and mother.

August 26.[1]—Garscadden, nine o'clock,—my aunt kisses the cold clay of her dear husband,—my dear uncle. What a sad return home. How changed; the head of the house away. Dear, dear dust to me. When I heard the news yesterday I felt at once alive to an event of the most

[1] William Connal, born at Stirling, 27th January, 1790, died suddenly at Glenmurchie, Forfarshire.

solemn import to me. I was not so much taken by surprise, as at once called to look at such an event in its bearing on my own change whenever that may come, on my own walk in the world, on the sanctification of the trial to us all. A long, sad run in the train to Meigle from four to eight, and then a drive in an open dog-cart to Glenmurchie. How dreary that wilderness of moor in the dark with the wind rising. Yet how bright the Milky Way. I reached the Lodge after a drive of eighteen miles. I hastened to look at the dear dust, and this morning (how beautiful) we took our way to the South. What a melancholy picture as the dog-cart with the coffin, sustained by the keepers, wound round the hill to the spot where the hearse stood—a distance of three miles.

September 6.—At Garscadden, where I have been ever since the funeral, which took place on Friday, the 29th August. I cannot but think that I have had much firmness in all this. Had I given way I might have been less useful to others. I am now placed in a more important position in life; I feel it so. O Lord, give me grace for it. Keep me from entangling myself with what will mar my usefulness. The newspapers are full of my uncle's death, and many friends continue to express regret at the loss of an old friend. Strange that on the Wednesday previous to his death he had an opportunity to speak of his fifty years' connection with business in Glasgow at young Colquhoun's dinner at Killermont.

September 7.—At church at New Kilpatrick. ——— showed me a letter that unsettles all the fancies I had as to taking Garscadden, which I thought I might have done to keep us all together.

September 10.—I pray for grace to follow in my uncle's footsteps in kindness and friendliness to others; in being able to be useful to old friends and connections associated with his memory; to get above and live above the petty jealousies and mean rivalries that embitter life. Attended a meeting of the Merchants' House Directors yesterday. The mention of my uncle's name affecting. I feel now as if an inheritance of a good man's memory had come into my keeping. I feel now as if far more was expected of me

—as if God were calling on me to act publicly for Him. With no one now to control me as formerly, to consult the wishes of, the health of—I have, on the one hand, to avoid the danger of becoming unsettled, slothful, without an aim, self-indulgent; and on the other to occupy creditably a position where my opportunities of doing good may not be so continuous and so apparently devoted.

September 13.—Petition to be served heir to my uncle this week, and designated as son of Michael Connal late of Parkhall.

October 4.—Left this morning for Ormidale to attend the funeral of Colonel Campbell. Arrived by the "Iona" steamer at the new pier at 11 A.M., and drove along that picturesque road to Ormidale House. William Connal chief mourner. The sad procession presented such a contrast to the bright day and the autumnal beauty of the landscape. The burial ground and the enclosure within a short distance of the house. Saw Major Warrand for the first time on this occasion. When last here William Connal was married. Strange that the "Iona" steamer should touch for the first time at the new pier on the occasion of the poor Colonel's funeral. Went to Edinburgh on Wednesday. On Thursday went to the castle and felt stirred on seeing the 34th Regiment on parade. Poor Ormidale's death on Tuesday, at 3 P.M. How sudden and so soon after my uncle's.

October 11.—Yesterday at Lochgoilhead at poor Archibald Campbell's funeral. A picturesque place of burial in the plot of ground occupied by Drimsynie. Saw Mrs. Campbell, his mother, on Monday evening. A most overwhelming trial. What a sad round of trials.

November 8.—Took farewell of Garscadden on Thursday morning. Walked up the low walk at top of park. A long farewell. Much affected by the thought that a man who had exerted such an influence on my happiness had passed away; one so kind and good. The house had lost its attractions for me, but the wrench at first was very painful.

December 15.—At a meeting to-day in the Council Hall of various parties—magistrates and citizens—about discharged prisoners. Proposed as a member of committee by Mr. J. Playfair. A subject in which I feel much interested. Had Dr. Wildman Whitehouse at dinner on Saturday, 22nd November. Showed specimens of shells drawn from depths of the Atlantic. Attended meeting about the Atlantic Telegraph in Council Hall on Wednesday, the 19th November. Elected President of Stirlingshire Society on 4th December.

December 27.—Spoke at meeting to-day about discharged prisoners. Good men's minds very much in difficulty about the matter of treatment. Anxious to prepare well for Stirlingshire Society's meeting. Wrote Mr. Buchanan, the President-elect of United States, about it. Claimed him as having a Scotch ancestry. Poor Hugh Miller!—a bright genius quenched in darkness. Overworking of the brain. . . . My uncle Eben. procuring particulars of the early family history of Connals, Wrights, etc., etc.

1857.

January 10.—At home after week of exhausting work and some excitement in preparation for the meeting of the Glasgow Stirlingshire Charitable Society. I feel it to be due to my uncle's [1] memory that it should not be a failure. Had a letter this morning from the Master of the Mint.[2] He joins the Society. I spent New Year's Day, the first for many years, at home with my mother. What a solemn year has passed away. I am entering on the great battle of life without that kind and friendly voice to warn and counsel me.

March 5.—Wearied with the excitement of electioneering on behalf of Mr. Walter Buchanan, who is to-day returned by a large majority—about three thousand. Felt it my duty to take some interest in this matter. The Maynooth question assuming in my eyes a different phase. I see parties so divided that nothing short of the withdrawal of State support from the Irish Presbyterians can accomplish that object.

[1] William Connal was one of the founders of this Society in 1809.

[2] Thomas Graham of Ballewan, Stirlingshire.

April 9.—Spent yesterday afternoon in attending a meeting of some interest in connection with the lodging-house movement. Afterwards went through my district, having had no dinner; had a piece of bread and beef in my pocket, and came home about eleven o'clock at night.

May 4.—Arranged for a suitable tablet for my dear uncle's grave.

July 22.—Home from Iona—34 of a party. The gun of the "Florida," one of the Spanish Armada, most interesting.

August 12.—Saw my Uncle Wright at Stirling on Wednesday last. My Cousin Hamilton anxious about her boys at Cawnpore. Have been in correspondence with Dr. Dickie of Belfast about the Natural History Chair. Saw the old Principal (M'Farlane) about it on Wednesday last; a wonderful old man—very polite.

August 29.—Oppressed with sad forebodings as to the Cawnpore massacres. On Wednesday out at Barlanark at the *fête* of the children of Hutcheson and Millar's schools.

The poor boys[1] at Cawnpore—it seems as if it was all up with them. Oh, the horrible butchery! "Vengeance is mine, I will repay, saith the Lord."

September 19.—At Dr. Andrew Buchanan's on Thursday night, 17th, to meet Dr. Livingstone, the African traveller.

October 5.—Walked into the Cathedral to-day. Stood beside my uncle's grave. Copied from the north wall of the Chapter-house, within a recess: "Farewell to all the vanities of time; oh, may all my friends be servants of the living God after I am mouldering in the dust."

November 11.—Felt more alarmed than I had ever been at the financial crisis. The closing of the Western Bank on Monday at two o'clock, the "run" commencing on the Union and City Banks and continuing up till to-day, leading this morning to the suspension of the City Bank, gave an aspect of peculiar gloom to the city. The whole of the difficulties not at once realized. The panic-stricken crowds in the streets opposite the various bank doors, the various cases of peculiar hardship, the utter destruction of confidence for the time being,—all sad features of the day,

[1] Robert and John Henderson, sons of Rev. Robert Henderson, Stirling.

—the fear of to-morrow. . . . Indian news to-day—Delhi taken, Lucknow relieved; but all at a sad loss of life.

November 21.—Two days of delicious weather; I do love this Indian summer.

1858.

January 1.—Rose, thankful to God for many mercies.

January 14.—Regret that from a dogmatical way of speaking to one of my brethren I betrayed a most imperious spirit. On Monday last made a director of the N. S. Savings Bank.

January 23.—At the dinner of the Stirlingshire Society on Monday—a pleasant evening.

February 5.—Too often out at dinner of late, and I am glad to avoid one more invitation to-night and be quiet at home. Had a strange hunt yesterday for a deed about the Molendinar fishings. Went with Dr. Wylie to the Hall of Faculty of Medicine: could not get the safe opened. A skeleton of a man who had been hanged before it. A run for the keys by cab, etc.; a smith to pick the lock, and after all disappointed.

September 20.—Old B—— at Parkhall dead. Strange thoughts come over me as to that place, once so full of associations to me. . . . Parkhall is to be sold. I find the constant tear and wear of business leaves me no time for leisure, and may eventually leave me without strength or spirits to be useful. I think it would be a noble thing to say that I have been [able after] thirty years, to come back again to a position forfeited in the hour of misfortune.

March 27.—My mother writing a note to Mr. Niven in reply to one from him unexpectedly received the other day about Parkhall. Strange that he and his wife, on B——'s death, at once seek to revive the past. I have turned over some old papers to-night about deeds, plans, estimates (1826). I was at Mrs. Campbell's (Drimsynie) funeral on Thursday. I felt the old lady's loss as one who had been kind to my mother and sister. The last link broken in a large connection. It is good to take a lift off the burdens of the poor. Met with Dr. Hetherington and Mr. N. Stevenson at dinner about ten days ago, and spoke about a prize of £50 for the students of three years' standing or so, for a digest of suitable illustrations from the fields of science, history, etc.

April 14.—Dined last night with William Ewing. Met a Captain Maynard there who was in the "Herefordshire" ten years. Strange that my father superintended at the building of her at Bombay in 1812. These revolutions in events constantly recurring.

May 8.—Went on Thursday night to Model Lodging House and saw thirty-five Russian sailors. Presented them with *The Book and its Story*.

May 17.—Last week had a hard week of it. Wound up with a fatiguing walk to Carmyle rather than disappoint the lads.

May 31.—Called to-night on Mr. West, artist, to see the copy of the miniature of my father.

June 28.—Had a glorious view of Loch Lomond, the Firth of Clyde, etc. Ben Lomond dark and majestic. The islands with their green livery and white circle round each in the dark blue water. The distant rugged Grampians seen through Glenfruin, where the pibroch thrilled in 1602 in the massacre of the Colquhouns by the Macgregor, rising peak above peak, bathed in the yellow light that was shed down on them ; a dark tempest cloud gathering between us and them, then a glorious rainbow over Dunfionn or the "Hill of Fingal." . . . Got Mr. Turner to give me to-night sanction to examine cartulary of St. Nicholas.

July 22.—At Arran . . . a solitary walk I had at 4 A.M. very impressive. The two giant sentinels at the entrance to Glen Sannox, seen through the mist and rain, most startling. A rough sea—and I am home . . . . Gave Moffat (St. Andrew's Square Reformatory) Hugh Miller's *Schools and Schoolmasters*.

August 4.—How often has the thought of Parkhall crossed my mind.

August 5.—News of the Atlantic telegraph being completed reached Glasgow this day. "A girdle round the earth."

August 9.—On Friday night at Botanic Gardens. Saw the *Victoria Regia* with eleven large leaves. Thought of poor Gourlie. Many thoughts of Parkhall, but if I encumber myself with obligations which may go far to abridge usefulness, and alter my course of life, I may be involving myself to grasp a phantom. I think of Haldane who sold Airthrey, etc., for the good of the church.

August 21.—I entered on my forty-second year on the 11th inst. Life, as it advances with me, appears to be truly a pilgrimage; I cannot seek to nestle here. I see other men let things go as they please, and appear to have no purpose in life but their own pleasure. Their very selfishness keeps them steady.

August 21.—This morning an advertisement appears as to the sale of Parkhall. I am satisfied, the more I think of it, that it will be a retreat for my mother, and that the opportunity has presented itself for resuscitating old recollections . . . The moon shone like a lamp over the eastern portion of the city. The Cathedral reared its huge picturesque masses before me, while the hum of voices and the merry shouts of children broke the silence of that solemn resting-place. Shall I live to myself? I felt what a noble thing it was to do good—higher than social position, higher than the achievement of uniting continents by the telegraph, [though] it is noble as a means of good.

August 28.—I feel that life is too short to be spent in the vain desire to amass a fortune, which I think I never shall, or to found a family. To do good in my day and generation is a higher and nobler aim.

September 2.—Visited with ——— the Catholic Apostolic Church. Symbolism run mad.

September 16.—Yesterday afternoon I completed, through Mr. Barr, the purchase of Parkhall. I put into Mr. Barr's hands the disposition in my mother's favour, drawn out in 1826, and I had the pleasure of being able to say that I would like the obligation fulfilled.

September 23.—The Council for the city have accepted Buchanan's gift for an institution for destitute children, and sanctioned the purchase of M'Phail's house. There will be brighter days for the Calton I trust yet. Men begin to speak about Parkhall.

September 25.—Walked up to the Cathedral burying-ground. Thought of those lying there and of one far away in the dust of India. How happy they would have been to see this consummation.

October 2.—Mr. Scott and his daughter left us to-day. Felt happy, after the kindness shown me by him twenty-three years ago, to show him and his some attention. At Kinross on Wednesday, the 29th, at the dinner to Mr. Williamson—Sir Graham Montgomery in the chair. Saw the comet last night, brighter than I could possibly have conceived. Relieved against the sky, dark but clear of clouds, it appeared like the scimitar of an archangel. What a revolution through space! How infinite is God!

October 18.—This morning struck with the notice of the death of Bryce Buchanan, Boquhan. Felt for a few minutes strange and tumultuous thoughts about the past in connection with it. Keep me, O Lord, humbly devoted for good. I knelt down in the counting-house room, before the lads came, and prayed. On Saturday with Laurence Hill, etc., at Kirkintilloch—the Peel, Gartshore House and its hospitalities, the Roman camp on Barrhill; felt strange emotions in disinterring the stones laid by Roman soldiers. The imperial grasp of their legions felt, as it were, paramount, now for ever passed away.

October 28.—Wrote Mr. Temple, Inspector of Schools, about Hants and Wilts Adult Education Society. Wrote also, after seeing the Rev. J. Craig, the young men of Templeton's factory about Bell Street Institute. On Monday last (25th) had a deputation from the Fourteenth Ward about offering myself as a candidate for the Councillorship. Declined peremptorily, on the ground of immaturity on some questions of great importance. Wrote the Hon. and Rev. Mr. Best about education (adult); hope yet to see the Universities examining mechanics such as the "Spout."

November 6.—Received volume from the Rev. Dr. Temple as to Oxford Associate in Arts Examination. Wrote him, etc., and also put myself into communication with A. M. Dunlop, M.P., and A. Hastie.

November 29.—Dined at the Dean of Guild's at Cadder on Tuesday, 23rd inst. Pitch dark from fog. Mr. H. E. Crum-Ewing, M.P., and Mr. A. Turner in the carriage with me. Two hours going. Dined at 8 o'clock; Sir James Campbell, the Provost, and others. The darkest day in the memory of Mr. Patrick, warden, High Church, a good and venerable authority. Asked out here and there to dinner how gladly would I remain at home.

December 17.—Named on Monday one of the Botanic Garden Council. I would wish to be useful as to this.

1859.

January 5.—A chair taken from the village of Little Boquhan—believed to have been in the possession of Thomas Buchanan, father of the celebrated George Buchanan, 300 years ago—presented to the Archæological Society on 3rd inst. On Saturday at Mugdock tunnel and castle. Looked across the valley of Strathblane in the direction of Parkhall.

January 10.—I started on a visit [to Parkhall] with my mother, etc., at 9.15 this morning. A fine, fresh morning. Strathblane beautiful and picturesque: Duntreath, the distant Ben Lomond, and other mountains. I had little time to realize the peculiar interest of my situation in going back to visit a spot once so bound up with my mother's happiness and my father's position, and now I was on my way to revisit it as the owner of it. How many changes since 1828. These have been over-ruled for good. My father's sailing for Calcutta, my mother's leaving his bones there, far up the country near Moorshedabad: he never thought that his son would get back the place where he once spent his life in peaceful occupation, and where he occupied the dignified position of a county magistrate. What a strange romance! Though I have had many struggles and trials—my mother's dependent position, my sister's death, my own battle with others in getting on—here am I at last with Parkhall in view! Welcome! . . . The house—the old familiar parlour and drawing-room; my mother through it all; much affected. Major Stirling not at home. Called on Dr. Graham of Killearn in coming home and shook hands with him. He still remains to recall those who are away. How peculiar my position. O Lord, give me grace to act aright as to it.

January 15.—Attended the funeral of Mr. J. R. Anderson . . . my old tutor. Dr. Graham of Killearn called on my mother yesterday. Old recollections and associations are reviving. Met Mr. Blackburn of Killearn on Thursday about the Stirlingshire Society's business. Parkhall marches with Killearn property. . . . I see before me a week of much pressure.

January 22.—To-night at Tom Richardson's; a musical party. On Monday found that I must act as croupier at the dinner of the Glasgow Stirlingshire Society. Mr. Blackburn, M.P., filled the chair. Appointed sub-convener of the Buchanan School Trust on Tuesday. Sent some things out to Parkhall for the garden.

February 5.—More than usually in public company of late. Met officials at Mr. M'Dowall's, Mr. Jamieson's, etc. Included in the list of a committee formed in Edinburgh about the Imbecile children, on the 3rd instant, in connection with a society. Joshua Paterson the only other Glasgow man recognized in it.

February 10.—I have just pressed a lock of my Uncle William's hair—silvery. It is a strange memento. How truthful, how conscientious, how disinterested!

March 2.—At J. D. Bryce's last night about the Buchanan Bequest. Discussed my views as to a general school, and the doing away with the opprobrium and the down-draught of a pauperizing institution. On Friday last met Mr. Pritchard of the South Seas. . . . Looking forward to Parkhall; think of planting a *Deodar Cedar* in remembrance of the past.

April 2.—I desire to see in all that concerns me, discipline. The present is a state of discipline.

April 30.—Heard Walter Buchanan and Robert Dalglish in the City Hall. On the 25th at the Necropolis with the Dean of Guild inspecting walls and Roman Bridge, etc. The Botanic Gardens, and more particularly the applications about the Buchanan Bequest, engaging my attention. On Wednesday, 27th, attended conversazione at the College; very brilliant. . . The Discharged Prisoners' Society heavy work, but prepared to work it out. Donald M'Donald, my father's old servant, makes his appearance after being in Australia, and claims my interest in him. I have had refreshment in the thought that though I may not live to see the issue of good now, I am encouraged to enjoy God in what I do. My power to do good may be limited, but it is my talent for which I must give an account.

May 7.—Young Captain Caton buried to-day.

May 23.—On Wednesday last, the 18th, drove out with my mother, aunt, Mr. Barr, etc., to Parkhall. My mother agitated a little; a noble drive and a fine day. Parkhall trees fresh and green; the fields beautiful. The house our own once more. Visited the farm, plantations, etc. I hope to see my mother quietly and happily settled there by next week . . . My poor father away, but my mother spared to come back.

June 17.—I have to note one or two things. On Saturday last I walked to Killearn and called on Dr. Graham. A splendid amphitheatre of country. I prayed to be useful to the district. The associations of the past came vividly before me. I have read my father's few and simple words, uttered thirty-one years ago: "I feel their kindness; say to them that Balfron has still a friend in me, and that if my poor endeavours have been of use to any of its inhabitants, happy shall I be if ever again I have it in my power to serve them."

June 18.—I walked with the lads to-night. It is my duty to foster their taste for what would improve their minds. Yet I regretted I could not be with my mother. Signed to-day what my poor father never could complete—the document conveying the life-rent of Parkhall to my mother. I have thus been enabled to fulfil the desire (out of respect to my father's memory) to give legal force to

the Barony of Cremanan or Crymynam, but now in the Barony of Buchanan, Parish of Killearn, are held *per chirothecarium*, for a pair of gloves, from the Crown.

October 10.—Have received an invitation from the Provost, Magistrates, and Water Commissioners to the inauguration of the Glasgow Corporation Water Works, on Friday, the 14th instant. Came in from Parkhall this morning. At church in Killearn yesterday. Lunched at Carbeth on Saturday. My spirit revived, wearied as I was, with a sight of the hills, the trees, the pure stream, and then home.

October 15.—Yesterday at Loch Katrine—heavy showers at intervals. Steamed from Balloch to Inversnaid. Mr. and Mrs. Buchanan, Carbeth, on board. Took in Duke of Montrose and party at Balmaha. Dr. Hill on top of coach to Stronachlacher. Boat to the point of interest—saw the Queen. Very interesting sight. Saw the two men—fine fellows—dressed in blue flannels with red trimmings, descend the tunnel in a boat. Helped to light their lamps, and away they shot in the waters of the loch to a point about one mile and a quarter distant in the cavern. Wet and cold passage down the loch to Balloch; not without danger. The Rifles looked well, the Celtic corps picturesque. Away to-day with P. Playfair and J. Dale looking at a house in the country near Shettleston, for our discharged prisoners.

October 22.—I am compelled to relinquish all claim to the membership of the Council of the University by not having matriculated for the fourth year. I am sorry for this. I might have initiated some important change in attaching to the University classes of men who have at present no connection with it. It is a check. I see in this a thing to make me humble; it recalls misspent time twenty-six years ago. . . . What a splendid sunset in the eyes of the world is that of Stephenson, the great engineer, buried in Westminster Abbey beside the illustrious dead, with no fictitious honour descending to the tomb with him. A plain commoner, of large mind, benevolent heart, and a master spirit of gigantic enterprises that have been successfully completed.

for Professor Grant, whom I met last night at Dr. Arnott's, *Herschell's Astronomy in Chinese.*

October 1.—Introduced myself to Emily Faithfull, who takes so much interest in female labour.

October 11.—Two events have occurred fitted to recall the past: the death of Dr. Fletcher and the dinner in memory of Dr. Dymock. The one reminds me of my father and mother going out to India in 1828, and my being lost in London, having been sent to Clapham instead of Clapton, and returning to London, wandering about Cheapside late at night, until a gentleman, apparently a foreigner, sent me out on the twelve o'clock stage to Clapton. He [Dr. Fletcher] has outlived early prejudices against him. The dinner of Dr. Dymock's pupils took place last night, Mr. Towers Clark in the chair. Thomas Dymock there. A very interesting meeting. I gave expression to the pain I felt in the remembrance of that misspent winter (1826).

November 10.—A new scheme projected to interest the lower classes—a combination of music and readings.

December 5.—The visit of the Empress Eugenie created excitement during the last ten days.

December 22.—I am more and more convinced that a man should use his wealth while alive, with a reasonable amount of consideration for friends and relatives.

1861.

January 1.—How important it is to make others happy while we have the opportunity.

January 26.—Had a letter this week from John Beatton, from Lowell, Mass., U.S.A., acknowledging the advantages of the "Spout" Institution.

February 16.—Spoke to Mr. Logan and Mr. Dalrymple about my father's tomb at Obia, India. Both had seen it, and the former had seen him. Have found interesting particulars about my paternal grandfather[1] in the Kirk Session records, Stirling, 1796. Time tries people.

[1] Michael Connal.

June 1.—At the opening of the new wing of the Royal Infirmary.

August 5.—The real enjoyment of the country and of natural objects consists not in possession. I have felt more relish and keen susceptibility of the beautiful, the interesting, and romantic, when I had no such thought in my mind as possession. How truly, then, may a poor man enjoy the common bounties of Providence—fresh air, green fields, trees, streams, hills—far beyond the owner of them.

August 12.—I entered yesterday on my forty-fifth year. I am in my prime. What am I doing? My opportunities are slipping past.

September 13.—Invited by the Provost and Clyde Trustees to the banquet given to the officers of the Fleet on Friday, 30th August. A magnificent affair.

October 1.—Dined at Carbeth on Saturday, 28th. Mr. Maitland of Whinfield there. Called on Mr. C. J. Tennant at Ballikinrain on 28th.

December 7.—Have been occupied day and night with the account[1] of St. Nicholas Hospital, preparing for the press.

[1] Paper read before Glasgow Archæological Society, 7th November, 1859; afterwards printed in book form.

1862—1867

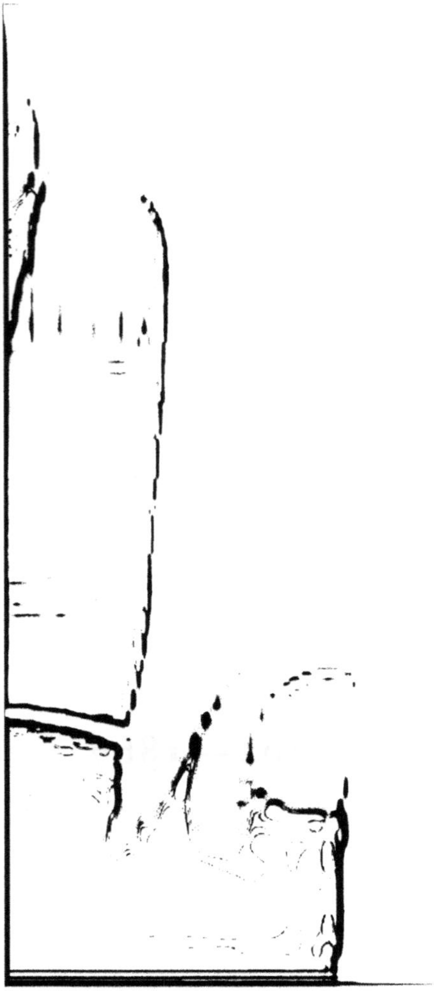

January 1.—Sad events have taken place since I last wrote. Prince Albert's death. The feeling generally one of deep sorrow.

June 5.—After a long interval I have a few quiet minutes to jot down my memoranda. My mother once more in the country at her old home—a peaceful and a smiling one. I took her there on Tuesday. A fine drive; everything beautiful.

July 1.—Mr. Findlay of Easterhill died on Friday last at Boturich Castle, Loch Lomond side. My uncle's old partner now away. He and I were born in the same house, in Miller Street.

July 31.—I spent a quiet Sabbath at Parkhall on the 27th. I was affected almost to tears, being alone in the Muir Park amongst the trees, that God should have spared my mother and me to be there again.

August 7.—At Parkhall last Saturday and Sunday. Sir Henry Moncrieff preached. Walked with him. A fine, open-hearted man. A beautiful day. Have now finished my little book, and I hope the memorial of St. Nicholas Hospital will be in the hands of friends by next week.

September 30.—On Wednesday, 17th, I started in the train for York. I felt it to be a duty to relieve my mind as well as to see the exhibition in London. I arrived in York early on Thursday morning in full view of the noble minster. I walked round it and heard the little boys chanting their music-lesson in one of the aisles. Then

I got entrance for a very hurried glance at it. The horn (Saxon times) curious, and also the cup and crosier. Some beautiful monuments and a noble window. Off to London by 10 train. I found to my surprise my cousin Michael[1] at the "Tavistock." The life, the roll of cabs and omnibuses, carriages, etc., overwhelming. Visited the exhibition; a wonderful place. The striking of the hours by a peal of bells interesting. I thought of the crowds that thronged the passages giving way to others in the course of nature, hushed in death; and yet these triumphs of man's skill! The horticultural gardens magnificent. At the College of Arms, St. Paul's Churchyard, to see James IV.'s ring, sword, and dagger. Had them in my hands. At Covent Garden Market one morning during my visit. Affected to tears with the goodness of God in the fruits, flowers, vegetables, etc.

November 20.—Last night I presided at the opening lecture on Natural History by Dr. Scoular in the popular class of the Andersonian University.

1863.

March 10.—The marriage day of the Prince of Wales. At the review on the balcony of the Buchanan Institution. A very grand sight from the multitude of people. The preparations for display in the evening very great.

March 14.—Took my aunt, Miss Ellen Ewing, etc., to see the illuminations on Tuesday night down towards the river. A dreadful crush at St. Enoch Square.

March 23.—I was with Mrs. Thomas, wife of Captain Thomas, on the 19th, endeavouring to get her money for destitution in Harris. A woman of great energy. Helped to get her £42 in an hour and a half.

March 30.—Saw Lord Palmerston arrive on Saturday night, 28th. The Premier of the Government of such a country; what a lofty position!

July 10.—The building of Stirling's Library commenced. On the building committee.

[1] Son of Patrick Connal.

July 22.—On Saturday, in expectation of the young men crossing the hills, went up with Mr. Le Febure to the top of the Earl's Seat. A magnificent panorama; Glasgow, Ailsa Craig, Arran, Loch Lomond, and the range of the Grampians, Lake of Menteith, Arthur's Seat, Tinto, etc. . . . . Looked down on Glasgow, with its manifold opportunities for good or evil.

August 27.—To-day, with a party of the Archæological Society, to Haggs Castle, with which I was very much pleased.

September 3.—When at Greenock to-day went out in a steamer to the fleet. Went on board the "Warrior." The moment I got on board I was struck with the spacious deck and the towering masts. The sailors fine-looking men. Then I thought of war. Wherefore such expenditure of men and material to defend and vindicate the honour of the country? The world is still a troubled world. Surely the time is coming when the splendid armaments will not be needed—when nations shall learn the art of war no more.

September 9.—On Saturday introduced by the Provost to Admiral Dacres, when on my way to the country. . . . . Went round with John and marked some trees for being cut down.

September 17.—Last night at Wemyss Bay with my aunt. Mr. Napier, ex-Chancellor of Ireland, to be her guest soon, on the occasion of delivering a lecture in this city. At first anxious to meet him, and then indifferent. Very likely to be lionized; but such a man as a quiet companion would be very acceptable.

October 17.—Elected vice-president of the Natural History Society on the 29th ulto.

October 19.—Spent the early part of this day at Parkhall. Went over nearly every part of the property. A beautiful morning, but the country assuming a russet-brown look. I am happy to see that place beginning to smile; happy that my mother has been spared to enjoy it.

November 13.—At Gourock at Robert Binnie's on Wednesday, 11th instant. The hills capped with snow, and the sun bringing out the purple and yellow-green shades of colour in which they were clothed. . To-day James Thomson sent me a memorandum, interesting to me as recalling the earliest thing I can remember. He called, on 7th February, 1822, at my uncle's house in Miller Street—the house in which I was born—in the evening, to show the Bible and Psalm-book to my uncle, aunt, and mother, to be presented to the Rev. William Anderson. I was standing by the fire-place in the drawing-room; I was then four years and six months old.

1864.

January 7.—Walked up on Monday to the Cathedral burying-ground. Stood, as I have often done, beside beloved dust, and there lifted up my heart to God in the corner of the old pile.

February 4.—Dined at Mr. Hugh Tennent's at Wellpark to meet Mr. Cosmo Innes on Friday, 29th January. Interested in his lecture, but only an elegant *résumé* of materials well known. . Professor Balfour asked me to act as sponsor to his little daughter, but I have declined. I cannot treat the obligation as a compliment and act insincerely.

February 26.—Last night at the annual meeting of the "Spout" young men. . . . A photographic album presented to me by them. A very acceptable gift, recalling many countenances that I feel an interest in.

March 19.—At Parkhall on Friday, the 10th. Very sad at heart, yet pleased to see my father's place smile under a course of improvement. Why sad? I may have pleasure that my dear mother has the prospect of spending the summer there; but except from the consciousness that I have been useful, and may be useful, to the neighbourhood, my vocation seems to be in this great city. I am to struggle away here.

April 9.—Elected a member of Assembly at the last meeting of Presbytery Have declined that others may get the opportunity.

May 16.—Took the oath of allegiance at Justice of

Peace Court Hall, as appointed to the Commission of the Peace on 12th May. . . . .

[Sir Michael was married 7th October of this year to Miss Helen Catherine Leckie Ewing.]

1865.

January 4.—At Ballincleroch; a large family party. Everything went on well.

January 19.—At Killearn, at Dr. Graham's funeral. . . At various dinner parties—Cadder, Yorkhill, etc.

March 4.—The death and funeral of Cardinal Wiseman is full of significance as to the pretensions and ambition of the Roman Catholic Church. There is a total absence of the idea of moral worth and simple greatness in the whole affair. It appears to have been a most pompous exhibition.

April 12.—At the opening of Stirling's Library last night; the Lord Provost in the chair. . . . Sat yesterday as a Justice of the Peace along with William Stirling, Cordale.

May 15.—The public news of the day is the assassination of Lincoln, the death of the murderer, and the surrender of the military power of the South, together with the policy of the new President—all absorbing.

June.—Have had some correspondence with Sir J. E. Alexander[1] about the manuscripts left by my Uncle Eben. He has been very much interested in them. I had a call to-day from Mr. John Mackenzie Lindsay[2] of Dundee wanting to see them; also a relation. Meditated a visit to London—went up 28th June. J. S. Fleming and I dined on a steak in the "Cock," near Temple Bar.

August 5.—The election for the county full of absorbing interest. In driving over to Drymen met Sir James Colquhoun; gave him a lift.

[1] Lieut.-General Sir James Edward Alexander of Westerton, eldest son of Edward Alexander of Powis, by his wife, Catherine Glas, daughter of John Glas, Provost of Stirling.

[2] Son of Provost Lindsay of Dundee, of the Dowhill family.

August 23.—Unexpected detention at Dumbarton with the procession of St. Crispin in laying the foundation stone of a hall. (Men big bairns after all.)

September 28.—My mother has made up her mind to make Parkhall her permanent residence.

October 21.—The death of Lord Palmerston this week, a sad event and the subject of general sympathy. Elected a director of the Merchants' House. Mr. and Mrs. Leckie Ewing with us at Parkhall on Saturday, the 7th.

November 16.—Mr. Gladstone's visits to Scotland remarkable as showing great aptitude to adapt himself to three or four different audiences—City Hall, working men, and Edinburgh University.

December 14.—The Archæological Society's meeting on Monday, the 4th. Mr. Stewart stayed with us. Mr. Smith of Jordanhill, Mr. Hart, John Buchanan, Sheriff Erskine Murray, and others dined with us. Tried hard to get Sir J. E. Alexander to preside at the Stirlingshire dinner on "Auld Handsel Monday," but he has declined.

1866.

March 28.—At the College conversazione with my wife on 22nd, in the Corporation Galleries. Mr. Gilbert Scott referred to his plans. Mr. William Ewing introduced me to a son of Sir John Herschell . . . More or less likely to be engrossed with the Merchants' House history. Rummaged out with W. H. Hill a good many documents from the safes in the House. I have been absenting myself from all scientific and literary societies as much as possible, as I am now more susceptible to cold than ever. I was at the flower show this afternoon in the City Hall. I was almost affected to tears by the sight of magnificent azaleas, hyacinths, tulips, etc.

May 14.—I returned from England on Wednesday morning with Helen. Linnacre a quiet English home—flowers in the hedge-rows innumerable. Visited Dover and the Castle on Thursday; then Mr. Fielding[1] and his

[1] Thomas Mantell Fielding, great-grandson of the novelist, married Jean Eleanora, daughter of W. Leckie Ewing of Arngomery.

daughters. The French coast very clear. On Friday went to Canterbury, the spot where Thomas à Becket was slain,—his shrine, the Black Prince's tomb, etc.; a quaint, quiet old town. The spires of the cathedral attract rain frequently; a fine undulating country. Saw in passing over the Medway the "Great Eastern" at a distance.

August 20.—I have never been able to sit down and note what has interested me in the interval that has elapsed since 6th June. I have come from Ballinclerach this morning with A—— R——, and Captain John Macfarlan. Mr. Ewing's funeral at Kippen on the 14th inst. The wrench of leaving Arngomery killed him.

October 18.—The Duke of Edinburgh's visit to the city to-day. Prince Consort's statue unveiled. On Tuesday last the great Reform demonstration in Glasgow. I think that Mr. Gladstone's measure should have passed; it would have settled the question for twenty years at least. These political questions inflame many minds, but they don't bear on the progress of the country. Education, economy, etc., etc., go quietly and surely on without this dangerous agitation. The tendency to physical force almost a necessity from the license of speech permitted and encouraged. Went out on Tuesday to Bally with Helen to meet Hugh Matheson and his wife. The Mauritius newspaper just received brings Michael Connai into notice by a scientific paper. I entered on my 50th year on 11th August.

December 8.—Tom Fielding's father died in November, and was buried 30th ultimo. A truly good man.

1867.

January 1.—Poor Mungo Campbell died on Saturday last. Went out to Parkhall on Saturday, 22nd ult., to a meeting of heritors in Killearn.

March 9.—See from newspapers that John Millar has been made Solicitor-General for Scotland. My old schoolfellow at Tillicoultry. His is a case of persistent hard work.

June 5.—Went to Edinburgh to the General Assembly. Saw the venerable Dr. Clason carried out apparently dead. Heard an address by a medical student in the Madeline

Church, where the medical mission is
place; the oak table round which the
identical table on which the body of t
lay after his execution.

July 4.—On Tuesday got a bell
search of, dated 1641. Have arran
Hill as to its being presented, on be
to the Glasgow Town Council. The
opened 1st July. This is very mu
property in Killearn and neighbourh

September 11.—What a change
College friend, Joseph Hooker, nomir
of the British Association for next y

October 12.—Tom Gawne and hi
Parkhall yesterday after spending a
feel more and more my duty to tha
(Bell Street), associated as it has bee
that will outlive the passing wants
to get James C. Burns interested in

October 31.—At the Justice of
Much exercised about doing more f
a Commissioner of Supply for Stirli

November 21.—Came round by Sti
Parkhall. Saw William Wright, Mr.
Mrs. Gibson, and Mrs. Donald Cam

December 22.—At Mr. Geikie's l
logical Origin of Scottish Scenery
Elected president for the second tin
Charitable Society, on the occasion
Sons of the Rock dining with then
accept it. Made a director by the
the Logan and Johnston Institutic
meeting of the Archæological Soci
A good many interesting things len
Charles I.'s cap, worn at his execut
a good many interesting books, p
Buchanan's paper on the stone foun
Kilpatrick, most interesting. Profe
"Ancient Astronomical Observati
One observation as to an eclips

August, 1042, as the time when the Danish fleet of Haco was at Orkney or Shetland. On Sabbath . the Green full of people; a great crowd in front of the jail. Everything quiet, but the display of force had its influence. Fenianism is the fanatical spawn of Irish-American rowdyism.

January 25.—On New Year's Day at the Buchanan Institution. Robert Gray lectured on "Birds." Drove out to Archie Colquhoun's afterwards. Dined at Archie Robertson's; had a party the next night; a very happy meeting. Presided at the Stirlingshire dinner on the 13th inst.; the Sons of the Rock there. On the whole a success. Sir James Alexander and Mr. Buchanan of Carbeth with us all night.

April 8.—Division on Gladstone's motion about the Disestablishment of the Irish Church one of the most striking evidences of the progress of opinion. Infinitely preferable to indiscriminate endowments.

June 4.—N—— preparing to go to Biarritz to visit her mother; my Aunt [Mrs. William Connal] accompanies her. The news of the dreadful loss of the "Garonne" on Friday, 22nd May, reached town on the Saturday following. It has altered the plan of sailing to Bordeaux; they now go through France. Went with N—— on Thursday, 21st, to Yorkhill to visit Mrs. Graham Gilbert. Went into the studio. Trying to interest members of the Stirlingshire Charitable Society and the Sons of the Rock in a memorial window in the High Church, Stirling.

June 17.—At home alone looking over old papers of my uncle. How truly kind he was; I shall ever venerate his memory. . . . E. Gilbert to go to Demerara by the "Cuyuni." I hope it may be blest to the recovery of his health. I could not see a valuable young man die by inches without an effort to save him.

July 31.—William Thompson wrote me about the death

of his mother, which took place at Brighton more than ten days ago. I remember with gratitude all the kindness of that family.

August 12.—Felt for a day or so a strange depression. I think it arises from a sense of being without an object in the country. W. Connal's welcome to the Stirling visitors at Hillfoot took place on Thursday, 6th August. The water-works and Mr. R. Dalglish's gardens visited—a success. The Sons of the Rock have had their opportunity; the Stirlingshire Society must have its own by and by. I thought of —— collecting around him all the sumptuousness of a fine residence. It may be a good thing for the country-side, and, no doubt, his hospitality commands influence, I believe, for good; but what about the abodes of poverty and neglect? The claims there will scarcely admit of large expenditure on one's self. . . . Sent —— to-day a photograph of the bell (1641).

October 12.—The grand ceremonial of the laying of the foundation stone of the College took place on Thursday the 8th. Mrs. M'Farlan and her daughter, Hamilton, Mary Ewing, and Mrs. Connal, all at 16 Lynedoch Crescent. Thankful, when it was all over, that there was no accident.

October 23.—Mrs. Hinds, Mrs. Alexander Connal, my mother, etc., all at Mrs. W. Connal's, 220 St. Vincent Street, at dinner. A more than usually large gathering of Connals.

1869.

January 6.—The announcement of the perversion of the young Marquis of Bute inexpressibly painful. Captain O'Connor died on Sunday morning, the 10th. At his funeral on Wednesday the 13th, and was one of the pall-bearers; a very sad event.

February 8.—The derivation of "Calton" referred to by me; from *Caltinua* (hazel).

March 13.—Arranged to let Mr. Ballantine go on with the window in the church in Stirling. The designs more to the point as illustrative of the objects of both societies.

March 25.—Mr. Niven made some remarks of a graceful kind in remembrance of my father. . The manuscript by Dr. Porteous of the records of the Glasgow Presbytery was very interesting to me, and I am happy to have it in my possession.

May 6.—The country beautiful. Spoke with my mother about the field called "Endrick Field" about to be sold. She appeared interested in my getting it. It was part of Parkhall once.

May 20.—Occupied nearly two hours each day for several days in the J. P. Court. . . . How often the pride and selfishness of men make business most trying.

July 9.—Have examined the call to R. Woodrow of Eastwood to Stirling (1717). I noticed several names with which I am familiar; probably ancestors.

July 14.—There are some political aspects of the times full of solicitude. The majority in the Lords for concurrent endowments, and the loop-hole by which grants may be given to Roman Catholics, apart from the national system of education.

July 28.—Left for Cupar on Friday afternoon at 4.20 *via* Edinburgh. William L. M'Farlan took me through the town before reaching home. Next morning left for St. Andrews—Archbishop Sharp's tomb, the castle, the dungeon, St. Regulus' tower, the tombs of Halyburton and Samuel Rutherfurd. Went in the evening to Magus Moor; visited the spot where Archbishop Sharp was killed. Brought away a slip of privet. Strange the interest that attaches to a deed of this kind. Visited St. Leonard's College on Monday, Queen Mary's thorn, etc. The links peculiar as a field for the sport of golf. The venerable aspect of the place fitted to impress and to cherish student-life. The country interesting, but wanting in picturesqueness.

August 18.—Saw to-day, in Mr. W. Ewing's, the proceedings of the House of Commons from the time of Edward VI. to 1745 in manuscript; most beautifully written. He asked me what to do with them, as they were offered for sale—seventy-five volumes. I got the published volumes with which they tallied, and I think I interested Mr. Ewing more in them. . . . Making a little walk for my mother at the burn at Parkhall, with

Much affected when passing Downshire Hill, where R. B. Forman lived, whom I visited again and again from 1835 to 1838. Left London on Monday night.

May 4.—Drove home with N—— from W. Connal's after the baptism of their child. On Monday night, 25th April, started again most reluctantly for London. Walked with Mr. M'Lure through the streets of London on Thursday night after dinner; a vast solitude, and yet a world of human beings. Enjoyed the boom of the bell of St. Paul's and the majesty of the dome in the clear morning sky, say at five o'clock. London, with its spires, in the morning light most imposing.

May 26.—Michael Connal gazetted on 17th instant as surveyor general, colonial engineer, and engineer for Government railways for the Mauritius.

June 27.—Took a walk with N—— on Saturday evening towards the Botanic Gardens. The College a noble pile, increasing in picturesque effect as it rises. Struck with the many changes which a walk on a previous evening brought us to see,—the bridges over the Kelvin, the demolition of North Woodside House, the quiet country road invaded by new thoroughfares. How the stream of time runs on! Thought of my dear uncle away. How much he was identified with Hillhead and the city, and now he is scarcely known. Man at his best estate is vanity, vanity stamped on everything. So much oppressed with this feeling the other night that I could scarcely shake it off. On the morning of the 24th spoke as delicately as I could to Mr. Buchanan, Carbeth, about buying a little ground, if he was willing to sell it, so as to preserve the amenity of the house in the country.

July 18.—On Saturday went to Stirling. Pleased with the window in the Old Church contributed by the Glasgow and Stirlingshire Charitable Society and by the "Sons of the Rock." Went to Callander, Loch Lubnaig;—arrived at Strathyre, went by a sheltered road to Balquhidder, Ben Ledi behind us; passed through the strath, and finally arrived at the site of the old church, beside which the remains of Rob Roy now lie. A most romantic spot. Loch Voil most exquisite in the distance,—the hills converging to the placid surface of the lake. . . . Stood for a moment on the tombstone.

August 18.—Much struck with a picture of Napoleon I. taken a few days before his death at St. Helena. A face expressive of great suffering, with a subdued kind of look. On the 11th entered on my fifty-fourth year. How solemn the present time, when nations are made to reap what they have sown. Prussia punished for her high-handed robbery of the territory of Denmark and Hanover and other States; France for ambitious designs, unsettling the peace of other countries. The declaration of war of 15th July was simultaneous with the declaration of the Pope's infallibility.

August 31.—On Friday night paid a visit to Carnock, a very fine old place. Beautiful trees, walks, and garden. A kind of magnificence about the garden in front of the house. The house several hundred years old—1543 on the door we entered by. An oaken bar, said to be of Bruce's time, slipped in behind the door as a barrier. The stone walls very thick. The rooms, leading from a common stair, are like cells. The family portraits in the dining-room very interesting. Met Mr. Park[1] of Airth at dinner—once Librarian of the College—revived old College stories.

September 15.—How pleasant to see my father's place smile. William M'Intosh, now eighty-two, once my father's servant, called on Saturday last. He spoke of my father having a tear in his eye when he bade him farewell on leaving for India. N—— and I dined with A. Orr Ewing on Saturday, 10th. Very lovely night, sunset beautiful; the drive home by moonlight exquisite. Present at the dinner given to Sir John P. Grant—the grandest affair I ever was at—on the 6th inst.

September 24.—Came home to-day from Dumfries. A most interesting line of railway along the banks of the Nith. I must study it. Burns often in my mind in his passionate love of nature. Visited on Friday the Greyfriars' Church and St. Michael's Church. The churchyard contains the dust of Robert Burns. Very much affected

[1] Minister of Airth.

by that monument. I was told Thomas Carlyle, as a boy, climbed the wall to see the spot. What a peculiar interest genius throws over a place. How wide that man's influence has been for good and evil. Visited the house where he lived and died. A little girl pointed to the corner where he breathed his last. A little low-ceiled room looking out on a lane. I stood and read the inscriptions on the graves of the two martyrs—William Welsh and William Grierson (1667). How we cling to the memory of men who have sealed their testimony with their blood. Trying to interest the public bodies about the Logan and Johnston School being near the Buchanan Institution.

October 13.—N—— and I returned to-day from N——'s wedding.[1] Yesterday a tempest. The previous evening (Tuesday) there were one or two rainbows, indicating unsettled weather. Very beautiful; the western sky lighted up with the glow of sunset and the moon shining calmly on the sea. There was a fair representation of both connections: H. M. Matheson and his uncle, General Matheson; General M'Donald and his wife and daughters; Miss Catherine M'Farlan, Miss Christian M'Farlan, Miss M'Farlan, Muiravonside, and her brother; Mr. and Mrs. J. Orr Ewing; Dean Hood, etc. . . . . Affected with the trials of the poor; yet they are happy in the midst of trials. How widely diffused is happiness. Looked at the ruins of the Hunterian Museum; probably I may get some memorial stone.

November 17.—Got some part of the frieze of the Hunterian Museum and sent it out to the country, as a memento of old College associations.

December 14.—How difficult to step out from the ranks in a career of true public spirit.

1871.

January 2.—I looked at my dear uncle's bust.
How considerate of others, how sensitively alive to the credit of the various branches of his family. I sent Michael Connal, Chesterfield, some notes about our family connec-

[1] Eleonora Leckie-Ewing married John Matheson M'Donald.

tion, which ha interested him. He had sent a
original of the marriage settlement of my great-gran
[Patrick Connal, 1749].

February 4.—The country beautiful even in its
dress.

February 16.—The Stirlingshire and Sons of the
Society dinner took place—the first dinner of the
societies. H. Campbell, M.P., in the chair. . .
window has cost me above £70. I have not had a
support in it.

February 20.—The Spring beginning to manifes
Walked round the little property. On Thursday,
at Edinburgh at Mr. Kirkpatrick's[1] funeral. Affecte
tracing up family history to interest Michael
Chesterfield. Where are they? How true, "the pla
knows us shall soon know us no more." The great
is to be living by faith in Christ and attempting
His strength.

March 25.—Much exhilarated by the sight of the
budding and the tokens of Spring. . . . I did
to the promenade in the Corporation Galleries on T
—the marriage-day of the Marquis of Lorne an
Royal Highness Princess Louise. This event has
happiness to a large proportion of Her Majesty's sul

April 20.—I am happy to find that the lads have
so much interest in their Greek. Gave —— 12s. to
Greek dictionary.

May 27.—We meet here for a little in the world
how solemn the responsibility to do good while we
the opportunity. At Glenorchard at dinner on Thu
25th inst. Paris the subject of conversation. I ho
of this baptism of blood, France will consider her
The future is very dark. Went the other night to s
wild beasts. These denizens of the forest, caged
our inspection, interesting, but humiliating. How fea
met with in their native haunts. "There is a lion
way" implies a sore trial. The little pony "Fanny"

[1] John Kirkpatrick, Supreme Judge of Ionian Islands, grand
Sir Thomas Kirkpatrick, third Bart. of Closeburn, married Jea
daughter of Captain John Glas.

better. The fields, the hedges, the trees, all beautiful. Alexander Connal home. He had been three weeks in Jerusalem. Bailie Watson appears interested in my remarks upon the old dial-plate in the Gallowgate, and I hope to secure it from destruction.

July 1.—N—— left yesterday for North Berwick with Miss Marion Kirkpatrick, where they have arrived safely.

July 26.—The papers to-day contain Thiers' speech about Popery, and the hold it has on France. The expression, "Whose assistance we accept in the moral government of France," is most suggestive. The reply of Gladstone to the Irish deputation most alarming, as showing the coming struggle with that system about to be renewed. These sentiments could not be brought so easily to the surface unless nations and statesmen were heaving under them.

August 16.—The papers full of the centenary of Sir Walter Scott. There has been some good speaking, and that in quarters where I did not expect it. The banquet in the City Hall a very grand affair. The speaking very good, particularly Jowett's, Sheriff Bell's, and Dr. Macleod's. Robert Monteith's was that of a man of culture. It took place on the 9th. There was a remarkable unity of thought between the speeches in Edinburgh and Glasgow. I believe Sir Walter Scott was pointed out to me in Edinburgh at St. James's Square. It was in the street leading out towards Leith Walk. It must have been in 1830 or so. How few have seen him. There are some things to do. The printing of the minutes of the West India Association, etc., and the writing of an autobiography, so that all my manuscripts may be utilized for whoever may care to preserve the record, and be benefited by it. . . The

on the 9th August. How strange that scientific men should discredit the supernatural. Went with N—— to the flower show in the Botanic Gardens on Thursday evening, 10th. Very creditable.

August 26.—The subjects to be brought before Lord Shaftesbury may be like a photograph of the condition of the city in its moral and spiritual state, so far as the means are in operation to elevate the masses, in the education of children and youths, and to alleviate the poverty and distress in all classes.

September 7.—I had the honour of being introduced to Lord Shaftesbury, and spoke for one moment about the Old Pye Street Refuge, Westminster. His remark to me about adult criminals—"They must be dealt with individually"—contained a great deal of wisdom. I was thankful the party had good weather on Friday and Saturday so as to make these days pleasant.

October 20.—I spent Monday last till 5 o'clock at Parkhall; very much the better of fresh air and occupation; trimming the trees in the Fintry Road. My mother wonderfully well. How sweet the little place looks in the gorgeous colouring of autumn. The meeting yesterday of the Technical College Committee; more like something definite. Its aim appears too grand on paper. It starts with what cannot be realized without enormous funds. It must be gradual.

November 18.—About this time took advantage of favourable weather to plant some trees (about 2500) in the high wood at Parkhall. I hope they may thrive. I have been promised the old dial-plate in the Gallowgate by Mr. James Watson, now Lord Provost.

December 16.—A great many demands on my time of late. None so unsatisfactory as responding to dinner invitations. These are a great waste of time. It has been a most interesting thing to observe the public anxiety as to the critical illness of the Prince of Wales.

1872.

January 17.—The Stirlingshire dinner came off on Monday, 15th inst., William Connal in the chair. William Corbett, the oldest living member, present. Mr. Robert Hart also present (James Watt's friend). A rather successful meeting; 38 new members. The son of William Campbell,

little. Wrote to-day to London about out-door pensioners of the Royal Asylum for Incurables. The bond over Stirling's Library shown to me cancelled. Things are getting into shape there. The Technical College programme agreed upon. I dined at the Dean of Guild's yesterday—an official dinner. Sat for a little in the dining-room with Dr. Norman Macleod, who recommended Elliot Nicol's Bible lessons. He appeared to think that the sceptical opinions of the present day should be met by young men who are teachers being called together in conference. Think often with pleasure of the "Spout" progressing. Surely it will do good to young men.

February 24.—I was asked to attend Miss Isabella Glas' funeral (last surviving daughter of Provost John Glas), on Tuesday, 20th, at Stirling.

March 9.—Went up to Lanark along with a good number of justices, to vote for a procurator-fiscal for the Airdrie district on 5th inst. The change did me good.

March 15.—Heard to-day that Mr. Buchanan, Carbeth, died yesterday. My mother's neighbours passing away. It may lead to great changes in that country-side.

March 30.—I think that some women may give themselves to the work of nurses without neglecting other claims.

April 20.—I went up to the old College yesterday. I passed into the library, about to be taken down, and into the Greek class-room. I felt for a moment a pang of real mental distress when I recalled my want of preparation one day, the fruit of ill-regulated studies and trifling precious time. I remembered forty years ago with a pang; I almost shed tears. . . . . I have been struck with a remark in the *Illustrated News*, in an article on Mr. Maurice. It shows how a train of thought was running in his mind that was also in mine in 1848, when the "Spout" took its rise. It is to this effect:—"The democratic agitation between Chartism and Socialism that spread to England from the French Revolution of 1848 was to be met with earnest co-operative efforts by the more affluent classes, to aid the working men to better their own condition. Wealth, leisure for recreation, and the means of good education were the objects most desired. The main result of the movement that originated in the autumn of 1849 was the founding of the Working-men's College." I have a few things to do, and I wish to do them well. The speculative mania in shares, mines, etc., is carrying men off from sober pursuits.

April 29.—Our pet dog very far through. How such a little companion steals in upon our habits and adapts himself to our wants. . . . The country beautiful, but the air keen.

May 29.—Mr. Russell, the chaplain to the Commissioner, secured me a ticket for the dinner at Holyrood on the 28th inst. I went into Edinburgh by the five train, drove to the Palace; servants in white and gold liveries; shook hands with the moderator, Dr. Jamieson, in the reception-room; Mr. Ramsay, purse-bearer, and Mr. Russell. Was presented to His Grace the Earl of Airlie. Sat on his right hand, Mr. Hannan being between me and His Grace; Col. Mure of Caldwell on his left. Dined in the long picture gallery. Pages, pipers. Very much gratified by the kindness shown me. Passed through Queen Mary's room on our way to the Banqueting Hall.

June 17.—Young's statue of Graham, the chemist, now in its place, but I have not had time to look at it.

July 15.—Poor T. Richardson died at Perth on 26th June. His hearty, shrewd character very attractive. . . . Michael Connal, Mauritius, gazetted within the last week as a member of the Legislative Council.

August 7.—On Saturday, 3rd, met Dr. Andrew Buchanan, and he showed me a letter from Dr. David Livingstone, of date 18th December, Ujuji.

September 6.—I am more than ever convinced that sticking to a principle ensures success in the long run.

September 26.—Saw Mr. Lowe yesterday opposite the Provost's house on my way home. Archbishop Manning in the City Hall on Tuesday night on the Permissive Bill. A great deal of good sense and good feeling in his speech. There should be more liberty than the permission of two-thirds of a community as to such accommodation of a public house.

November 11.—Walked round the Green by myself; thought of being useful to that district if God spares me. The Buchanan Institution and the Logan and Johnston School already great blessings. . . . Recommended young men to keep note books.

December 7.—Very happy in my mother being with us since Monday, 2nd December, and apparently quite well. Had Major M'Farlan and his wife, Sheriff and Mrs. Erskine Murray, and Andrew Melville at dinner yesterday.

1873.

March 1.—Before I left the country Dr. Guthrie's death mentioned to me.

March 29.—After a period of excitement, extending over a fortnight, I have been returned for the Glasgow School Board as one of fifteen. I felt very calm all along, and I had some hope of success till the afternoon of Thursday, when some information transpired that implied I had only a chance. The result has overturned all calculation. I accepted the invitation to stand at the close of last month. I consulted ——, and though warned on all hands of the difficulty and trouble of the office, I have seriously given my mind to it, in the hope of doing good to my native city, and in a way that will tell for the future above all others. At dinner at Dr. Rainy's on Thursday, the 20th. Met Dr. R. Buchanan, Principal Fairbairn, and Sir W. Thomson.

April 12.—Busy this afternoon at home with the ordnance maps of the city to assist the School Board. The first meeting on Tuesday, 8th April, courteous and business-like.

April 26.—The choice of a clerk a serious matter. I hope the Board may be rightly directed. On Friday morning in Mr. Whitelaw's office examining the testimonials of candidates. J. A. Campbell, Mr. Kerr, and Mitchell present with Mr. Whitelaw.

June 23.—Paid up the balance of the Stirlingshire Society window. Think that I have paid enough—about £80 out

July 17.—With Whitelaw to-day at Springburn looking out for a site for a school. We exchanged opinions as to the great difficulty we have before us in the religious question. I hate Limited Liability Companies.

August 7.—The dreadful railway accident at Wigan makes one almost timid in travelling.

August 25.—At Wemyss Bay with my aunt. Lord Shaftesbury there. I hope that great and good man may be spared for a great work yet. The Archæological Society goes to-morrow to Crossraguel Abbey. I cannot go with them. As I have been writing a thunderstorm has swept over the city.

September 8.—At Parkhall from Saturday till this morning. The moon rose in most resplendent majesty above the hills immediately behind Ballikinrain. God has given us good harvest weather. . At the School Board; took notes of all that was said. The impression left on my mind is that Page Hopps has overdone his part. He has ridden his hobby to death and to the disgust and alarm of all right-thinking men. The Roman Catholics have stood by him in direct opposition to their own convictions of the necessity of religious education in education worthy of the name. Oh Lord, give me grace to work while it is day. How prejudices vanish when we look at the eternal realities, the petty disputes and heart-burnings of life.

September 23.—The sale of Carbeth a very sad thing to the family and neighbourhood; about four hundred years in the Buchanan family. I have never so much as got an opportunity to look at it. Motives of delicacy always withheld me from asking questions.

October 13.—N—— and I heard the Jubilee Singers in the City Hall on 9th instant. I was very much struck with their plaintive melodies, and interested in their appearance.

October 25.—At Janet Ewing's funeral at Kippen yesterday. . . . No wonder the affections of the family cling to that happy home. Dr. Candlish's death a solemn event. His funeral on Friday last.

November 10.—Feel more than ever the value of Dr.

Buchanan and Mr. Whitelaw in the School Board. I have not gone near the musical festival this week. I feel some repugnance to the Word of God being sung for amusement; yet it is the alliance of genius and high art in illustrating the sentiments and ideas of Scripture. Met Dr. Bryce of Belfast, and spoke of his lectures in 1841.

November 22.—Disraeli to-day in the City Hall. At the Corporation Galleries on Thursday, 20th, at the luncheon given by the Provost. Very much pleased to see him (Disraeli) admiring Pitt's statue. He must have regarded it with much interest; the living and the dead statesman; the politics of the past and of the present must have been floating in the mind of the living one. Heard his voice in a few sentences and then left. His appearance most peculiar . At the Miners' Mission Conversazione. . . . The roughness and yet warmth of heart of the miners dwelt on; their low domestic state and yet high wages. Bought Disraeli's *Sybil* to-day, that I might read about the Queen's accession to the throne.

December 23.—The drowning of Sir James Colquhoun in Loch Lomond on Thursday last (18th) the subject of wide-spread sorrow.

1874.

January 3.—The Provost spent an hour on Saturday evening last reading a defence against Walter Smith's attack on the School Board accounts. Tried to advise him to forbear and let the matter drop, which eventually he has agreed to do.

January 14.—I almost wept yesterday, everything was so dark. At the banquet to Sir Bartle Frere on the 8th January. His remarks very good and interesting to Scotchmen. . . . . I have been looking over my Uncle Eben's manuscript [family history]. How we all do fade as a leaf!

January 24.—On Monday, 19th, at the Stirlingshire Society dinner, at which I have dined regularly, with two or three exceptions, since 1839. On Friday morning went into Edinburgh with Mr. T. A. Mathieson and Mr. Warren.

Met the Endowed School Commissioners, etc. Hope that a good impression was produced. Previous to this went into the Parliament House and had a long talk with R. Horn, advocate, about old stories. After dinner at Mrs. M'Farlan's, 28 Stafford Street, went out with her and her daughter to see the illumination on the occasion of the Duke of Edinburgh's marriage (23rd January). St. George's Church dome lighted up; castle with lines of fire; gardens sparkling; orderly crowd; Princes Street magnificent.

January 31.—The country in a turmoil with the elections. Whitelaw a candidate, well supported. The community have been taken by surprise by Gladstone's dissolution of Parliament. His financial speech a masterly address to the Greenwich electors.

February 16.—The Buchanans leave Carbeth to-morrow, apparently finally. How sad! A stranger occupies their home. Shook hands with them in church yesterday. The window now erected in Kippen Parish Church to Mr. W. L. Ewing, and very satisfactory as a work of art. . . . I would rather have painstaking, persistent attention to preparation for the pulpit than erratic evangelistic effort. I look with much solicitude to Whitelaw leaving the Board for his duties in London. It would imperil our position to have another election under the vacancy. The duties of this Board more and more engrossing.

February 25.—On the 17th met the Parochial Boards and spoke, probably inadvisably, about the education of pauper children. Tempted sometimes by the excitement of the moment to speak when I should keep quiet.

March 4.—Yesterday went down to Mrs. Col. Campbell's funeral along with W. Connal and his two youngest sons, the oldest being on the Continent, having been with Mrs. Hunter at Florence. Fletcher of Dunans on board, to whom I had afterwards an opportunity to speak about Miles Fletcher of Parkhall. He told me that he was a rather distant relative; that Archibald Fletcher, the [illegible] his father as a boy. . . . . I was forcibly reminded of the Colonel's funeral on the 4th October, 1856. Laid the old lady in her grave in the same romantic spot, amongst the trees close by the stream that flows into the Ruel. The picturesque hills very beautiful from their being partially covered by mist. A vague grandeur all up the loch, particularly about South-Hall. Colonel Campbell of South-Hall at the funeral. Mr. Gordon, the Lord-Advocate, was to have been there, but was summoned to London to be sworn as a Privy Councillor. Mrs. Col. Campbell had held him up in her arms as his godmother. She was of the Munros of Teaninich,[1] about Ullapool. The season of the year and the extreme distance prevented older friends of the family being present. . . . Mr. Story of Rose-neath there. . . . There is a vague anxiety about news from Coomassie; a disaster is feared.

March 21.—Sir Garnet Wolseley arrived in London to-day. The victory over the King of the Ashantees complete.

March 28.—I visited the graveyard round the College Church, so soon to be removed; a neglected-looking place. The date, 1699, is cut on the lintel of the door. Elected a member of the executive committee of the approaching Social Science Meeting (September next).

May 9.—Stephen Mitchell's gift of £70,000 for a library announced.

May 23.—Mr. Caughie dead; the prince of infant teachers. On Monday, 18th, looked again for the stone lost in the *débris* of the Principal's house in the University—the stone about the Blackadders of Tulliallan.

June 5.—On Monday, 25th ult., arranged to get the lintel of the old Grammar School, with the date 1601 on it. The Patronage Bill of the Government may prove a stumbling-block to many in the Free Church. Tannahill's memory celebrated in Paisley on 3rd June. I think it a vain thing to exult in the association of the poor poet with Paisley, when they did no good to him during his life.

[1] Mrs. Campbell was the elder daughter of Thomas Warrand of Warrandfield, Inverness-shire, by Catherine, only surviving daughter of Captain James Munro, R.N., of Teaninich, Ross-shire.

His lyrics may be specimens of genius, but that a whole community should be turned out for a holiday is too much. Probably a holiday on other grounds came opportunely.

June 15.—My mother has been suddenly taken ill. Went out immediately by 4.40 train; got Dr. Morton to accompany me. The gravity of the attack arises from her advanced age. She had written me the day before in such a good, firm hand, I was quite unprepared for the stroke. Dear, dear one, she is better; but I must prepare for separation ere long. I felt I must sit loose to the world; it is passing away. May this impression never leave me.

June 26.—Was struck with a remark of a woman about the boys on Wednesday on the Gourock road—"That there were a great many little minds there, and that we did not know what they might come to." One generation goeth and another cometh.

July 6.—Got to-day the old dial-plate from the house in the Gallowgate—a memento of thirty-five years.

July 14.—Met Dr. Rainy and his daughter in Woodside Terrace. He said that he hoped soon to meet my mother in a better world. I was very much affected as I left him.

August 12.—Cosmo Innes died within the last ten days. I have often thought of the probable effect of the Patronage Bill on the Free Church. The arrangements for the Social Science Congress are thickening. Captain Stirling of the prison and Mr. Quarrier at me; notes from Dr. Gairdner and John Burt. Oh Lord, make me more and more useful. The vanity of everything here presses on me as I sit beside the feeble form of that dear one in the little bedroom at Parkhall.

September 9.—On Wednesday, 2nd September, I went down to Cardross, Dumbartonshire, to visit the Watsons. Walked round the cliff of that beautiful promontory of the Firth of Clyde. Lost my luggage; a great source of discomfort to me. It is believed to have been stolen.

September 28.—The aspect of the country very sad from bad weather and the sombre tints of autumn. The little burns full of water. Lord Craighill and Mr. Warner-Wright to be our guests during Social Science Congress. On Monday, the 21st, had a prolonged meeting at the School Board. Did not get home till seven o'clock. The masters of the High School at last managed to accommodate themselves to the new order of things. At the distribution of prizes in the City Hall on Friday, the 25th.

October 12.—Came in from the country very early this morning. My dear mother feeble, and not so cheerful as I used to leave her. I was beside her a good deal yesterday. I am rather more anxious about her. O Lord, into Thy hands I commend her dear spirit. Shall I receive good at the hands of the Lord, and shall I not receive evil? Exposed to all the bustle of receiving friends during the Congress from Wednesday, the 30th September, to Thursday, 8th October. Very glad to renew old friendship with John Millar, now Lord Craighill. Mr. Warner-Wright, from Norwich, a very fine, frank young Englishman. The reception in the College interesting, but the room insufficiently lighted. . Introduced J. Millar to great many friends. Glad to get home. Took my place in the "Repression of Crime" Section and never left it. The Corporation Gallery conversazione rather tame. Introduced by the Provost to Lord Rosebery. I hope that good may result from all this. The Provost introduced me to Sir Joseph Napier on Wednesday morning. The men that I got to write papers all made their appearance in time, which was very satisfactory. The country very beautiful in its decay. . Elected a director of the Merchants' House.

November 2.—Came in from the country. The dreadful storm of wind has blown down a good many trees, particnlarly a fine beech and an oak, besides some poplars, and started others. Walked round the place. Up in the high wood this morning; the trees thriving.

November 21.—Wrote Joseph Hooker about the death of his wife.

November 30.—Came in from the country to-day; the aspect bleak. There was a sad tinge over my mind, for I left my dear mother weak, and not so strong as she was ten days ago.

December 16.—I had to go to Mrs. Connal's to di
Dr. L. Lockhart there. Spoke of his father and old t
Had a letter to-day from R. Horn, advocate, abou
father-in-law's bust. I noticed in the newspapers
William Cullen Bryant, the American poet, had his ei
third year celebrated. I remember when Dr. Guthri
on his Manse Scheme, going down to Ayrshire,
anxious I was to introduce him to Bryant. I am
looking after the College stone—Blackadder of Tull
memorial stone.

1875—1878

January 6.—I am more and more impressed with the sweeping away of one generation after another.
The servants to have a party to-night.

January 25.—The Stirlingshire (dinner) passed off well. Sir William Edmonstone in the chair. Replied for the office-bearers. Very weary in my business, and I think, before I lose all my energy, I should devote the remaining years of my life to more congenial work. Went to M'Clure's to look at the picture by Miss Thompson—"The Roll Call." It is not a picture to get into raptures about, but it is touching and simple. A sad, business-like look about it.

February 6.—My dear mother continues much the same. How pleasing to think that she takes interest in everything. She saw "Gracie" from her bedroom window with the cart, taking away leaves from the lawn. At the Prisoners' Aid Society. A great deal of good done modestly and economically. Walter Paterson's influence had brought people not usually attracted to such meetings. Mr. Whitelaw passed through the ordeal of seconding the speech yesterday pretty well. He is a man of mark.

February 22.—At Stirling. . . . Looked at grandmother's old house. Arranged with Mr. Chrystal that if it ever came into the market to let me know.

March 1.—Refused to accompany —— to the meeting with the Magistrates about singing saloons. There is a class of men who think that by social influence they can put down things. The meeting may be useful in calling attention to what is indecent in the performances and music, but there may be a difficulty in parties being harmonious as to a remedy for this state of things.

April 17.—Dr. Robert Buchanan's death embodied in a minute (School Board), with some suitable expression of regret. I feel his loss ; it stunned me when William Speirs told me on Wednesday, 31st March.

May 6.—Read to-night some interesting notices of the residence of the Fletchers at Parkhall in 1817 in Mrs. Fletcher's autobiography. Came in from the country on Monday ; my dear mother wonderfully well. She was on the sofa in her room for an hour on Tuesday, and saw the old pear tree in blossom. How bright and green everything is in the country, and how full of melody the bushes and hedges, and how busy the crows. The ponies, the little dog, all full of life and interest.

June 2.—Last night at the conversazione in the Corporation Galleries. Had some pleasant talk with MacNee the painter about the pictures. . . . Went round the South-Side schools with J. A. Campbell yesterday ; the new schools are all princely buildings. Felt gratified to-day by the venerable Dr. Rainy asking for my mother.

August 25.—My mother very much exhausted. Can I doubt the mercy of God when I think that since 1830, when she came home a widow from India, He has upheld her? It is thirty-four years since Fanny was taken away, and we were left alone in the world. . . . Wrote Mr. Graham Gilbert, thanking him for his kind present of grapes to my mother.

September 6.—My mother died at 2 A.M. on the 2nd September. . . . Thought frequently to-day of the happy years I spent with my mother. . . . O Lord, give me grace to be useful and to seek to be guided by Thy holy providence.

September 8.—The funeral started at 10.30, and we arrived at Lynedoch Crescent just as the company were assembling. Pall-bearers—Alexander Connal, Dr. Gibson, J. C. Gibson, William Wright, George Henderson, R. Leckie Ewing, Sir James Alexander. Mr. Johnston presided ; touching prayer. Principal Douglas followed. In the evening reached Parkhall by 4.40 train.

This morning opened her desk, and read what my mother wished in the memorandum left in her own handwriting. I shall try to fulfil those injunctions, as if she were beside me. . . . . Many kind letters of sympathy.

October 4.—Went to the Grammar School to look at the stone which Mr. Paton described as quite a feature of the building. Felt cut to the heart when ascending the stair to old Dr. Dymock's class-room (1826-7). The thought of the folly and trifling of youth comes back again and again in the race of life.

October 7.—Went into Edinburgh with J. A. Campbell and W. Kidston, etc., to consult counsel [School Board business]. Saw Mr. Rutherford Clark (Dean of Faculty) and Mr. Watson (Solicitor-General). Then visited Normal Seminaries; went into two or three of the old rooms of Moray House.

November 4.—Interested in the death of Dr. Forbes, Bishop of Brechin—an old college companion. I could not have fancied him turning out a dignified ecclesiastic, with such high notions of his own communion.
At the School Board to-day. Mr. Galloway, writer, told me that if it had not been for the vigorous hold taken by Mr. Whitelaw, etc., at the first, we must have paid more money to-day for sites—probably by many thousands.

December 19.—J. E. Mathieson wrote me about some-one to represent the China Mission. Thought of Mr. Sloan.

1876.

February 5.—The Stirlingshire dinner took place in M'Lean's Hotei—Mr. Bolton in the chair. I sat next Sir William Edmonstone, and we had some pleasant talk together. I gave "The Imperial Parliament." Sir William had been absent from only one out of 248 divisions last session. He said he intended to stick to his work as long as he could crawl. This was rather ominous for Bolton, who is the future Liberal candidate for the county. Sir James Alexander stayed with us that night. Had

Mr. Whitelaw at dinner, with members of the Board, on Monday, 31st January; very pleasant. Mr. Whitelaw, in taking leave of the Board on Thursday, 3rd February, made a most feeling allusion to Dr. Buchanan's and Dr. M'Ewan's removal by death, while thanking the Board for their consideration and kindness to himself personally. That man has a great many amiable qualities. On Thursday evening attended the opening of Centre Street School. It is a great honour to have to do with such institutions and such a movement. . . . Affectingly reminded of the past by having to declare that my father had died in 1829, and that he had left my mother nothing. This to satisfy the Inland Revenue Department as to my mother's estate. Miss Cooper, Ballindalloch, our guest from 25th to 29th January.

February 26.—The election of members of School Board the subject of public discussion. I attended one of the first meetings on the 9th inst., presided over by Professor Berry, when Kidston made a statement, and J. A. Campbell declined to stand, which led to a shower of compliments from Dr. Jamieson and others. No doubt Mr. Whitelaw's withdrawal and his is a loss. I did not like the complexion of the meeting; it appeared to be too much of a conclave, which might give offence outside. I honestly stated that I intended to stand as a candidate, but that I did not wish to be the nominee of a conclave. I think that I may be useful to the Board, and I don't think it would be fair to desert it in such a crisis, for on the continuance of the present arrangements much depends as to the future success of the Bill. There may be fresh legislation before the next term of office expires. I visited my dear mother's grave on Sabbath morning, the 20th. On the 22nd I sat for my photograph, for Mr. Whitelaw's album, for the School Board. . . . I feel the responsibility of the position I am placed in as before the community. The prospect of a settlement of the question as to the complexion of the [illegible] interested. On Thursday was at the dinner given by the School Board to Mr. Whitelaw. I think the meeting was a success. Mr. Whitelaw was presented with an illuminated address, and he made a most feeling reply. We had a good many books to show, and Kidston had some knick-knacks. It was a snowy night; a severely protracted winter. The three daily papers, on different grounds, appeared rather to slight me. The poll satisfactory. I think Whitelaw should not have hazarded Mr. Dodds' candidature; he has injured Mr. Cuthbertson. The summation of the votes must have heen most fatiguing. Whitelaw at it all night and up to the last.

April 5.—Met at School Board on Tuesday, the 4th. I was elected Chairman. I feel more than ever the necessity of devoting myself to this work. Congratulations on all hands. Miss Helen M'Farlan with us for a few days. Talked with us to-night about what took place on the 18th May, 1843. Her father was a leading man in the movement.

April 27.—Was present at Sir William Stirling Maxwell's inauguration as Chancellor of the University. At breakfast in Queen's Hotel in the morning at J. Cleland Burns' invitation. At the opening of the Museum in Kelvingrove Park on Tuesday, the 18th instant.

May 6.—Saw accidentally in the *Stirling Observer* the death of Robert Johnston Brown, late Colonel of 14th Hussars, in London. Strange to have been in such complete ignorance of that man's whereabouts for so long a time, when we were thrown together in youth.

May 22.—I cannot tell how sorry I was at the loss of my little cat. I had bought some medicine for it, and it was away. It must have crept into some hole and died. And poor little "Trim" has been amissing in the country for more than a week. These things wean me from pets. . . . I cannot be a party to Disestablishment, as, on the other hand, I cannot join the Establishment. I believe that the hand of the civil power will, after some years, find its way to humble her, for she has reaped an advantage at the expense of the sufferings of others without acknowledging it. But for the existence and prosperity of the Free Church she never would have got rid of Patronage, and the State has never acknowledged the wrong she did to the party who left in 1843.

June 8.—Dr. Eadie's funeral yesterday. His death and the notice of him in the newspapers call up the remembrance of Tillicoultry. A kind note from Joseph Hooker on the 5th instant.

July 3.—On Thursday I distributed the prizes to the High School boys in the Queen's Rooms. I tried to say something about Natural History and about Caius College (Cambridge) and its entrances. That same evening I distributed the prizes in Kennedy Street, and on Wednesday at Finnieston. . . . It was very gratifying to see the children. A very affecting thing took place at Oatlands. A poor mother received the book intended for her boy, who had died suddenly—I put it quietly aside into her hands. The great James Baird's death has occurred, and his will rather disappoints me: *he* might have left a good sum to the University.

August 7.—At the laying of the memorial stone of Hutchesons' Grammar School, and afterwards at the dinner. The display of plate and flowers very fine; the hall quite baronial. Replied to a toast as to the School Boards. Interested in seeing Sir Daniel MacNee there. Came in from the country on Monday, 31st July, in the same train with Thomas Carlyle; recognised him from his photograph. He had been the guest of the Arbuthnots at Old Ballikinrain. Mr. Jeffray, of the Mills of Balfron, invited me to make an offer for the piece of ground that formed part of Parkhall, Endrick Field. . . . I try to be content with what I have. My father had no more ground than I have. I may not set my heart on anything here. It certainly would be a pity if he (Mr. Jeffray) created some dis-

September . . . Have invited Sir Thomas M'Clure

is now two years since I met him (Dr. Rainy) walking in Woodside Terrace, and when he expressed himself so solemnly and affectingly as to the meeting with my mother in a better world. At the School Board for a little, and then met Mr. Jeffray and closed with him for the ground—Endrick Field. I was quite calm and decided.
I would have reproached myself had it passed into unfriendly hands. After Dr. Rainy's funeral took Professor Grant down to look at the dial from the Gallowgate. He is to direct me as to its position on the wall of the school in Græme Street.

September 1.—At the opening of Henderson Street School on Wednesday night. Said something about North Woodside and its associations with the Hamilton (North Park) family, Sir Thomas Munro, etc. On Tuesday evening at the opening of the third British Workmen's Public House without drink. Heard Dr. Wallace and Bailie Torrens speak. Said something which Mr. S—— M—— thought to the point about Dr. Norman Macleod's saying: "If I were a working-man, unless restrained by higher motives, I would go to the public-house for excitement."

September 12.—On my way to examine an exhibition of Natural History objects, N—— overtook me with news that Mr. Angus Turner had been drowned at Wemyss Bay. He had gone in to bathe at the rocks beside Villa Clutha. He travelled with me on Tuesday last from Stirling with Mrs. Caton and her son, and was as full of intelligence as usual on all subjects. I went down yesterday . . . and made some arrangements as to the funeral. On Tuesday went to Stirling by mistake for the 6th of September. At Lieutenant Cameron's lecture in the evening. On Wednesday went to the College reception room. Mr. Sherman Crawford, his sister, and young Dr. Balfour dined with us. Called at Mrs. Campbell's, and saw Dr. Hooker and his wife and lunched with them. At the President's Address (Professor Andrews) in the evening; moderate and sensible. Some interesting things in the Archæological cases. Thursday evening at the conversaziones in the Royal Exchange and the Philosophical afterwards. Professor Hedges dined with us on Thursday, and Dr. Laing on Friday. At

Professor Tait's lecture on "Force." . . . Sir James Campbell died on the 10th at Stracathro.

October 2.—Just in time for the presentation, in the City Hall, of the freedom of the city to Richard A. Cross, Home Secretary. Then went to Great Dovehill to see about the Sun Dial, 1708. How gratified I am to see such a noble building in that part of the city, and on that spot. Had a deputation of pupils of Buchanan Institution of 1861-63, inviting me to preside at their annual soiree on 1st December. How anxiously would I avoid these things; but I must encourage them. At the conversazione in the Garden Palace on 12th September. Professor Macnab and Mr. and Mrs. Russell dined with us. On the morning of that day heard an unpleasant discussion on Spiritualism in Section D (Biology).

October 18.—Very wet weather. Thankful that the Prince of Wales' visit is over, and that the city has sustained its credit in a loyal welcome. Loyalty needs to be expressed now and again to cherish it. . . . The tie between master and servant very slight. A small increase of wages will entice one away.

October 20.—Went to Edinburgh, and, after passing through the garden around Scott's monument, visited the exhibition of Sir Henry Raeburn's works in the National Galleries. Most interesting. Then met Mr. Middleton and Mr. Kennedy at 2.30 at the station, and accompanied them to the office of the Board of Education, and met Sir John D. Wauchope and Dr. Taylor on business. Compared with Glasgow how quiet and beautiful as a city. Affected to-day with the sad news of Sheriff Dickson's death. I saw him beside the Prince on the platform on Tuesday. How fleeting is life! Came home with Middleton and Mr. John Knox, of the Parochial Board, etc. Very pleasant talk about total abstinence and the licensing system. The people cannot be forced. The desire to be social lies at the bottom of a good deal of drinking. The man who went to Moir's Tea Shop would not give a "free claver over a glass" for all the tea in his shop. I return to Raeburn's pictures ere the impression passes off. A few lines—bold, rough—and a likeness is produced most life-like. The attitude of some pictures graceful in the extreme. A very sad and subdued feeling came over me after visiting the exhibition. They have passed away, and live only for their children in these pictures.

October 28.—Went to St. Enoch Station this afternoon to bid good-bye to Alexander Connal on his way to Nice. Roger Hennedy gone; poor fellow! How unhappy he was sometimes. I hope that it has been otherwise latterly. He took a fancy to me and introduced my name in the preface of his *Clydesdale Flora*. Witnessed on Saturday, the 18th, the launch of the "Northampton" (war vessel); magnificently and smoothly gliding into the water opposite Yorkhill. I feel weary sometimes; I want the elasticity of former years.

December 23.—Went to the Lord Advocate's on Tuesday, the 19th, as to some provision in future legislation for destitute and neglected children. The meeting considered a pleasant one, and so far satisfactory. At Sir James Watson's at an official dinner, as Dean of Guild, on Wednesday, 20th.

1877.

January 1.—I got a kind note from Lord Craighill, inviting me to the *levée* of the Judges on Circuit on Tuesday, 26th ult. He introduced me to Lord Young. I went to the court and witnessed the opening proceedings. I dined in the evening at Maclean's Hotel, and sat next Adam Paterson. I met a deputation of the Industrial School on Wednesday in the Board room, and on Thursday evening I presided at the meeting of evening classes in the City Hall. Upon the whole I was not satisfied with the result; it was too uproarious.

January 20.—I have been pained all day in recollecting that I had acted impatiently last night with ——. Went to the City Hall to hear Captain Markham lecture on the recent Arctic expedition—Sir William Thomson in the chair. The flag which he planted in the highest altitude ever attained by a ship was hung from a rod on the platform. It was interesting to see him as having passed through such a perilous expedition.

January 25.—Unveiling of Burns' statue in George Square. Read two columns of a note on his writings and the principal events of his life in the *Herald*. Very sad; so sad, that when the procession blocked the streets and I could not pass, I could scarcely look at it. Surely the whole thing is overdone. Burns gave graphic and beautiful expression to what thousands feel; but as for the man himself, he appears to have wasted life. It was not that he had nobler thoughts than many men who have shown heroism, courage, patient endurance, intensely pure affection, but who never gave expression to them; yet I cannot but feel the power of his genius.

February 10.—Went to Edinburgh—Dr. Duff and J. A. Campbell in the train with us. Talked with Dr. Duff about the Mohammedan College just started in India. Their exclusiveness is giving way. On Monday, 29th January, at the conversazione in the Athenæum. A bad night. Went there to show face; reluctant to add to my engagements. The School Board occupies a good deal of time, but it is hopeful kind of work. I am more than ever reluctant to accept invitations to platforms, etc.

February 25.—I think it was on the 13th that I went to Edinburgh to visit the classes of Mr. Schneider at Moray House, and at the High School. It was very interesting to visit these places of education. Afterwards went to the Scottish Board of Education to prepare the way for a grant of £100,000. I feel more than ever that I am getting up in years, and that it is more than ever incumbent on me to work while it is day. My paths of usefulness are now pretty well mapped out.

March 31.—Distribution of prizes. . . . It was interesting to see so many intelligent young persons—the hope of the city.

April 26.—Dined, at Lord Craighill's invitation, with Lord Adam on Tuesday, 24th; Sheriff Fraser, Sheriff Clark, and Principal Caird there. The removal of the Academy, Elmbank Street, westwards, and the High School to the Academy premises, the subject of discussion in the newspapers and University Court. We may yet find difficulties cropping up. There was an indication of the School of Art and Design looking out for premises in the East-End. I indicated the Buchanan Institution. It has been a long cherished dream of mine to have a branch in the East-End.

May 19.—At Ferniegair on Thursday evening, 10th inst., to visit the Kidstons. A beautiful sunset scene from his billiard-room window. Invited to dine at a State dinner on Thursday, 24th May (Queen's birthday), by invitation of the Provost. On 5th May, Mrs. Connal, W. L. M'Farlan, Keddie, etc., etc., at dinner. The story of Ure of Shirgarton came up.

June 28.—To-day I presided at the distribution of prizes at the High School. There was a "lining" of friends round the front gallery. It was very interesting to be brought so closely into contact with young and ardent minds. What a wholesome, elevating thing is this widespread interest in education.

July 12.—Hunted up yesterday the old stone that was embedded in the wall of the Principal's Court, old College. I have an impression that someone said, who had some knowledge of the locality, that in all probability it belonged to the old Blackfriars monastery, which once gave shelter to the University.

August 1.—Struck with the beauty of the Luss hills—bright green, with a crown of purple as the morning sun lighted them up. Sent out to-day to the country, three stones from Blackfriars churchyard, and one stone from the Principal's Court. These may serve to stir up a train of reflection now and again.

August 13.—I see the death of Charles B. Findlay, Boturich; very sad.

August 24.—Visited Dunblane Cathedral and Archbishop Leighton's library. Put my hands on a volume, very old—*Origen on Celsus*—in all probability handled by Leighton. . . . Kippenross trees very stately. . . . The little burns at Parkhall foaming and rushing from the heavy

September 10.—I think that I have a great taste for tracing out old places and family histories and weaving them into an address, and giving life and interest to what would otherwise be dry.

September 21.—The moon very bright, and Mars a very beautiful object in the firmament. Fine weather after a very rainy season. Had the opportunity of witnessing the opening of the Queen's Dock; a magnificent sight. The monster bridge, 800 tons in weight, swung sweetly round, admitting a large Atlantic steamer. On Thursday at the presentation of the freedom of the city to General Grant, and afterwards at the banquet. When speaking of old John Mitchell, now in his 90th year, the Provost was so kind as to introduce me to him [General Grant].

October 3.—Elected an extraordinary director of the Athenæum. Poor Cunningham Monteith dead.

October 16.—Presided at Dr. Logan Aikman's lecture on Monday evening, the 8th, on "Dr. Samuel Johnson." Said a few words, which apparently interested the audience, on his appearance and visit to Glasgow, 1773.

October 25.—Emily,[1] after a protracted illness, died at Solsgirth on Monday, 22nd inst.

October 31.—invited to be at the opening of the Mitchell Library to-morrow.

December 3.—W. Connal's daughter married quite privately to Mr. Warrand.

1878.

January 1.—I was present at the unveiling of Thomas Campbell's statue on the 28th December. The dinner was postponed.

January 11.—The marriage of A. Orr Ewing's daughter Edith, to Major Hazelrigg, celebrated at Ballikinrain on Wednesday, the 9th; a most glorious winter day. The was an interesting sight. The death of Robert Horn, Dean of the Faculty of Advocates, reminds me of old days.

January 26.—Miss Ella Orr Ewing so ill on the 22nd that there was no hope. . . . Shook hands to-day with James Stewart of Garvocks as the member for Greenock. A most severe struggle; the Liberal party divided; and Sir James Ferguson a man of great address and experience. Went out on Monday morning and looked at General Wolfe's house in Camlachie. How powerful association is!

February 14.—On Saturday morning last (the 9th) went out to Parkhall to attend the funeral of Miss Ella Orr Ewing. How very sad to be met in the magnificent corridor that was filled with a gay company on 9th January—just one month before—by A. Orr Ewing in deep distress. The service unusual: a hymn sung (66th paraphrase), and then all knelt (Dr. Charteris and Mr. M'Naughton). The interment was within the walls of the picturesque ruins of the old church. . . Rev. Dr. Dickson of the College called yesterday afternoon suggesting Sir Joseph T. Hooker as Chancellor of the University, and wanting me to sign a memorial to keep the office out of the region of politics. I declined; not that I did not sympathize, but I felt an incongruity in doing so—as if I were so influential in matters of that kind. I told him that I wished to keep to my own sphere. . . . Sir J. E. Alexander flourishing in the *Illustrated London News* as one of the chief parties to the rescue of Cleopatra's Needle from neglect. The war crisis saddening everyone. The institution of the Scotch hierarchy—the last act of the Pope—full of significance as to the growing pretensions of the Church of Rome.

March 2.—I was rather reluctantly put in the chair on Tuesday night at Professor Grant's lecture at the Athenæum. Delivered with clearness and freedom. He told us there were now 184 asteroids.

March 11.—Went to the soiree of the natives of Lewis on 8th. H. M. Matheson[1] presided, and said some good things about the necessity of the people coming in greater numbers to the mainland. The extraordinary attachment

[1] Hugh [illegible] Matheson of Little Scatwell, Ross-shire.

thought on my own leaving the world, that dear one away to the eternal world.

August 26.—Came in from the country to-day. At 7.30 on the brow of the hill where the plantation was. The whole field purple with heather in full bloom, the mist rising off the Lennox Hills, but quite enveloping the mountains to the north. . . . On Friday heard Lord Rosebery pay some compliments to Glasgow in presenting cheque at the Loan Exhibition, and at eight o'clock presided at the opening of the Garnethill School. I believe I made the meeting interested in the associations of the spot. . . . Had some interesting intercourse with Professor Grant and old Robert Hart (now in his ninetieth year) on the observatory on Garnethill. . Sir James Alexander wrote me about the Back Walk of Stirling. . . .

September 4.—At the School Board every day this week. On Monday I was at Anderston School from 10.30 to 1.30 with defaulting parents. Some very distressing cases. Went to the opening ceremony of the High School. I was happy in getting through this with comfort. The meeting is considered a success. The Lord Provost and four of the Magistrates came in their robes with the halberdiers. A fair representation of the community.

September 18.—I went to-night to the Queen's Rooms to hear Miss Faithfull lecture on "Extravagance." The Lord Provost presided, and I was unexpectedly called upon to propose a vote of thanks to her. I referred to the past relations with her father, etc.[1]

October 4.—[City of Glasgow Bank]. . . . There has been an unscrupulous use of facilities too lavishly bestowed on some men of enterprise. What a calamity! Many friends involved whose resources must be abridged, if they are not ruined.

October 8.—The meeting about the disposal of ground to Hutchesons' Hospital by the Buchanan Institution held to-day. Should it issue as I expect, how strange that my day-dreams will be realized in the erection of an important

[1] Mr. Faithfull, Vicar of Headley, was very kind to Sir Michael when

for it ten years ago.

October 18.—I left Parkhall [redacted]
(14th) with a rather heavy heart.
beautiful in the decay of the [redacted]
have duties here.

October 22.—I have come ho
my own personal comfort with [redacted]
hands of the law, friends and [redacted]
the charge of fraud in the police [redacted]
last made me dumb with [redacted]
Oh! what a wreck of character, [redacted]
city. . . . The Free Church
teaching is sneered at because [redacted]
the City Bank stood prominent [redacted]
I met Dr. S——, and told him [redacted]
and church courts being cautious,
lost. . . . I learned that the
the directors were in the police o
one. Monday's newspapers discl[redacted]
What infatuation, what facility, an
ruin.

November 7.—At the meeting
mittee of the Relief Fund yesterd
of the Merchants' House. . . .
November, left with Mr. Kenned
After reaching Westminster Palace
A—— waiting for us at breakfast
Francis R. Sandford, wandered dow
Embankment. I regarded it with i
sense of reverence, and yet that m
antiquity. Interview with Sandfo
and satisfactory. . Went
the seals, etc. The acrobatic perf
did not care to look at them.
or ten minutes into Westminste
crowded with monuments; the
Impressed with the grandeur of

[1] Henry Craik, C.B., M.A. Oxon., LL.D.,
Department.

Hyde Park to see Albert Memorial; magnificent. The gloss taken off London for me. On Sabbath morning wandered over Westminster Bridge to Stamford Street. Remembered the stifling heat in my lodgings forty-three years ago and more. Came over Blackfriars Bridge and went to St. Paul's. As Mr. Kennedy and I said, there could be little more cultivated there than a devout spirit, for the place was too large to hear distinctly. The singing fine, but on the whole I felt it was foreign to spiritual worship. The altar decorated with flowers and cross, and the existence of a side chapel perplexing and almost Roman Catholic. . Saw a Roman Catholic woman, with a thick cable round her neck, preaching against Martin Luther, under the arches of the railway. I came down from London on Tuesday morning, the 5th November.

November 16.—Charles Randolph has gifted £60,000 to the University; a noble but eccentric gift. . I have refused for the second time, after the interval of a year, to give the *Bailie* a photograph. I wrote the editor that I shrank from public notice.

November 23.—The revelations of the examination of W. Scott of J. Innes Wright & Co. most distressing and unaccountable. The minds of men otherwise honourable must have been lulled to sleep as to their responsibilities.

December 5.—At School Board work from ten till three or four. At St. Rollox School, and visited the mother of a boy in Middleton Place who had been breaking windows.

December 21.—Sent Mrs. Buchanan, Dunkyan, to-day three Christmas cards, with thanks for so promptly sending my keys which had been left at her house on Thursday last. . . . Mr. H—— on Sabbath afternoon last delivered an address about total abstinence as intemperate as could well be conceived. . . Mr. Campbell, Clerk of Supply, wrote me that I had been added to the roll of commissioners for the county of Stirling. . . . On Friday, 14th, induced John Guthrie Smith to accept chairmanship of Stirlingshire Society.

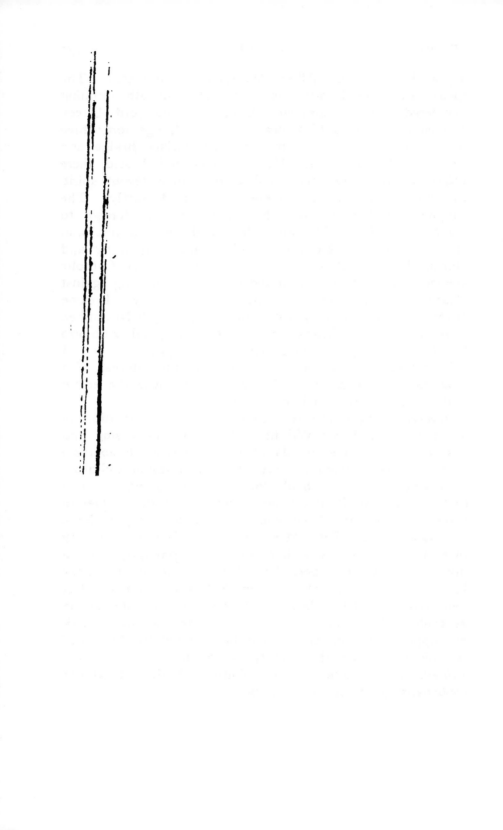

1879—1881

January 1.—O Lord, keep me that I may not be left to dishonour Thee in my profession, nor make religion to be scoffed at!

January 4.—Heard to-day from Lady M'Clure of the death of the sister of Sir Thomas M'Clure.

January 17.—I attended the dinner of the Stirlingshire Society on Monday, 13th, under the chairmanship of Mr. J. Guthrie Smith; a most successful meeting; the Chairman's speech most interesting.

February 1.—I have been sad all day. The verdict of the jury waited for by a crowd in the Royal Exchange last night at six. To-day the sentence is announced. On Monday, 27th January, went into Edinburgh with P. Clouston; not called. Saw the court through a window; asked to speak for J. Innes Wright. On Tuesday morning, 28th January, again in the Parliament House. Spoke to James Morton, who had come down from London. Arranged with Counsel (J. Guthrie Smith) to witness for John Innes Wright. . . . . Followed P. Playfair into the witness box. Lord Craighill administered the oath to me. I saw nobody in the court but the advocate who examined me. A great variety of opinion as to the sentence. By many considered too lenient. I am satisfied that it is not harsher. It might have prolonged bad feeling had the five been acquitted.

March 1.—I feel indications of failure of strength, and less elasticity of body and mind.

March 8.—There are great red and yellow bills out to-day with our tender of service to the community as

School Board members. I got Sir James Watson and Dr. Patrick to nominate me. Had some talk with Sir J. E. Alexander about the Zulus. He showed me a sketch how the troops could have entrenched themselves behind their waggons.

March 15.—The *Herald* and *News* very fair in their criticism; the *N.B. Daily Mail* is unjust and ungenerous towards the Board. . . . I wish to see the Education Bills of 1872 and 1878 a success. O Lord, keep me humble and true to what is right!

March 29.—My name has been prominently before the public in the illustrated periodical the *Bailie*. Mr. Buchanan Hamilton of Leny is to meet me next week about the Buchanan Society bursaries. I am getting photographs of the members of the late School Board not hitherto taken. . . . Sir James Lumsden's funeral was on Thursday.

April 12.—The committee meetings of the several departments of the School Board passed off so far well; so much so, that I was not prepared for a most unpleasant meeting on Thursday last when the four ratepayers' candidates, leagued with the Roman Catholics and Mr. Martin, outvoted us and carried their point, arresting further payments to teachers and reviewing the whole expenditure. This cannot be overtaken *per saltum*; six years' work cannot be compressed into the experience and information gathered in ten days. These men seem determined to crown their successful candidature by showing the citizens good grounds for their rash assertions. Cuthbertson resigned his post as Convener of the Property Committee, but has since been induced to retain it. I felt so heavy at heart that I would willingly, but for the call of duty to the community, and the great cause of education in the country, have retired from the Board. The community may come to see that the post cannot be filled eventually by men of liberal views as to remuneration. They must take more interest in the election for the future.

April 19.—I feel more and more the pressure of the School Board as to the money responsibilities of it. The

munities. The narrow question of saving the rates may lead to arresting the expansion of ideas as to remuneration of teachers and as to accommodation, which has been shown in working out the act hitherto.

April 26.—Old Robert Hart died (I think on Monday last, 21st) in his 91st year. I hope some suitable notice will be taken of him as the last link of Glasgow who knew James Watt.

May 3.—The deputation to the School Board on Thursday, headed by Professor Veitch, as to the spending of some of the Haldane Academy money in connection with the schools, is the realization of ideas I entertained long ago.

May 10.—Poor little Gracie, the old pony, probably forty years old, my mother's favourite, was found dead by John Colquhoun in the stable on Tuesday morning, 29th April. She had taken her mash pretty well the night before. . . . . Went to the Archæological Society meeting held in the University. . . . . William Ramsay's son referred to the first chemical society of Glasgow; I had the minute book in my hand, date 1801. I was struck by the majestic situation of the college and the pile of buildings as relieved against the western sky. . . . The death of Dr. Charles Murchison, on 23rd April, noticed in the *Illustrated London News* of 3rd May; born, July, 1830. Can this be the young lad of promise in Balfour's class whom I knew about 1846, appointed three weeks ago to be physician to the Duke and Duchess of Connaught? His previous career a great success. Balfour's son, Isaac Bayley, appointed Professor of Botany, Glasgow.

May 17.—I looked forward to the week that has now passed with much solicitude. I have been carried through it. There is more anxiety before me. I have to face the crisis of increased taxation of the School Board. . . . . On Friday, 16th, the "Spout" meeting passed off well—Dr. Marcus Dods in the chair. . . . Several people are always drawing me out as to the School Board: Mr. R—— to-day expressed surprise that I subjected myself to the bother of it, and the contentions arising from the new members. I said life was short, and we must put the Board on the rails.

May 24.— . . . Received an invitation through Dr. Russell, Chaplain to His Grace, to dine at Holyrood Palace on any one of three days of next week. . . . J. N. Cuthbertson is a candidate for the Kilmarnock Burghs. It takes me quite by surprise. Very anxious work at the School Board both on Monday as to salaries of teachers and on Wednesday as to finance. There has been far too much crowded into three months since the new Board began its labours. The strain upon my own mind has been very great. . . . What a blessed change of weather! the grass will surely come on fast now.

May 28.—At the meeting of the Mechanics' Institute, Bath Street, last night; I said a few words as to "Harley's Byres" and Dr. Garnett. He suggested Dr. Birkbeck as his successor in the Andersonian about 1801 or so. Walked home with Professor James Thomson and his son, who had just taken his degree at the University.

May 29.—I feel a sense of relief, but I am conscious of great fatigue as the result of the finance meeting of the School Board to-day. I had no support from the professed friends of liberal management. I showed them that a rate of 5d. was necessary, and they agreed to it. I expect that they will fire off this rocket at the public meeting on 9th June.

May 31.—I met Mr. Weir (of William Baird & Co.) some days ago, and he told me that he had seen Mr. Whitelaw on Thursday, the 22nd May, and his talk was about the School Board, and he expressed the hope that I would continue in it.

June 5.—Mr. James Robertson, U.P. minister of Newington, has passed away. He died as he lived—gentle and pathetic. His career at Tillicoultry gave promise of what he eventually proved to be.

June 17.—The grain field is very beautiful. Watched

I began this memorandum book with notes about my dear mother's death. Here, after nearly four years, I am alive, and still able to fill a place in this world's business. Oh, how brittle the thread of life! Oh, how much need of always living above the world, while living in it!

June 26.—Went to the Kelvinside Academy to see the prizes distributed by Sheriff Clark. The boys were comparatively few, but all of the better classes. I was asked to say a few words, and referred to the contrast presented in physique and bearing to what I had seen within the last twenty-four hours; but warned them to remember that the maps, drawings, penmanship I had seen yesterday, while by a class socially below them, were in every way creditable to the young persons; and that they must remember that with their advantages they were expected to occupy the front rank. . . . I went out by the 4.40 train to Parkhall to prepare for the visit of the Buchanan Institution on Tuesday, the 24th. . . . As the children arrived at the wicket leading to the high wood, there was a flash of lightning, and a thunderstorm began. It travelled by Loch Lomond on to the north and N.E. It alarmed us, and there was a retreat to the byres and yard of Redyett. The rest of the day was on the whole pleasantly spent by the boys in football, swimming in the Endrick, etc., till they left at a little after six o'clock. The *picea nobilis*—a beautiful pine—was planted by Bailie Miller, above the spot where old Gracie the pony was buried, and where the splendid beech died down. . . .

I am becoming alive to the work set on foot by the first School Board. We see the result in thriving schools. Glasgow has taken a leap by ten years in education under the Act of 1872 in school buildings, in systematic supervision, in attendance.

June 30.—With much solicitude met the committee to-day on the emoluments of teachers. It will be a difficult matter to harmonize contending opinions. O Lord, give me wisdom! . . . I am sometimes taken by surprise by people speaking of me as in my old age. . . . How fast time flies! Nineteen years since the Buchanan

Institution was last at Parkhall. The death of the Prince Imperial in Zululand, which is so sad, has brought to my mind Napoleon's reception of my father in St. Helena, probably in 1818. The particulars are lost now. What an influence that family has had on the destinies of France!

July 10.—I cannot express very well how depressed I feel in coming into town from Parkhall. It must arise from the complete change; the want of occupation to my mind is the great difficulty in the country. No sooner am I in town than a great many things, from which I otherwise would shrink, occupy me. I feel that I am helping things on, though it is more rest in the country.

Whitelaw was buried upon Saturday, the 5th. How short, but how useful his career has been. I hope that I may not have any personal ends to serve in my relation to the School Board. The consolidation of the system is a most important matter for the community, and well worth all patience and trial of temper and labour.

July 30.—Attended Mr. Bell's funeral to-day. I suppose I was invited officially from his being the English master of the High School. The grave of Christian was in a garden surrounded by the flowers of hope. . . . . I felt a repugnance in going to the School Board to-day. There is so much difference of opinion about things of no great moment.

August 4.—[At Kinross.] How beautiful the whole country! Castle Campbell looking down from its gloomy recess on the hills. More and more impressed with the vanity of everything here to satisfy the soul. I have thought of Psalm lxxxiv. 6, making a well in the Valley of Baca, serving God cheerfully in the way of duty. . . . At Kinross Churchyard saw the obelisk to the memory of the three Misses Stedman, who perished in Loch Leven.

August 11.—Went to the meeting in Balfron on the occasion of opening the reading-room and library in connection with the coffee-room—A. Orr Ewing, M.P., in the chair. I took the opportunity to show the snuff-box presented to my father fifty-one years ago, and expressed the hope that the generation now cropping up would not belie the character of that which has passed away. . . . This is my birthday; I have entered on my sixty-third year.

September 10.—Monday last, 8th inst., quite a field day at the School Board. I prayed for grace to do what was right. I was engaged from 11 to nearly 4.30. The new men are too overbearing.

September 19.—Went to Parkhall on Saturday morning, the 13th, and stobbed off the ground for the stables, etc., with William Simson, the mason.

September 22.—Came into town sad at heart about School Board business. The work most uncongenial to me now, yet I may do good by hanging on.

September 25.—Went into Edinburgh to-day to Mrs. MacFarlan's funeral.

October 9.—At the Deacon Convener's dinner last night in the Trades' Hall. An old blue flag over the chair was carried by the Hammermen at the Battle of Langside, 1568. I sat beside James B. Mirrlees, and not far from Charles Tennant of the Glen, M.P.—all three educated at Tillicoultry, all three under Dr. Eadie as tutor. I took notice of this. I heard Rev. C. H. Spurgeon in St. Andrew's Hall at 3.30; a crowd of four thousand people. His text on Numbers xiv. 11. His voice filled the hall; it sounded sometimes like a bell. The treatment of his subject was plain but forcible; I do not wonder at his popularity. His whole bearing easy and natural, yet earnest. I was at the Buchanan Institution on Tuesday night . . . I do not care for Mr. ——; he is pawky, yet troublesome.

October 10.—Went to the opening meeting of the Christian Institute in Bothwell Street—Lord Shaftesbury in the chair. . . . In talking with Canon Macdonald of Lincoln, heard his opinion of the Bishop of Manchester as to stage plays.

October 13.—I was very reluctant to leave the country to-day; I had a feeling of deep solicitude as to the issue of the proceedings of the School Board. Yesterday was a most beautiful day. The trees were gorgeous in their autumnal dress. The hills were clear, and the light sometimes thrown on the distant hills was exquisitely beautiful. Walked up to the high wood, then down by the Endrick. Brought in little Princie to town.

October 19.—I went to-day to the High Churchyard to stand for a little beside the graves of those dear ones. I tried to recall their love and kindness, I thought of being forgotten by-and-by.

October 25.—On Wednesday at Mr. John Campbell's marriage to Miss Minnie Robertson. . . . The School Board in every one's mouth. . . . I pray that I may have strength to do what is right. . . . I cannot live always, and I am beginning to feel as if I would not wish to do so. I wish to follow out some things before I leave the world, if the Lord will.

November 1.—Visited with Mr. Johnston the site of the old church at Lecropt, built 1300. The country exquisitely beautiful. The foliage of the trees all hues, from pale to dark green, yellow, orange, brown, red.

November 15.—Gave the stones out of the quarry for the foundation of the new hall at Balfron.

November 29.—At the meeting of the Stirlingshire Society yesterday, and suggested Sir J. E. Alexander as chairman for 1880. . . . I was very much affected by seeing our old house in Abbotsford Place. I thought of my dear mother and of Fanny's death there.

December 6.—Invited to meet Mr. and Mrs. Gladstone at Sir James Watson's, but declined. Gave my ticket to Mr. Kennedy for the Rectorial address, and found out afterwards that a special seat had been reserved for me on the platform at the Kibble Palace.

December 20.—I went to the meeting presided over by C. Tennant, M.P., at which Dr. J. Dodds advocated the establishment of a high-class girls' school. I dined in the evening at 7.30 at the College, Dr. Gairdner's; met several men I had not seen before. Young Dr. Balfour there and the Lord Provost. . I met Sir Philip Cunliffe Owen at the Lord Provost's at dinner on Wednesday, the 17th. At the Corporation Galleries on Tuesday, the 16th, at the conversazione inaugurating the Exhibition of Prince of Wales' collection. Very much fatigued, but gratified to see so many tokens of interest in him, and of loyalty on the part of the native princes. On Monday, 15th, opened Abbotsford School—a splendid building. Apparently interested the people in an account of the Gorbals, of the Lennox family, and of the Stewarts of Spot and Blackerston. Brought into requisition Pinkerton's Iconographia and the parchment 1605 with Sir George Elphinston's signature. . . . Affected to think how soon a generation springing up forgets those who have been prominent in the past, say within twenty or thirty years. How humbling! Dr. Gemmell, at Dr. Gairdner's, brought this strikingly before me, in the case of medical men, such as Pagan, Laurie, M'Farlan, Burns, not known by young men entering the profession.

1880.

January 1.—On Monday morning saw from *Glasgow News* the news of the awful calamity of the Tay Bridge. I went to Stirling and thence to Gartness to Mrs. Buchanan-Kincaid's funeral. Travelled with John M'Farlan (Postmaster, Calcutta), Mr. Scott Moncrieff, Sheriff Lawrie, Dr. Gibson, Rev. Mr. Muirhead, Captain Ford. Received by Colonel Stirling of Gargunnock at Dunkyan. The service in the church—a good attendance of country gentlemen and of Balfron and Killearn people. . . . After the funeral drove to Parkhall.—Many trees blown down,—still such as could be spared. The storm on Sunday night must have been terrific. . . . Went to the conversazione of the Educational Institute of Scotland. A fine thing in all the arrangements. Went to the platform at 8.45 or so; I read the paper prepared by Mr. Kennedy, and made use, as the starting point, of Phinister's census. Dr. Donaldson very good as to getting out of routine.

January 10.—Presided at the supper to the poor in the City Hall on Monday, 5th inst.; about two thousand present—rather lumbering, but serious.

January 24.—I have had a busy time since I last wrote

in this book. The principal thing was going to London to see Sir F. Sandford about School Board business. Left on the morning of Wednesday, the 14th, with Dr. L. Aikman and Mr. Kennedy. A beautiful route—the sun shining sometimes on the hills in the Midland counties—trees, streams, hedges, fields, cottages, mansions. What a glorious country, if representing the cause of truth and righteousness . . . . Saw Sir Francis at one o'clock on Thursday, the 15th. . . . Wearied and rather sad. . . . Left on Friday night. In the early morning before sunrise looked up to the heavens. How brilliant and numerous the stars; sunrise very beautiful. . . . Heard Mr. Adam in the High School conduct a class in Latin and Greek. . . . At the Commemorative Supper Party of the Geological Society in the Alexandra Hotel on Friday evening. Very much gratified by statement of Mr. Barr as to his having had the idea of the society suggested to him in an excursion with the "Spout," probably in 1855.

January 26.—Went this morning to the Humane Society House, and rowed down the river to the island, opposite Commercial Street. Saw the canoe embedded in the mud and stones. Afterwards at the meeting of defaulting parents in Rumford Street School.

January 31.—Went with N—— to Professor Tait's lecture on "Thunderstorms."

February 7.—Wrote Mr. Thomas M. Barr (Geological Secretary) to-night, about the excursion to Kelvinside (Mr. Montgomerie's grounds), 18th June, 1853, as the likely one in which he accompanied the "Spout." . . . Gave eighty tickets for Prince of Wales' Presents Exhibition.

February 18.—The telegram announcing Mrs. Leckie Ewing's death at Devongrove on the 15th reached me on Monday—the funeral is to be at Kippen to-morrow, and I am to meet the company at Stirling. . . . Walked up Miller Street on Saturday afternoon, some day it will be for the last time.

February 25.—On Thursday morning, 19th, went by train to Stirling, then drove to Kippen. Though misty, a fine day on the whole. The funeral procession formed at the entrance to the picturesque old graveyard; Mr.

Wilson, Parish minister, read the service at the grave. . . . At the Archæological meeting on Friday, 20th, though very much fatigued, and was interested in Rev. Scott Matheson's paper about circles on stones, cup and rings, etc.

March 11.—Saw to-day West Watson's son's funeral—a military funeral—pass along Bath Street. Killed by the explosion of the shells at Irvine.

April 10.—On Monday went to Stirling to vote about the abolition of tolls in the county. W. Connal's son there as the Laird of Meiklewood.

April 24.—On Thursday, 22nd, went to Dr. Jamieson's Jubilee dinner. Though the proceedings were protracted till 11 o'clock, there was a great deal of interest about it. The happy domestic common-sense life and diligent discharge of duty in his study and pulpit very noticeable.

May 8.—The 550 volumes in the High School library came into my possession yesterday, and I gave them to the "Spout" last night at the Annual Meeting—the thirty-second anniversary of the Bible Institute.

May 15.—I see by the American illustrated papers that a beautiful casket with an address has been presented to Dr. Potter (Horatio), Bishop of New York; that same Dr. Potter, who, as Bishop-elect of Massachusetts, spent an evening with us in Dixon Street in 1838. I took him to hear Dr. Chalmers and Dr. Wardlaw. He had been in London immediately after the Queen's coronation.

June 9.—I left for London on Wednesday night, the 26th May. Went to the Treasury about the loan and the cost of examination of the High School, and saw Lord Frederick Cavendish. . . . Walked out to Fleet Street to get Scotch papers. Heard the result of Professor Robertson Smith's case. . . . I went out to Kew to call on Sir Joseph Hooker. I walked through the gardens, museums, etc., and I was much pleased. It is a noble thing thus to collate and systematize the wonders of the vegetable creation. . . . Found my way into the city: a great seething ocean of human beings. On Monday, Mr. Venables made a noble speech. Mr. Pope's could not compare with it. Mr. Venables is a fine-looking man; he is understood to be the prototype of George Warrington in *Pendennis*. Lord Houghton has dedicated a book to him as the first Greek scholar in Europe.

June 11.—I was so wearied that I did not go into Westminster Abbey or the House of Commons. I determined before I left London to satisfy myself as to Dr. Morrison's translation of the New Testament having been brought over to this country about 1813-1818, and by whom. I have always understood that a copy was entrusted to my father by Dr. Morrison when in China, to be presented to the India House. Through J. E. Mathieson got introduction to Mr. Carruthers of the botanical department of the British Museum, and through him to Dr. Rost[1] of the India House Library.

June 17.— . . . "Wee Princie" showed his happiness at seeing me. How kind of God to plant in such creatures such companionableness.

June 25.— . . . I have felt Robert Dalglish's death more than that of any public man for a good while: he died 20th June. A man of remarkable geniality of disposition and a great deal of good sense. A most useful public man.

June 28.— I am very much saddened by the whole aspect of the Bradlaugh case.

July 12.—On 7th inst. went with aunt to the launch of the Russian Imperial yacht at John Elder & Co.'s. At the launch aunt and I stood quite close to the Prince Alexis and other great folks: a wonderful sight. The Greek priests were striking features in the ceremony.

July 27.—I have a note from Professor Ramsay from Alyth, about the views of the Glasgow Board as to endowments. He did good service with Lord Spencer when the deputation met with him in June.

August 24.— . . The country in its leafy glory very beautiful. The hum of insects fills the shade of the limes.

September 21.—Came home from Wemyss Bay yesterday morning: W. B. very attractive. The sermon in the Episcopal chapel in the evening very evangelical and

[1] Dr. Reinhold Rost.

graphic. A dreadful pelt of rain on leaving chapel. Lord Shaftesbury there—the guest of John Burns. I was struck with the restlessness of the sea; how different from the repose of the country. Mr. Young of Kelly came up to town in the same carriage with us, and showed us a stick —a pepper tree, a gift from Dr. Livingstone—a piece of paper with the doctor's name on it.

September 30.—On Monday morning last, 27th inst., at 7.30 in the high wood tracing the springs; a most beautiful morning. The bright purple bloom has passed away from the heather,—the black-cock was making his peculiar cry. I was struck with the growth of the trees —the trees which I had myself planted.

October 14.—Walked home with J. A. Campbell. Saw the death in the *Glasgow News* of John Middleton in his sixty-second year, at Kinfauns Castle, on the 12th October. I remember when we used to gather fossils out of the shale in the quarry at Burnbank.

October 19.—In the morning with Mr. Kennedy inspecting John Bell's pictures at North Park House—a most princely mansion; the collection of a life-time. Every public room full of articles of vertu; here and there curious articles of furniture.

October 26.—Dr. Jamieson dead. I believe him to have been a true standard-bearer of the Cross.

October 29.—Drove to St. Paul's to Dr. Jamieson's funeral; the services were very solemn. The representation from the University, headed by the mace-bearers; the School Board, preceded by six officers, attracted the attention of the crowd lining the street. It was altogether a very striking mark of public respect to a venerable and worthy citizen and minister of the gospel.

November 15.—John Ramsay the great obstructive as to a liberal interpretation of the Scotch Act.

November 30.—I have returned from Parkhall to-day, having gone out to be present at the laying of the foundation stone of the new parish church. . . . I have been told that I was at the laying of the foundation stone of the old church in 1826. The stone was laid by Mr. Blackburn. I thought as I sat in the little parlour of all God's goodness

I thought of my passing in childish playfulness under my father's limbs as he stretched them over the mantelpiece.

December 20.—On Monday, the 6th, at a meeting about a duplicate portrait of Mr. Whitelaw in Mr. Whyte's office. On 7th, at Buchanan Institution; on 8th, went to the R. C. demonstration of song by children of St. Andrew's Schools. Dr. Munro very friendly, and the singing good.

1881.

January 3.—William Thompson's letter received on Saturday morning, thanking me for the window I have put in Kippington Church. . . . On 29th ult., at the presentation of Mr. Whitelaw's portrait to the Corporation. Mr. Whyte's remarks very good.

January 22.—I wrote Wyllie Guild to-day again about the missing MSS. about the old grammar school of 1460, having seen in the newspapers the death of the widow of Principal Barclay. . . . Mr. Alexander Moore, accountant, interested me by telling me how his success in life began by a suggestion of mine. . . .

February 7.—Carlyle's death the subject of some absurd remarks in extravagant laudation.

March 19.— . . . The terrible news of the Emperor of Russia's death (Alexander II.) proclaimed on Monday morning.

April 16.—On Wednesday evening at the Philosophical Society. How truly diverse are the pursuits and tastes of men. . . A most interesting charter by the Earl of Mar, 1619, to James Ure of Shirgarton deciphered for me by W. H. Hill.

April 25.—Anxious about the question involved as to teachers' salaries, and after a good deal of preparation was in a position to-day, so far, to arrange matters towards a satisfactory settlement. Then went with Mr. Cuthbertson and Mr. Keyden to see ground in Fir Park Street. Spent an hour below the Exchange, looking in the *Times* for W. Graham's speeches, 1866. Got a copy of an essay on the birthplace of St. Patrick, from the author, J. A.

Turner—a perfect stranger to me. On 21st, at the meeting for the higher education of women; Mr. Jebb spoke. In the evening went to the Archæological Society. Introduced the charter about Ure of Shirgarton from the Earl of Mar, which interested them. . . . The account in the *News* of the removal of Lord Beaconsfield's remains to Hughenden Manor in the dead of night very touching.

May 2.—I had to stand up and enter my dissent against the changes proposed in Stirling's Library at a meeting of the directors on the 28th ult. I resigned my chairmanship of the library.

June 6.—Wearied to see Parkhall during my illness.

June 16.— . . . A dull but dry day; the larks were singing very sweetly in the fields. Have tried to get young Bayley Balfour to come to Parkhall; I owe his father thanks for much kindness. . . . Met the magistrates (three of them), and spoke about the robes at the distribution of prizes on the 24th inst., High School. Saw the Lord Provost also on Friday last. They are most reluctant to put them on. There is nothing out of place in a due regard to ceremony on public occasions.

June 9.—We were at Mr. William Wilson's marriage to Miss Turner, at 2 Victoria Terrace, Dowanhill.

June 28.—I have not seen the comet yet. What a strange thing, this celestial visitant i

July 8.—Dr. Samuel Miller's funeral was to-day. I respected him very much.

July 20.—I met Professor Balfour near the College to-day on my way to call on him. We fixed 6th August for a visit to Parkhall. I was struck with the magnificence of the buildings and the surroundings. As a student said to me, they will have their associations in the course of time like the old College in the High Street.

August 18.—Saw Lord Craighill this morning at the George Hotel at breakfast for a moment. I attended the levee on Tuesday to meet him. I have lost all that desire for honours which at one time possessed me.

August 30.—I felt most solicitous and uncomfortable to-day dealing with the school teachers' salaries. Some of my colleagues want a generous spirit. Four hours at School Board business.

October 15.—Handed over to Dr. Marwick the papers relative to St. Nicholas Hospital, lent me by Dr. Scouller fifteen years ago from the Andersonian Museum. He wrote as if they might be of use in obtaining a charter to facilitate the collection of the revenues of the hospital.

October 19.—Busy with School Board matters to-day. Yesterday afternoon, after School Board business, went to the Cathedral at three, where Mr. Honeyman pointed out and described the various features in the architecture illustrative of the history of the Cathedral. I felt very much affected by thinking of those old architects and masons; of the beauty, and more or less ornate character of their work. On Monday night presided at the giving of prizes and certificates to those who had passed satisfactorily in the examination instituted by the London and City Guilds Institute.

November 5.—Met on Wednesday, the 2nd, with Mr. John M'Clure and Mark Bannatyne as to the giving of a portion of the school fund for a day industrial school. Opposed it with all my might.

November 12.—I arranged with —— as to the payment of £1000 to assist in cancelling the bond on the church buildings.

November 19.—I hinted to J. N. Cuthbertson about his being spoken for as to a degree to Dr. Dickson of the College.

December 6.—A painful meeting (at least to me) of the directors of Stirling's Library. There appears to be a settled purpose to destroy its individuality by those who have to do with the Mitchell Library, and I broke out upon them as the meeting was drawing to a close.

December 24.—There is no doubt constant engagement with the business of the Board, and it is sometimes irksome, but I believe it lies at the bottom of a vast social revolution.

1882—1884

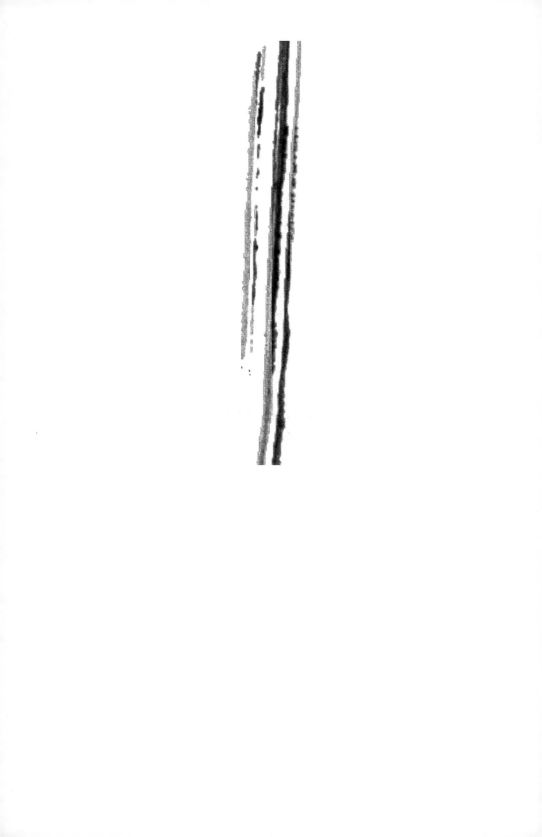

1882.

January 7.—A dreadful gale yesterday. I hope that I may have no bad news from the country as to the fine old trees.

January 14.—At the Philosophical Society on Wednesday about the gas affair. Matters are getting into shape for a solution. Sir W. Thomson stayed behind the rest to exchange friendly greetings with me.

January 21.— . . . . I have been away two days with lumbago; I think I got it while under the Exchange Room, examining the *Glasgow Heralds* of 1831, when Charles Stirling[1] was president of the Stirlingshire Society. The dinner passed off very well; there was a large turn-out. I said something about the year 1831 being a counterpart of the present. Daniel O'Connell arrested on the 18th January, 1831. . . . It is a great matter not to overbear others, and rather to let the light dawn on them. . . . A riot in Duke Street in the Reformatory took place on Wednesday night. It is very sad, when everything has been done to improve and interest them.

September 28.—I went yesterday forenoon to fulfil an engagement to speak in connection with the Training Home for Nurses. I visited the Home along with J. N. Cuthbertson on 25th inst., and was very much pleased. It supplies a real want. . . . At six o'clock went to the centenary dinner of the *Glasgow Herald* in the St. Andrew's Halls. A great crowd of people; representative.

[1] Colonel John Stirling of Gargunnock, son of Charles Stirling, of Stirling, Gordon & Co., was president, 188

The vestibule was crowded. Sat down at 6.30: dinner protracted till ten. Sat beside Dr. Paton, Rector of the High School, and Mr. Alex. Allan. I am most anxious to keep out of the eye of the public now for some time. I am rather inclined to think it is my duty to go forward again to the School Board. Archbishop Eyre appears to be anxious to take a lead in public matters; he rose up to shake hands when I entered the room.

February 11.— . . . Sometimes at the cost of feeling and the interruption of courtesy I give expression to what I think if my aim be a good one. The result is better in the long run; again, I should not be hasty in word or deed. On Thursday night at Sir William Thomson's, the College, to frame a report for the Council for Wednesday, 15th. Sir William full of interest about the first lighting up of his house, from top to bottom with the electric light.

February 25.—I bought, through Mr. Keith, at an auction of books, an interesting volume, in which Patrick Connal's name occurs, in opposition to the settlement of Mr. Robert Campbell at Stirling, 1764. P. C., my great-grandfather; Rev. R. C., great-grandfather of John Campbell, my partner. Went in the evening to hear the lecture by Principal Dallinger on the lower forms of animal life. I am very happy to see some daylight into the stern and harmful officialism of Poor Law relief. Spoke to Dr. Dickson about Mr. Kennedy getting a degree. Affected with a sense of the vanity of everything here in the dispersion of the treasures of Hamilton Palace

March 4.—Madam Celeste dead within the last few days. I remember at Edinburgh long ago—probably in 1832 or 1833—being carried away with the romance of the character she personated on the stage; she was the wild North American Indian girl. What a fool I was but it showed the witchery of the performance. . . Met Sir Henry and Lady Moncrieff last night at 220 St. Vincent Street. N——'s mother used to go with her father to his grandfather's on Sabbath evenings to supper.

and then prayers—a patriarchal custom. Sir William MacKinnon came in to tea. Had some talk with him about the Disestablishment question. He agreed with us that Providence had not opened the door for such a change, and that the people of the Free Church could not be said as a body to be prepared to follow the ecclesiastical leaders.

March 11.— . . . . I was rather saddened yesterday by a complimentary letter in the *Mail*, but suggesting, as I was advanced in years, I should be relieved from being on the Board. Am I then getting old in the judgment of others—I who feel like a young man still?

March 18.—The sight of young people, however fatigued I may be, always gratifying.

April 1.—H. M. Matheson has been receiving the King of Spain.

April 22.—At the Archæological Society meeting; Wyllie Guild was very good on Glasgow Directories.

May 13.—Last Sabbath morning (8th inst.) stunned by the news, which I learned from a stranger, of the murder of Lord Frederick Cavendish and Mr. Bourke by assassins in Phœnix Park, Dublin. Unhappy Ireland! Those agitators have much to answer for. . . . . The funeral on Thursday at Chatsworth very affecting. Took notice on Monday at the public meeting of the Board of Cluny M'Pherson's death.

July 3.— . . . I said to ——— on his return to this country, that old Richardson said it was an easy thing to make money, but a difficult thing to keep it. Called on James Mitchell, LL.D., about the Gillespies.

July 6 (*Wednesday*).—N——— and I have come home from the wedding at Solsgirth; Emily Connal married to Nathaniel Spens. The saloon carriages full of friends. I was pleased to renew my acquaintance with the Ochils and the villages at their foot. W. Connal's house commodious and purpose-like. The country-side beautiful. It is a strange thing to see him a grandfather, and his family leaving him.

July 7.—Saw Colin Gillespie's portrait, and refreshed my memory with particulars of the old mill, Woodside.

Then went down towards the Kelvin and inspected it. Came through the West End Park; struck with the beauty of the grounds and the situation. Truly the city is a magnificent city, and has even a finer future before it. Seen in the gloamin', there was an impression of grandeur—the towers, the spires, piles of buildings, trees, and river—all partly under shadow.

August 1.—Went to the cattle show (Highland and Agricultural Society) on the Green before going to Larbert. Very much affected by the sight of the bees at work, and of the horses led round the ring.

August 8.— . . . Mr. M'Naughton gave me a letter of my father's to Dr. Graham about the Parish Church gateway, dated 16th February, 1827.

August 11.—This is my birthday. I have completed my 65th year. What a blurred life, yet how full of mercies! Had a visit from J. O. Mitchell and Mr. L——, Woodlands Road, on Wednesday night about interesting features of the district. They told me that the old mill was taken down within the last few days. I saw it just in time; I now find that it was built in 1784.

September 13.—A great load off my mind by the news as to the defeat of Arabi in Egypt. What an awful thing if it had been otherwise. . . I was very much affected on Monday morning to hear the chirping of chickens in the old stableyard.

September 18.—I was much struck with the advertisement in the *Herald* as to Arngomery. I thought over it, and again and again dismissed the idea. It would be a serious step to have anything to do with it; still I return to it. I have a great deal yet to do to Parkhall. The affections of N—— and her sisters still twine around Arngomery. The property has some claims of a special kind on the family of William Leckie Ewing. It is a pity that these should not be conserved. I have written Mr. M'Lachlan of Auchentroig, asking some particulars. I felt so undecided that I took the letter out of the post-rack, and, after showing it to Mr. Wilson, put it back again. . . .

September 20.—This morning Mr. M'Lachlan sent me a statement about Arngomery. I felt that the time had come when I had to make up my mind. I lifted up my heart to God. . . . I at once telegraphed to Mr. M'Lachlan offering the upset price of £33,500. . Got an interesting letter from Duncan M'Naught about the meaning of the names of some mountains seen from Parkhall.

September 21.—Mr. M'Lachlan called about 10.30. I found that I must offer more, as another offer had been made. . . . I offered £500 more, and there the matter rests.

September 26.—I am satisfied that I have done right. On Friday, 22nd, Mr. M'Lachlan made his appearance and closed with me; others were after the place. Received letters to-day from Lord Craighill and Mr. L. Ewing congratulating me. . . . I took Mr. M'Lachlan at once to John Hill, who was very glad to hear of the purchase. The missive was written out in pencil, and Mr. M'Lachlan, to prevent all mistakes, took the train at 11 o'clock to Edinburgh and came back at 3.30. All was right, and I then wrote out the offer which was accepted. Archibald Robertson came in and satisfied himself that all was right, and he said that William Leckie Ewing sat at Mr. Hill's left hand in the same chair in 1864 and signed the missive that bore away his relation to the property and then burst into tears. . . . "All Kippen," said A. Robertson, "was in a bleeze." . . When I told N—— she said it was like a romance. The day her father (at dinner) told her and J——, probably M—— and their mother, that the place was sold, they said it would be a relief to him; but every stone was dear to him, and when the carriage eventually drove him away, some months afterwards, and the last boundary of the property was passed, he said that his heart was broken.

October 12.—Invited to the Corporation luncheon on Saturday, in the Corporation Galleries, to meet the Duke and Duchess of Albany.

October 28.—Went by 10.45 train to Lochwinnoch. The day was very beautiful and the landscape. The lake had a fresh, living look about it, with swans and wild fowl.

December 2.—Dr. Laing, the little vivacious teacher of mathematics, died yesterday.

December 9.—On Thursday wrote Mr. Mundella in reply to his note to me hoping that he would come to Glasgow in the third or fourth week of January. Dr. Donald Fraser a superior style of man, but with more action than I liked. How like the outcome of London dissenting circles. Striking in appearance, and obviously the pet of a circle of admirers. . . . Missed by half an hour seeing the transit of Venus.

December 19.— . . . Yesterday evening met Mr. W. E. Forster at dinner at Mr. Stephen's, Dean of Guild. Said a few words to him about his speech on Saturday and about the ninepence a week limit. Pleased with his devotedness and earnestness.

1883.

January 20.— . . . Entered as a member of the County Club, Stirling; proposed by Mr. Blackburn of Killearn, and seconded by Colonel Stirling of Gargunnock.

January 23.—Went to Edinburgh by 11 train. . . . Went to the Parliament House and saw Lord Young in a side room. He appeared to be quite ready to comply with our wishes to open John Street and Dennistoun Schools, probably about the middle of February.

January 26.—Very anxious about the meeting of the executive committee of the "City of Glasgow Shareholders Relief Fund" to-day at 12. . . . During the four years the committee have met month by month. Sir J. W—— applauded a remark of mine, now that the liquidation of the bank has been brought to a close and the relief committee settling down to a steady course of action; it was, that the lesson should afresh be put forth to the community, that, in "the first wrong step in a course of policy, there should be the moral courage to retrace

Queen Street station and drove with him and Mr. Russell to Dennistoun School, then to John Street, Bridgeton. Then we lunched in the lesser City Hall, and at two o'clock the meeting was held at the large hall. Lord Young's address sensible.

February 16.—A day of comparative freedom from engagements. Ransacked some drawers and revived old things, interesting as forming part of my life. Gazed with affectionate composure on a photograph of my mother and her little dog, at Parkhall. . . . The paper about the Parochial Registers of Cambuslang, anterior to 1688, by Mr. J. T. T. Brown, very interesting. Dr. Alexander Patterson gave me a ship's log-book, 1758, from Clyde to Barbadoes. On Wednesday went in the morning to the Loan Exhibition of Italian Art. . . . I can scarcely appreciate the expenditure of so much wealth on decoration and artistic beauty when so much has to be done in philanthropic and educational matters. On Tuesday, 12th, at the Lews Relief Committee. . . . The whole question of the Hebrides a problem ; I have an impression that there must be something very attractive in the free life in the open air, no matter how poor the crofters' abode is, that indisposes them for the patient industry of our towns ; and that an ever-recurring period of distress, at intervals of a few years, may be the normal condition of things until education makes more progress. Emigration on a great scale will throw the prospect of the cultivation of the soil and the amelioration of the social condition of the people that remain further back. They must be trained more and more to make the best of the condition they are in, so that their self-support may be more confirmed.

February 23.—Went to Lochgoilhead to attend the funeral of Mrs. Donald Campbell—the aspect of the coast very beautiful even in winter. . . . The new laird of Drimsynie in the steamer with us. . . . The old church contains an imposing monument to the Arkinglas family.

March 1.—At Mr. King's at dinner to meet Professor Abel, who lectured in the St. Andrew's Halls on "Explosions." Sir W. Thomson at the dinner, Professors Jack and

Ferguson, etc. Chemistry not even in its infancy. The French chemists more imaginative than the German—not so sound.

March 10.—Dined at Dr. Wallace's with the Philosophical Society Council. Interested in James Thomson's (F.G.S.) remarks about the value of oatmeal as food; he has traced the proportion of bandy-legged children throughout various districts of Lanarkshire and Glasgow, and where oatmeal is an article of diet, the proportion is less than where loaf bread is used.

March 17.—Drove out with N—— to the Observatory at the invitation of Mrs. Grant, but the night very cloudy. Very much impressed sometimes by the vastness of creation, in thinking of the starry world.

March 24.—Heard to-day on my way home that little Atta[1] had passed away at 12 o'clock. . . . I went to the St. Andrew's Halls on Thursday to hear John Bright on the occasion of his installation as Lord Rector of the University. With all the noise of the hall—the effervescence of the students in their animal spirits—I was much impressed with the sight. There was something sad yet grand in the sight of so many human beings—young, handsome, full of hope, capacity for the business of life, and yet only on the threshold of it, the men of the coming generation, in whose hands were to be placed the interests of the country, at least in so far as they formed an important factor in it. The speech of John Bright made me sad; it wanted something for the occasion; it showed me that Quakerism is a principle defective in its views as to our relation to God and man; there are far more complicated elements in the questions touched on than he gave expression to. This country is in the hand of God a power for good. . . . There may be war to chastise the grasping and disturbing

hurried to fully appreciate what he said, but he looked at Education for the mass of the people from the English standpoint. I was indebted to Charles Tennant, M.P., for the introduction. . . . On Wednesday, at 12.45, met the Technical Education Commissioner at lunch in the Western Club. Much interested in Mr. Swire Smith's remarks as to John Bright's plan of making his speeches.

March 28.—Went to little Atta's funeral. Ballancleroch looked very pretty. The hymn, "How bright these glorious spirits shine," sung in the drawing-room by the company, and a hymn by the children of the clachan at the grave.

April 4.—Went with Lord Shand and John Ramsay, M.P., to John Street School, Bridgeton, and the Buchanan Institution. Then went at 6 o'clock to the Banquet in the City Hall to the convention of Royal Burghs—a magnificent affair. Sat beside the Town Clerk of Elgin and Mr. Melville of Edinburgh; both full of life and spirits, the former, though the factor for Lord Fife and other landed gentry, holding most revolutionary views. They may be sound at bottom, but they are most unpalatable to those having landed property. Lord Balfour was very frank in the ante-room. Monday was a day of very great pressure. . . .

April 7.—Went to the Home Mission Association meeting, and said something about the Parochial system of relief being administered by the churches—the divorce between the church and the poor brought about by the Poor Law Acts and Organization. Dr. Chalmers' plan the best.

April 28.—Interested to-day in Professor Roberton's information about Dalmarnock ford and the surroundings. Spent more than an hour looking over the *Glasgow Heralds* of 1820 and 1821. Some interesting events especially to myself in these two years—Dr Muir's settlement in St. James', Sir W. J. Hooker's appointment as professor, and Sir D. K. Sandford's appointment. Wrote an apology to John Kirkpatrick, Edinburgh, as to the funeral of his sister, Christina, on Monday. . . . Tuesday 24th, dined in George Hotel with the Judges at 8.30, Lords Deas and Adam. Sat next Rev. Mr. Dickson, the minister who officiated at the Circuit Court, and the Pay-master of the "Warrior," who had seen service in Peru and Chili and other parts of the world. Lord Deas angry with the trumpeters interrupting him when proposing a toast. I was struck with the look of the young advocates—shrewd-looking fellows—unmistakable self-confidence. . . . . Matthew Cruickshank, Summerlee Works, told me to-day that he was with Beaumont Neilson when he caught the idea of the hot blast at Muirkirk Ironworks.

May 5.— . . . On Thursday, 3rd inst., waited on Dr. M'Vail, along with Dr. Stirton, in his consulting-rooms, New City Road, to induce him to withdraw the requisition which was the subject of discussion at the Council meeting of the Philosophical Society on Wednesday. It is a very serious responsibility to interrupt the harmony of the society, where professional jealousies may be aroused, by the suggestion of St. Andrews being an examining University without residence being required of the students. These medical men have keen antipathies, and the special privileges of the University here are regarded with jealous feelings by extra-mural teachers. I was thrust into the chair on Wednesday night, and I am a little afraid that I expressed myself too strongly. . . . Went to Mitchell Library to consult Keith's history (Spottiswoode Society). Saw Mr. Hannan in the afternoon in his own house. Went down with J. N. Cuthbertson to Springfield. A good meeting at the opening of the school. They say a street running in front is to be called Connal Street. . . . On Sabbath, in the afternoon, Dr. Marcus Dods read a closely reasoned paper, but it was not fitted for a popular audience—"Christianity for the Million." . . . Thought over in the drawing-room before dinner of Dixon Street associations forty-five years ago. My dear mother and sister, my dear uncle William, my uncle John, my ambitious thoughts

gift of the Tree Fern at Arngomery, "Cyathea dealbata." . . . Met Dr. James A. Campbell and Dr. Cochran-Patrick in the Western Club, along with J. N. Cuthbertson and Mr. Kennedy, about Mr. Mundella's new Educational Bill on Friday morning.

May 26.—Men that I have known are passing away, Walter Buchanan, once M.P., died on Monday at Chester, in the house of his son-in-law, Mr. J. George Smith, who was once in the counting-house. . James Stirling of Cordale died on Saturday in the Alexandra Hotel. . . . I reflected that when Lord Deas bade us good-night at the Circuit Court dinner he said that there was serious and important business on the morrow. The trial of the two men then took place, and now they have paid the penalty of wrong-doing with their lives.

June 6.—On Monday came in from the country. Went out on Friday afternoon, 1st June—the trees magnificent. Went from one end of the property to the other,—from the High Wood to the Endrick. The place that knows me now shall soon know me no more for ever.

June 18.— . . . Went on Saturday to Edinburgh to attend Mrs. Buchanan's funeral; Bailie Thomson, Bailie Dickson, Dr. Roberton, and Dr. Candlish were in the same carriage—Roberton full of life as to battle-fields and old stories of Scottish history. . . . The country very beautiful—the red and white hawthorn, the laburnum and lilac in their glory. What beauty in the red fiery sunset, and the moon like a lamp through the trees!

June 25.— . . . Poor old "Major" died on Thursday night—faithful animal; he was buried where the large beech tree was blown down in the avenue.

June 28.— . . . Feel wearied and fatigued sometimes, the strain on me is continuous and the demands are incessant.

July 4.—The awful calamity at Linthouse shipbuilding yard in everybody's mouth. I pity the Stephens very much. How unconscious we are of danger from long habits of security. How humble I should be. . . . Disgusted with the will of ——; after all, he wanted true love of science, —he was an earthworm.

July 23.—Came into town to-day,—Mr.
of Craigbarnet with me in
entailing the property. I thought of the sister of John
Glas (Mrs. Dr. Wilson)[1]
deed of entail.

August 22.—Dined at the George Hotel
Lords Young and Craighill spoke and shook
Edward Colebrooke there.
looking set of young men

August 24.— . . .
the High Church; I wept
brance of the dear ones lying there.

September 11.— . . . I sat in the garden at Parkhill for a little, thinking over the past. I thought but for the associations of this place and the power to influence others for good, I might be happier with less to distract me.

September 19.— . . . I have had present to my mind of late that being useful in giving of my substance for good objects is redeeming labour from the curse, that what is put into my hands is from God—it is His, not mine.

September 24.—Went to the chapel at Duncrub;[2] Lord Rollo read the lessons. . . . There is an impression that it is against the whole genius of the country that a great man should thus worship as it were alone and apart from the sympathies of the people by whom he is surrounded,—of course, extending the courtesy to friends and neighbours to worship with him.

September 28.—Went to the lecture by Dr. Richardson on "Felicity as a Pursuit." Very much disappointed—bordering on materialism.

October 20.— . . . Went to the dinner given in honour of Sir A. Allison—a very grand affair. Sat next Sheriff Murray at the croupier's table. The appearance he had made in the forenoon very good. . . . The pipers in the street struck me very much as they passed the hall after dinner.

[1] Mary Grey Glas, wife of Dr. Wilson, R.N., and daughter of William Glas of Stirling by his wife Janet, daughter and co-heiress of John Grey of Loss.

[2] At Pitcairns, Dunning, on a visit to Mrs. Watson, sister to Lady Connal.

October 25.—Fast Day. . . . Kept my mind free from worldly distractions such as reading the newspapers.

November 17.— . . . Thursday, 15th, at the lecture by Professor Ball, Astronomer Royal for Ireland, on "Comets and Shooting Stars"—a most luminous exposition.
I could not get to the Luther Commemoration Meeting in the St. Andrew's Halls on Monday from fatigue.

November 24.— . . . Unable from fatigue to go to the Archæological meeting, but to my surprise re-elected a vice-president.

December 22.—At the presentation of the badge and chain of office for the Chairman of the School Board—a very pleasant meeting. Yesterday wrote Mr. Mundella again, inviting him and Miss Mundella to make our house their home from the 9th to the 12th January.
On Wednesday, 19th, with Mary L. Ewing at the French Art Loan Exhibition. Shook hands with Sir Philip Cunliffe Owen, who recognized me as having seen me at Sir William Collins' house. The Honourable Massey Mainwaring's remarks very good. On Tuesday present at the gift of the freedom of the city to the Marquis of Lorne, and in the evening at the Christian Institute to hear his remarks on Canada.

1884.

January 7.—At the School Board to-day making final arrangements for Mr. Mundella's visit. . . . I pray that good may come out of this visit for the future of Scotland as to its educational progress.

January 9.—I met Mr. Mundella at St. Enoch Station at 7.45 A.M.

January 12.—On Wednesday, 9th, dined at Professor Ramsay's at 7.30; Professors Veitch, Jack, Gairdner, Dr. A. B. M'Grigor, Dr. Cameron, Dr. Dickson, James A. Campbell. . . . The meeting in the Queen's Rooms a success. Dr. Caird spoke to the point with some force and animation. Mr. Mundella very good, though professedly not anxious to give an address. On Friday, 11th, the evening meeting in the City Hall splendid.

The whole effect of this visit will do good, not only to the community, to the teachers, and the School Board, but the views as to the future under discussion will have an important bearing on the progress of education throughout the country. What am I, O Lord, that such opportunities of usefulness should have been put into my hands!

January 26.—This morning went to the City Girls' School to see the pupil teachers get a lesson in cookery from Miss Robertson of the Dovehill; very much interested.

What a round of engagements. Mundella's letter to me published in the newspapers.

February 2.— . . . Yesterday evening went with N—— to the opening of the Bute and Randolph Halls.

February 22.— . . . The fearful gale of Wednesday night and Thursday morning has blown down more trees at Parkhall. Alas! I shall never see the growth of their successors to the same size. The beech near the milk-house, at the foot of which I played when I was a child, blown down in January by the gale.

March 7.— . . . Yesterday, at twelve, at the Chamber of Commerce to meet the parties who wanted a change on the system hitherto pursued. They were ungenerous in supposing that the Chamber picked up its information loosely; this attitude was presumptuous.

March 27.—Last night at the Christian Institute distributing prizes; spoke probably in too high a strain as to the discipline of life under the moral government of God—that it was education for eternity.

of the Commissioners on Reformatories and Industrial Schools.

May 3.— . . . I have looked on the possessions of life as most uncertain in our hold over them—we must not set our hearts upon them. How everything is undergoing scrutiny in the present day. The right to the soil which has been purchased is openly denied. Those who engage in these leagues for land restoration are not likely to do much good to themselves, while they make a great noise. There appears to be a spirit abroad that all privilege must be beaten down, a restless desire to attack everything—every institution that does not square with the most levelling-down ideas.

May 17.— . . . On Thursday at Kelvinside and Glasgow Academies. . . . Magnificent buildings and appliances. I hope that they may be full to overflowing in the course of time.

May 24.—On Thursday at the dinner in the Council Chambers; the Queen's Birthday. . . . Replied to the toast of the School Board. Bret Harte sat on the left of the Lord Provost (M'Onie). Struck with the fine military look of the volunteers as they passed down Hope Street on Saturday afternoon.

June 2.— . . . Prayed in the room where my dear mother died. Thought of that very room where I fell off the chair on the chest of drawers when I was a child, I suppose, of nine years. . . . I am looking forward to the breakfast I have to give to the School Board Clerks'

June 16.— . Had a call this last week from a sculptor wanting me to sit for my bust. I gave him no encouragement. He did not want remuneration. He thought that it might bring him into notice.

June 24.—Went by train from College Station to Hamilton at 2.35. Thought of Dr. Beveridge and Captain Vaughan. Passed into the grounds near the Palace, and found the Buchanan School children in a field in front of it. What a contrast, that noble pile without a tenant, and recently bereft of its treasures of art, etc., to meet the necessities of the Duke! What an unhappy man!—and

1795 on it, No. 41 east side of west wall. The tomb of the Leckies and of W. L. Ewing very well preserved at the south-east corner of the street. Met Dr. W. M'Kinlay looking for Dr. Anderson's tomb (the founder of the Andersonian); noticed David Dale's. The list given in the newspapers this morning awakens my reflections as to old citizens who have passed away. In Ephraim Gardner's house in Charlotte Street my Aunt Frances was married to my Uncle William. . . . The search after the materials for introductory remarks at the opening of Springbank School has a fascination akin to sport. It sticks at nothing. Affected to find that Robert Marshall, who died in Sutherlandshire, one of the managers of the West India Royal Mail Steamship Co., London, was the man who, when a boy of thirteen, wrote out on parchment the address to my father in 1828, when he left this country for India. The address was presented with the silver snuff-box in my possession.

July 28.— . . . I would wish to see everyone happy about me.

August 12.— . . . Went to the opening of Springbank School. I may have wearied the meeting a little with my long story about the Stirlings of Keir and Margaret Napier; some of the audience seemed specially interested. . . . Mr. Douglas, the Fiscal, died at about twelve o'clock last night.

August 15.—To-day I was put forward to propose a motion as to the raising of funds for the Society for Preventing Cruelty to Children. I was not anxious to put myself forward in the case, as I was content with the opportunities I had in dealing with defaulting parents at the School Board. Lord Glasgow was in the chair, and made a very good speech.

August 18.— . . . The Finglen burn a raging torrent on Saturday. The train stopped at one side, and the passengers passed by planks to the train on the Strath-

September 4.— . . . On Monday came in from the country; the pure bracing air does me good. How affecting to think of a hen bringing her chickens to the back door; hatched somewhere, and unable longer to do without the help of man. . . . Have had the pleasure to identify the old house in Castle Street, the house of Mr. Bryson of Neilsland, and, if so, the manse of the Prebend of Provan. Mr. W. H. Hill helped me as to the two properties, Hartfield and Neilsland, having belonged to the same family, and Hartfield through the Record office as occurring in the sasine of that property in Castle Street. I would like to throw some fresh light on that part of the city when preparing for some remarks at the opening of Townhead School. It is very striking, the death of Mr. Cooper of Failford (nephew of H. R. Cooper) and of T. Dunlop C. Graham of Dunlop occurring on the same day—27th of August—their properties being within five hundred yards of each other. They both appear to have been useful men.

September 11.— . . . The wild plants by the roadside very interesting—the stream, the trees, the hills, all beautiful. . . . Saw on passing over the moor above Balfron a tortoiseshell butterfly clinging to the whin dyke, far away from house or habitation. The whole road through Buchlyvie onwards an avenue of trees. Beautiful prospect on the left. Called at Drum.

October 10.— . . . Mr. James MacLehose has asked me to write memoirs of my uncle and of Tom Richardson for the *One Hundred Glasgow Men*.

October 19.—Walked to the High Church burial ground. Could only get a peep of where the grave was that held the dust of those dear to me, the gates to the Cathedral being shut. Thought of God, how I cannot fly from His presence. What a fearful thing it is to fall into His hands! What it is to be out of Christ! Could not shut my eyes to a woman and a little girl going down the High Street, following a young fellow,—evidently a quarrel. I touched him on the shoulder—"What's wrong?" "Don't be too inquisitive." I said, "My good fellow, I could not shut my eyes to what I saw." This, however, seemed to settle him, and he walked quietly back with them.

October 22.—Went out to-day to bring N—— in from the country. The variegated woods very beautiful.

October 25.— . I will miss the Fast days, as they have been a breakwater in the swelling of the tide of the world. I am now on the eve of another Communion season.

October 29.—Went down this morning to Wemyss Bay to see aunt. The peaks of Arran sprinkled with snow. The aspect generally bleak.

November 15.— . . . At the meeting of the Geographical and Ethnological Section, and found that I had been suggested as a vice-president. I was most reluctant to accept, as I cannot go out to meetings in the evening.

November 22.—Most reluctant to accept presidentship of Society of Sons and Daughters of Free Church. A note from Dr. Anderson Kirkwood must be answered about it. At the distribution of hyacinths and crocuses to children to-day in Bishop Street School.

November 27.— . . Hunted up Mr. Copland.[1] . . . He was very courteous, and showed me presses full of documents. One press full of charters in abbreviated Latin, all beautifully bound in folios.

November 29.— . . . What a burlesque on public business is the ease with which the Franchise Bill has been passed by a mutual understanding. Where is the shock of the contending parties? I think the giving seven members to Glasgow will lower the status of members of Parliament.

December 13.—At the meeting in St. Andrew's Halls, where Stanley was addressing a large meeting. Lord Rosebery presided. I helped Mr. Paton, who had a telegram from Lord Aberdeen, to get access to Lord Rosebery.

December 27.— . . . Sent a large number of old copies of the *Illustrated London News* to Belvidere Hospital, and an unusually large parcel for Christmas-tree, Larbert. . . . On Tuesday evening, 23rd, at the social meeting of School Board officers and their families. Said something about the management of the poor in continental countries. On the whole a good meeting.

[1] Register House, Edinburgh.

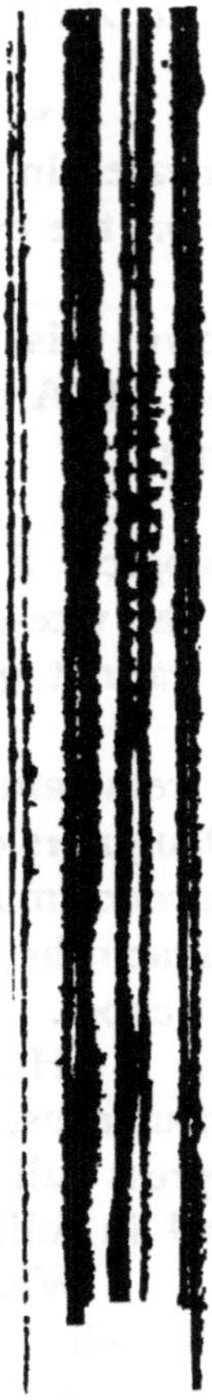

1885.

January 17.—Last night with N—— at the opening of Queen Margaret College. A crowd; probably successful on the whole, as an inaugural meeting. I hope it may be a good thing. I have not been able to attend the Philosophical and Archæological meetings this week. On Wednesday morning at the Dovehill meeting of defaulting parents; some painful cases, but not puzzling. I have been going about that district since 1838 and 1839—forty-six years.

January 24.—Came home at the end of the week's work very sad. News had reached the Exchange of the attempt to blow up the Houses of Parliament; and grave solicitude expressed as to the safety of the army in the Soudan. . . . Went down to the Stobcross docks to-day. Struck with the immense size of the steam vessels. . . . The world will roll on, advancing in everything that swells the volume of human happiness and comfort, in the mastery of man over the world, whether material or moral. Did not care to speak at the Stirlingshire Society on Monday, 19th, but carried my point as to printing the records of the Town Council from 1598-1658, which was left to the Directors with full powers. On the whole a very agreeable meeting. The provincial reporters mutilate speeches and miss the point of them. . . I may yet have a good deal to do in the world. I would not, on the one hand, shrink from labour or responsibility; but, on the other, I feel as if I would like a breathing time ere I passed away—a rest to put things in order. Visited Sailors' Home at the docks, and was very much pleased.

January [illegible].—Last night with R[illegible] at the opening of Queen Margaret College. [illegible] was [illegible] presently successful [illegible] the whole, as an inaugural meeting. I hope it may be a good thing. I have not been able to attend the Philosophical and [illegible] meetings this week. On Wednesday [illegible] at the [illegible] meeting of defaulting parents [illegible] some [illegible] cases, [illegible] not [illegible]. I have been going [illegible] that [illegible] 1841 and 1842—forty [illegible] years.

[illegible] the week's work very [illegible] had [illegible] the attempt to [illegible] attitude expressed as [illegible] the [illegible] Sweden.

[illegible] What [illegible] the [illegible] today

[illegible] with [illegible] we [illegible] everything that [illegible], and [illegible] in the [illegible] over the world [illegible] material or moral. [illegible] the Philosophic Society on Tuesday [illegible] point as to proving the results [illegible] 1695-1696, which was left to [illegible] the whole a very agreeable meeting. The [illegible] reporters [illegible] the point of their [illegible]. I have not [illegible] good deal to do at [illegible]. I would [illegible] to look [illegible] possibility [illegible] breathing [illegible] order. [illegible] very much [illegible].

one o'clock. We have always erred in under-estimating our enemies; and these tribes of the desert have been trained to the use of rifles. Went down to Helensburgh to see William Kidston about School Board matters. Full of interest about the election. . . . As Kidston said to-day, our time—his and mine—in this world is short now, and we must look out for suitable men to fill our places at the School Board. Work while it is to-day. "Sufficient unto the day is the evil thereof," he said, when I was forecasting difficulties. . . . The sudden death of the brown horse from inflammation, on the morning of the 18th, at about four o'clock, very distressing. . . . Had a very friendly letter from Mr. Mundella on Tuesday morning.

March 4.— Very much struck with the decidedly Christian remarks in the address of Principal Sir W. Muir to the students of Edinburgh (*Scotsman*, 2nd March). It is a new thing for such men to speak out for Christ so decidedly.

March 7.— . . . Professor Ramsay on the field as a candidate for the School Board. . . . What a pressure of things—the parliamentary boundaries, Charity Organization Society, Evangelical Alliance, George Anderson's public services, and other things.

March 14.— . . . Examined with much interest the *Glasgow Directories* for 1821 and 1822, lent me by Mr. Irving Ferguson of the Caledonian Railway. Presided at the meeting in Victoria Halls, West Regent Street, under the auspices of the Kyrle Society, and gave the prizes to children who had grown plants—principally hyacinths. A good meeting; Professor Lindsay, Messrs. Cuthbertson, Morison, Fife, and Kennedy spoke—an affecting sight. Mrs. Erskine Murray and her family and young friends gave some instrumental music. . . . I am called venerable, surely the term is inappropriate! I feel young, though I am not buoyant as I once was in walking; I am conscious, however, of being more easily fatigued.

March 21.—Saturday. . . . Got a note from Mr. Thomson (R. L. Ewing's brother-in-law), now in India, about Obia. Probably may hear about my father's tomb; most people say that it must have been carried away by the river many years ago.

March 24.—Tuesday. Invited by Principal and Professors to the luncheon at the University, on the occasion of Lushington's installation as Lord Rector.

March 26.—Went to the College to the installation of Lord Rector Edmund Law Lushington. A noisy uproar among the students for half-an-hour in the Bute Hall. They would have quieted down if Lushington had been heard, but for an hour the proceedings were very much a dumb show. The fine things he may have said will no doubt be in to-morrow's newspapers. Those invited to the luncheon met in the Randolph Hall. Saw Balfour from Oxford for a little; taken in by Edward Caird, and sat next Dr. Roberton and opposite the Professor of Chemistry. The mace talked about as having been found in Bishop Kennedy's tomb in St. Andrews. The most noteworthy thing was the loving-cup—passed round as the sun goes—a mixture of claret and seltzer water. I came away gratified by the hospitality of the Senate and impressed by the dignity of a place of learning. Lushington, seventy-three years old—brother-in-law of Tennyson—living at Maidstone in Kent. . . . Yesterday morning at Springbank School at a defaulters meeting. Surely by kindly counsel we are doing good. The schemes under the Endowment Act will involve additional trouble and fatigue.

March 28.—Saturday. . . . I see nothing before me but fatigue for the next three weeks; it is too much to go through this.

April 4.—Busy with letters and despatching circulars about *Stirling Burgh Records*. . . . The death of Sir J. E. Alexander in the newspapers yesterday, and of Mr. Bryce Buchanan of Boquban in to-day's. . . . I attended the farewell meeting with George Anderson, late M.P., in the Council Chambers. It was in some respects a painful sight to see a man who for seventeen years had been serving the community, leaving it confessedly very ill off. His appearance very true and modest, very much fitted to conciliate.

April 11.— . . Went to Parkhead public meeting at 3.20. A good meeting—Free Education formed the most important question; tried to meet it; very wearied. Last night at Springburn, in the U.P. Church. J. N. Cuthbertson and his friends in another hall in the neighbourhood. Spoke about the Minister of Education being an Imperial minister and not a Scotch minister only. . . . On Thursday, 9th, went out by 9.40 train to Parkhall. Country beautiful, though still bleak; the mountains majestic. Thought of those who have passed away.

April 18.— . . . The election takes me by surprise, Mitchell and Morison so far down, and Long at the top of the poll. Martin (as he deserved to be) is thrown out.

April 21.—Received a letter this morning with enclosures from Mr. Walter Thomson, Bengal, as to my father's tomb at Obia; no satisfactory or reliable information from any one. The factory is in a heavy, dense, impenetrable jungle. An obelisk or plinth on the bank of the river, but without an inscription, has been broken into on the east side, apparently by the natives in search of treasure. The platform is really immense on which the obelisk is built. The monument is a very fine one, quite imposing if the jungle were cleared away from around it. There are only two graves, according to native testimony—the obelisk and the grave of a child. Mr. A. Farquharson's note of 12th March is addressed to Mr. Thomson from Surdah.

April 25.— . . . Separated two boys fighting behind the Bodega; the exertion was too much for me, very wearied. Going over some old letters and papers. I may have opportunity some day to sit down and arrange them. There are interesting passages in one's life that would be entirely obliterated but for them. May my life be more and more a consecrated life.

May 9.— . . . Had some talk with John M'Gregor about some memorial of Sir J. E. Alexander. The idea of Cleopatra's Needle forming a part of it suggested. . . . The obligations at this time of the year press upon me. Arngomery a heavy thing; and yet I cannot regret having secured the property, whatever trial awaits me.

The landed interest of this country passing through a crisis.

May 16.— . . . Declined invitation to the dinner on the 21st in the Council Chambers; I feel more than ever disinclined for such things, and besides, I may stand in the way of others.

May 29.— . . . Wrote A. W. Grant about his wanting me to acknowledge myself as the author of a pamphlet about St. Nicholas Hospital before Sheriff Spens in the case of a railway dispute about a casualty on property in or near Nicholas Lane, Shuttle Street. It is singular how things crop up. Reconciling myself to a rate of twopence increase in School Board rate. It is a painful surprise; the effect on my mind is depressing. . Joined the Regality Club, an archæological movement that may pick up the fragments of Glasgow matters worth recording.

June 1.— . . . The crosses and trials of life are fitted to loosen the affections from worldly things, yet how many sources of comfort and blessing. Patted "Wee Fannie" in her stall; the little dog so happy in riding to the station; the little lambs how full of life, bounding here and there; the little kitten never at rest. The place dear to me from old associations. At Endrickfield cottage this morning; the stream beautifully clear.

June 8.—Came in from the country to-day. Anxious for the last few days about the school rate. It is a serious responsibility to face hostile opinion; still I believe that we have been doing a great work, and the community must pay for the necessity involved in the erection of buildings and the acquiring of sites to the extent of £700,000. My mind burdened with this thought on going out to the country on Saturday.

June 15.— Bade T. M. Fielding good-bye; he has been a week with us. Lord Salisbury appears by the newspapers to have accepted office. What a difficult task! But evidently the Gladstone Party have not been blessed in their administration of the country. Brought into town a good many flowers and blossoms. . . . At the demonstration (musical) of School Board children in the Wellington Palace on Friday evening, 12th. Spoke about the Duke of Wellington. Dr. F—— spoke in bad taste about Gladstone to the audience.

June 22.— . . . A gentleman whom I knew only by sight, said to me that it was surprising that the community were seldom at fault in fixing on the right man in a great work. Poor Arthur of Barshaw buried on Saturday. A remarkable man. . . . At the High School on Tuesday, 16th, about the arrangements for the 25th. What a republic the playground is. Professor Kirkpatrick there examining the French and German classes.

June 29.— . . . Surprised and dumbfoundered in finding a letter from Mr. Mundella, intimating that, at his instance, Mr. Gladstone has obtained the permission of Her Majesty to offer me the honour of knighthood. The letter of Mr. Mundella was accompanied by one from Mr. Hamilton, Mr. Gladstone's private secretary. I thought that as this was a matter affecting the family relationships, I should mention it to Archie Robertson. He advised me to accept the honour, also Mr. Cuthbertson. I told Mr. Campbell and Mr. Gibson; Mr. Wilson being in Bute, I wrote him. . . . This honour will draw me out of the retreat that I would fain creep into, and where I might quietly direct the business of the School Board along with others. I hope that it may not hinder me finishing up some things to my satisfaction. It will occasion remark, and involve a good deal of complimentary congratulation amongst friends; it may excite criticism. I feel that it is an honour out of all proportion to what I have attempted to do for education. . . . I would rather have been let alone and let others get honours. Still there would have been pride if I had at once declined. These honours help to conserve the interests of the country; to undervalue them is to put the Queen and her Ministers to shame, as if the distinction conferred was worth nothing.

July 1.—I received a letter from W. Wilson, but no letter from N——, which gave me great uneasiness. The telegrams which passed between us to-day explained the cause, the letter—through Sandy Stewart's oversight—not having been posted yesterday. I framed a letter of acceptance, and it is away to Mr. Mundella, and no doubt will have a passing glance, amongst other pressing matters, from Mr. Gladstone. I regard the change, from one of comparative obscurity to the glare of public notice, with some shrinking of mind, but I take it as a token to try and be more useful than ever. I now sit down to write several friends who would take my silence amiss.

July 9.—I received an invitation to the funeral of the wife of Lord Craighill. I wrote him a note of condolence. How sad to have grief and congratulation commingled.

July 14.—Went into Edinburgh. Called on Lord Craighill; he was prepared to meet me in the drawing-room —very much affected. Had some interesting conversation about Dr. Love and Dr. Balfour. He gave me a passage to read about Dr. Balfour in the funeral sermon by Dr. Love, which he said was one of the finest he had ever read—about his meeting him again in the eternal world.

August 4.—What an eventful period has elapsed since I last wrote anything in this book. . . The journey from London comfortable. The country appeared like a garden, too much cut up by hedgerows—some fields red with poppies; a great want of rain. The farm steadings snug, but wanting in cheerfulness; the brick gives a sad look. The spires of the churches pleasing objects. On Sunday went quietly to the Temple Church; looked with interest on Oliver Goldsmith's grave; beautiful lilies (Egyptian) at either end of it, placed there by some who admired his genius, and who determined that he should not be forgotten. Got access to the Temple. The service, though High, very beautiful. It was a fine thought to think of so many lifting up their hearts to God. Dr. Vaughan preached, "Arise, let us go hence." He referred to the great increase of political power to be conferred on the masses, and what changes it might bring about. He spoke too of the conflict of opinion as to the truth revealed in scripture. After service, an old man took me to the hall where the Benchers dined, and where the armour of the Knights Templars was displayed. . . . On Saturday morning, 1st August, went to the Waterloo

Glasgow. 7th July 1885.

My Dear Dr Gibson

I thank you kind note—

The distinction which is proposed to be conferred is bestowed, more with a view to bring into prominence School Board work, not only here but in Scotland—

It is very interesting to find that those in high

appearance in good time, and I shook hands with him. By and by Mr. Bryce, private secretary to Sir R. Cross, and several gentlemen appeared, and seven of them got into a saloon carriage with me. At first they occupied themselves with their newspapers; then they appeared inclined to talk, and some interesting conversation took place between me and the two men on either side of me as to the tenure of land, the Scotch Communion office, and the support of the ministry in the Free Church. When we got to Portsmouth a steamer was waiting for us. There appeared to be, on the way down, a good deal of waste ground. Saw hops growing, and lavender (I think),—an unusual crop. The harvest begun, fields rich with golden abundance. Arundel Castle—the fortifications of Portsmouth. Sir Richard Cross appeared more relieved when he got us all on board the steamer. I understood one man was wanting. He was very frank with me about the education clause in the Scotch Secretary Bill. Saw the *Victory* (Nelson's ship). The waters of Solent green-looking. A fine fresh sail to Cowes. The quiet equipages were drawn up at the pier. The royal arms scarcely visible on the panels. Struck with the quiet, business-like style in which we were driven up. The postilion, with black jacket and hat and white doeskin trousers, the very model of a servant. The people all very respectful. At the entrance, servants in scarlet livery ready to receive us. Ushered into a room, where lunch was served. . . . Honourable Colonel Ponsonby and Honourable Mr. Cust at the bottom of the table. Then we signed our names in a book, putting down my signature under the 11th August. Then ushered into a corridor which led to the Queen's apartment. Sir Richard Cross came out and said to several of us, "Put your hand under the Queen's hand, and kiss it, but do not touch it." When my turn came, I made two low bows, and then knelt on my left knee; and the Queen took from Colonel Ponsonby the sword, and touched my left and then my right shoulder with it; then put out her hand, which I kissed, and she said in a quiet, sweet, musical voice, as I rose from my kneeling posture, "Sir Michael Connal." I then retreated with my face towards her till I got to the door. There was no one in the room but the Duke of Connaught and Sir Richard Cross. The Queen's back was towards the window. . . . Sir Richard Cross said in a clear voice, "Mr. Michael Connal, ex-Chairman of the School Board of Glasgow." The fountain of honour, the sovereign of a great empire! What am I that I should be called forth to such distinction! Saw the Duke of Edinburgh, Marquis of Lorne, and some others of the Royal family. Beautiful view of the sea, fine terraces with flowers. Honourable Colonel Byng in attendance in full uniform as equerry. Came away in same carriage with Sir Richard Cross. I would like to have known what the men were distinguished for. Sir Henry Edwards, M.P., appeared to twit Sir Richard with the luncheon being more like a farmer's than a royal exercise of hospitality. I was too glad to get something to eat to criticize. I do not think the criticism was just. The voyage back was pleasant. Talked with Sir James Parker Deane. . A tedious journey from Portsmouth; Monday 3rd, being a holiday, may have increased the traffic on the lines. Arrived at my hotel about 9.45; wrote to N—— and Mr. W——.

August 11.— . . . Had some talk with Sir James Watson, telling him how I got on at Osborne. He is now in his eighty-third year; I told him he had kept abreast of everything going on.

August 24.— . . . Met Mr. Spofforth and walked with him to Kent Road School; incidentally referred to Forbes Campbell as frequenting a club in London of which he was secretary. Went up to the grave in the High Church burying ground where dear ones lie. Ascertained the date of my father's death for the County List of Families.

August 31.— . . . Dear wee "Princie" was nearly worried by four collies yesterday morning. . . . Sir C. Tennant came down to speak about Free Education in

September 9.— . . . N—— returned to the country. Great storm of wind and rain. Read Eadie's life by Brown; it brought back a good deal of the past. I cannot say that Mr. Browning on the whole, however sturdy in his independence of character, was one who inspired a love of learning. There may be great injury done to a boy in placing him under a despotism such as his method was.

September 16.—Yesterday morning at the Duke Street Reformatory from 10.30 to 11.30—very much pleased. . . . Still receiving the congratulations of friends, all couched in much the same terms—too personal.

September 25.—Returned from the annual meeting of the Y.M.C.A., Marquis of Ailsa presiding. Very interesting reports and addresses. Met Campbell Whyte and Mr. Somerville (late of Broughty Ferry) on my way home, and told them my mind as to the aim of the Association being guarded from running to seed. I did not approve of young men being enlisted as it were in a religious crusade. Met my old school-fellow, Henry Anderson of Partick, and exchanged remarks about old times.

September 28.—On Saturday, the 26th, left by 9.10 train for Kinross. A beautiful day. Affected when I thought of my uncle, John Wright, as I passed by Stirling. The Ochils majestic: the well-known villages. A sad feeling in passing Tillicoultry: woods, streams, villas, harvest operations. . . Mrs. Williamson in her bed and very feeble, yet quite acute; it was sad to see her thus prostrate: said to be ninety-four years of age. Called on Mrs. Beveridge. She showed me over her house, purchased for her by her sister—a marvel of accommodation and neatness, with a handsome plot in front. Unable, however, to articulate; her left hand and limb paralyzed. Mr. Burns-Begg and Mr. Stedman, banker, at lunch. Before I left, Mrs. Williamson gave me a copy of Mr. Burns-Begg's book on *Angling in Lochleven*, and wrote, supported on the bed, an inscription on it. Gratified I had made the visit out. These old friends of my dear mother must soon pass away. I am pleased that I have seen them. A glorious western sky. Passed Arngomery, and looked with some interest at Drum steading.

October 12.—Hard frost in the country. . . . The mountains rose majestically from the uplands, some distant peaks covered with snow. Walked in the High Wood; the heather was thick in some parts. Meditated while thus alone on all that has passed, and how God has blessed me. The harvest operations very pleasing. . . . In the evening, Friday, 9th October, at the meeting of the past and present members of the Spoutmouth Bible Institute in Free St. James's Hall—most interesting; about 110 present—Andrew Gillespie in the chair. . . . Altogether a most successful meeting. Paragraphs in the three newspapers next day; I hope that it may do good. On Tuesday, 8th, at the meeting in Queen's Rooms; Lord Polwarth and Marquis of Ailsa very fair in what they said, both apparently serious men. . . . Had some talk with Admiral Sir W. King Hall, K.C.B. ("Bulldog" Hall, to whom Boomersund was surrendered), and his lady. Nemesis Hall, the officer in the picture of the signing of the Pottinger treaty, and whom I knew, dead seven or eight years ago. Spoke to Donald Matheson. Dr. Andrew Thomson, who was to have been my guest, not well, and unable to read his papers. Said a few words at the breakfast; sat between Dr. Cairns and J. A. Campbell; spoke of Krummacher, Kossuth, and D'Aubigné. Heard Newman Hall and Oswald Dykes in the evening, Sir W. Muir in the chair. My intercourse with Mr. Stark very pleasant. Received a very complimentary address from the Headmasters of the schools under the Glasgow School Board. A kind note from John Cowan. Yesterday as I sat contemplating from the seat under the trees the glorious expanse of mountain, heath, trees, ferns, etc., I sought to give my heart to God. "What is man that Thou art mindful of him, and the son of man that thou visitest him?" My heart amidst all His bounty strongly unsatisfied; God alone can fill the heart, and the works of His hands are helps to praise Him.

October 15.— . . . At the dinner of the Deacon Convener (W. MacLean, Jr.) in the Trades' Hall. As a man said to me to-day he heard there was quite an ovation when I rose to speak. . . . Busy yesterday with

School Board matters and unable to attend the meeting of the Regality Club; appointed president.

October.—Visited my district, and called at every house.

October 23.— . . . . Mr. James Nicol, the chamberlain, in his *Vital and Economic Statistics* of the city, takes notice in very flattering terms of the honour conferred on me (page 187).

November 7.— . . . Elected a member of council of the Scottish Geographical Society, Edinburgh, and sent back to the Buchanan Institute as a director by the Merchants' House on the 3rd November. . . The only thing that reconciles me to the constant strain in connection with that property (Arngomery) is that I may leave it better than I found it.

November 21.—A great strain upon me for ten days past. This morning at Crookston Street School distributing hyacinths to the children, also at Centre Street, then drove with Barlas to Kay School; much pleased with the young men pupil teachers; prizes distributed by J. N. Cuthbertson. Recommended keeping a note-book; then went to cookery class, John Street, Mrs. M'Leod, teacher; cookery for the sick. Met George Buchanan about J. Chrystal's case of the Bannockburn widow. . . . Went to Lieutenant Greely's lecture in Queen's Rooms. Shook hands with him; I must read about his privations in his Arctic travels. Went to the Archæological to hear Mr. Boscawen on "Primitive Culture in Western Asia." How wonderful that we should be digging into the records of a time that brings us close to the history of nations that inhabited Palestine in the time of the Hittites. On Wednesday at defaulting parents' meeting in Springburn; nearly all Roman Catholic. Kind words go a long way. . . . Monday, 16th, in the evening dined at Professor Ramsay's to meet Sir F. Sandford. Had some talk with Sir W. Thomson about admission of children to Board Schools—there is mischief brewing about breaking down "use and wont." Pushed very much by Ramsay about printing notes of the reminiscences of school sites. Got from Mr. Renwick notes about Stirling extending back to 1519, gave them to Guthrie Smith: he says they are

very interesting. The conversazione in the Fi
Institute to meet Sir F. Sandford on the 13th
success. Introduced N—— to Lady Sandford, a
day gave her a photograph of the house in Mille
that belonged to her grandfather, and where her fat
born in 1784.

November 28.— . . . The result of the poll y
not satisfactory; J. N. Cuthbertson thrown out of St
district for the sake of a total stranger. The
remark as to Parliamentary seats—Glasgow throw
Political partizanship the rule, character standing f
ing. . . . Went to the College Library on We
morning to consult Kenrick's *Roman Sepulchral Mo*
about the tablet found at Lanuvium (nineteen mil
Rome, Via Appia). Met Professor Candlish; had sc
about secret societies and about a Bampton lecture

December 3.—Went to Larbert by 12.35 tr
Tuesday, 1st December. Pleased with the chil
dinner, everything cheerful. Mr. Cowan at the
but not so animated as I have seen him. The f
off the Ochils very exhilarating. At Buchanan In
in the evening. On Wednesday at a defaulters'
in Lister Street—these meetings do good. To-da
School Board; felt careless, and prone to say w
indiscreet: in fact, off my guard. The sense of r
bility removed from my shoulders has so far abrid
feeling of self-restraint. I pray that I may ever
mind my duty to God and to my fellow men w
provocations arise in my intercourse in the busine
I may note the death of James Morison (once i
coultry) within the last few days.

December 12.— . . . In the evening we
some reluctance to the festival of the Ancient Sh
in the Waterloo Rooms, A. B. M'Grigor in th
Sheriff Guthrie, Mr. Baird, M.P., and Mr. Gilbert B
M'Grigor's address very good. . . . On Mond
dined at Hugh Brown's, Clairmont Gardens; surp
find the Earl of Breadalbane there. Bolton pushe
little as to my having voted for Shaw Stewart. S
Badenach Nicolson. It is useful to mix with men

world,—it widens the sphere of your sympathies and interests. Expressed myself strongly to both W. M'Ewan and David Guthrie (vice-president Chamber of Commerce), and said that within eighteen months we would have a very decided movement in business relations with China from the conquest of Burmah. Mr. Blyth bought up at my suggestion the remainder of the issue of the *Evening News* of 7th—400 copies—containing the account of Orphan Homes.

December 19.— . . . On Monday, 14th, accompanied Mr. W. Mitchell to Gorbals School to introduce Mr. Robertson as headmaster at 10 o'clock. What an important step the occupation of that large school with children. What an element of social elevation. Spoke to W. H. Hill at the Directorate of the Merchants' House, about reports from representatives of institutions.

December 26.— . . . Received a nice letter from Principal Brown[1] about the bust which reached this on Monday afternoon, and which was placed in the Hall, St. James's Church, next day. On Monday heard of James MacLehose's death. Came into contact with him of late. He had put his finishing touch to the book to which he invited me to contribute.

[1] Principal Brown was for many years minister of St. James's Free Church.

1886

[redacted]

January 1.— . Had to go to St. Andrew's Halls to show face at the conversazione of the Educational Institute of Scotland. Intend to go into Stirling to-morrow to the funeral of Duncan M'Dougall.

January 2.—Went to Stirling by nine o'clock train. The funeral service held in the church. Mr. Lang, assisted by a U.P. minister, read and prayed; he pronounced a eulogium on Mr. M'Dougall. . . . Rev. John Russell's remains have been disturbed in clearing away the ground from the foundations of the West Church—the John Russell lampooned by Burns.

January 9.— . N—— got notice to-day of the death of her cousin Helen, daughter of Dr. Patrick MacFarlan. A truly good woman gone home. . . . Severe weather! At Mr. Ker's, at dinner, on Wednesday, 6th; met Principal Caird, Mr. Bottomley, Dr. Blackie.

January 16.— . . . Initiating a system by which the points of interest in pictures might be pointed out by a commissionaire—a step which I urged at the meeting of the School of Art on Monday night, 11th inst., when I was called to speak. Sir James Watson presided, and Mrs. Elder distributed the prizes. Sir James full of life for his years; read a long paper. Met at dinner at Sir James Watson's, Sir W. and Lady Thomson, Sheriff Clark, Lord Provost M'Onie, and Mr. Newberry.

January 23.—On Monday, the 18th, at the Stirlingshire dinner—C. M. King in the chair. Brought under notice (following up Guthrie Smith's remarks), the Stirling

Records as requiring immediate attention for publicati Yesterday finished the docketing of the Sch Board accounts for 1884 and 1885. In the even went with N—— to the conversazione in the Athena —Sir W. Collins in the chair. Dr. Marshall Lang everything worth saying. Have been in co spondence with William, Robert, and Henry Thomps very kind letters from them, and also from Mr. Muirh Kippen, about Ure of Shirgarton. . Receive kind letter from Mundella acknowledging the receipt the "Spout" report.

January 30.— . . . At the meeting of the Infirmary I was called to the chair. It was an interes meeting. I examined the reports, 1824-25, also the I mary (Royal) reports from 1794. No adequate repo what I said; the newspapers have no room for more a few facts as to the Institution in its present position necessities. Received this morning a copy *Reminiscences of Yarrow* from Mrs. Russell. . . . is a discipline, and in the removal of useful lives, bowing to the Divine will, we are called to realize God's work can be carried on without us, and that has a purpose of mercy in each individual case.

February 6.—Came home to-night very weary from meeting in the upper room of the Corporation Gall after Mr. Newbery's lecture on "Painting." I had preside. Many points of interest in it, but rather too fl It is a good beginning, however, and it may develop in first-rate school of instruction in Art. . Paid subscription yesterday and became a member of the I School Club. . . . Principal Nero (a negro), to w I gave £1 on 26th June last, has turned out an impo and been sent to prison. . . . On Tuesday morn went to Edinburgh with J. N. Cuthbertson. Walked up to Parliament House. Met Mr. Ma advocate, who showed us the library, etc., and took into the Courts, the Outer and Inner Division. Saw L Justice-Clerk Moncrieff, Lords Craighill and Young; L Advocate Balfour pleading before them. In the Co presided over by the Lord-Justice General, saw L

Shand, who evidently spied us and drew the attention of the President to us.

February 13.— The replies I get from several friends to whom I have sent copies of the "Spout" report, very pleasing. On Wednesday, 10th, after Lord Trayner's lecture, seconded a vote of thanks proposed by Professor Berry. A very interesting lecture on "Entails," etc.' Advised the young men to apply themselves to commercial law.

February 20.—Saturday. Came home from a tussle in the Exchange with a Canadian, introduced to me by Kincaid. He talked about a confederation of the Colonies with Great Britain, but it was evident he wanted this country shut out by tariffs hostile to other countries—the confederated Mother country and the Colonies. We cannot go back to protection. The Colonies have an eye to their own interests, and so far as Canada is concerned, except for some sentiment, it might join the States. No doubt the coalition of Canada and the United States would be a blow to this country, as it would hand over to a Republic the whole northern part of the western hemisphere. On Wednesday in the evening at the congregational soiree of Dr. Marshall Lang in the City Hall; sat between the chairman and Dr. Scott of St. George's, Edinburgh. The people seemed pleased with what I said about the Old Barony. Heard to-day from Mr. Caldwell of Paisley as to the family of Knox of Ranfurlie, and sent his letters to Rev. P. T. Muirhead, Kippen.

March 6.— . . . Requested Mr. David Dick to abandon the idea of putting a sketch of my career in the *Christian Leader*. On Wednesday, 3rd, at 2.30, with Finance Committee and Compensation to Teachers Committee, General Endowment Board. Obliged to take up a less liberal position than the rest of the Committee. In the evening went at nine to Cabmen's Amateur entertainment at the invitation of Mr. and Mrs. John Burns. Introduced to Lieut.-Col. Thompson of the Royal Scots. Drew from Mr. Underwood (U.S. Consul) a promise to get me the statistics of the State of Massachusetts. . . . On Thursday, 4th, at Sir James Bain's. A most sumptuous entertainment. Wrote Sir Joseph Hooker in anticipation of the opening of the Kent Road School, on the site of the old Botanic Garden, and had a meeting, preliminary (Dr. Joshua Paterson in the chair), about Dr. Somerville. The meeting inclined to a portrait by a first-rate artist. . A most protracted winter, snow during the night and severe frost this morning.

March 13.— In the forenoon had to speak at the meeting of the "Cumberland" Training Ship in the Market Hall; quite at a loss what to say; referred to Southey's *Nelson* and gave the boys a copy of it. Probably referred too freely to my father having run away to sea, and to the "Herefordshire," and the unexpected coincidence of meeting a gentleman who had sailed in her, at Mr. Ewing's at dinner. Some people seemed pleased. I would have been quite happy to be less prominent. . . . At the Presbytery meeting from 12 till 4.30 on Thursday, 11th, listening to the discussion of the overture on proposals affecting the Constitution of the Established Church. . . . The idea to my mind was that there was a party who had committed themselves to carry the voluntaries along with them in their desire for union, and that they must get rid of State support to do so, and that the present Establishment was the obstruction. Mr. Scrymegeour and Dr. Candlish practically admitted that there was no trusting to the interpretation of Acts of Parliament, and that after falling in with such an arrangement as Mr. Finlay's Bill, the difficulty might again arise and force on another disruption. The Free Church, in my judgment, should let the Established Church get the Bill securing the interpretation of statutes in favour of spiritual independence. It is churlish to refuse it to that church if it wants it. It may be an uncertain possession, as Principal Douglas brought out, from the democratic preponderance of political opinion in the country, or rather the tendency in that direction. I think that the Church of Christ will not be welded together till the yelp of the wolf drives the flock of Christ

substantial union without incorporation. . . . Surprised to get an invitation to attend a mass meeting of unemployed on Glasgow Green to-morrow (Sunday) at 4.30. Who could think of me as likely to sympathize with the Social Democratic Federation ?

March 15.— . Saw Mr. Kennedy, and consulted about Lord Moncrieff's visit on 27th. . . . The newspapers to-night indicate difficulties in the Cabinet about the Irish question.

March 20.— . Busy all day with circular about Dr. Somerville's portrait. . . . Received a very pleasing note from Sir J. D. Hooker about his father and his relation to the old Botanic Garden, I think on the 17th inst.; I intend to make use of it when the Kent Road School is opened formally. . . . Went in the evening to the Archæological Society; J. O. Mitchell read a paper on James Stirling, mathematician, who was presented with a silver kettle by the River Trust about 1750.

March 25.—Thankful to have got two engagements over. At the Bellshill Bazaar at 12 o'clock, in the Crown Halls; said a few words in opening it about Bothwell Haugh, Bothwell Bridge, Orbiston, and Owen the socialist. I hope the Rev. W. M'Donald's efforts to clear off debt may be successful. He needs £800. The people apparently pleased to see me. Handed round six purses with fifteen shillings in each. . . . A favourable sketch (not sarcastic nor hostile) of myself in the periodical *Fairplay* of 20th March. Quite inaccurate, however, in many particulars. Gave Colin Brown my subscription for Dr. Somerville's picture.

March 27.—Yesterday went to the dinner to Professor Veitch. Glad I went, as the numbers were so few. On the whole the meeting fitted to do good to the [Archæological] Society. Referred to the printing of the deed in 1856; part of the Town's title to the Sub-Dean Mill, date 1446, and to the circumstances of the times when the Society was cradled on 3rd March, 1855.

April 2.— . . . Ascertained that the two Egyptian boys in Anderston Public School, who got prizes for complete attendances, were Mahommedans, but getting all the advantages of Christian education not only in school but in Sunday Schools. . . . Received from Mr. Underwood (U. S. Consul) the State papers of Massachusetts as to wages and prices since 1752.

April 3.— . . Definitely declined to have anything to do with the proposal of a portrait as a present from friends in Free St. James's. Michael Connal's [Mauritius] daughter played at a concert last night in Hillhead Burgh Hall, given on behalf of the unemployed at Partick.

April 9.—Mr. Gladstone's Home Rule Scheme unfolded in a three and a half hours' speech; I have read it so far as to see the drift of it. He does not realize that he is placing the country at the feet of the disloyal and the fanatical. Mr. Trevelyan's speech good; Ireland will become a poor country; capital will flee from it. His safeguards as to checking extravagance in measures by an Irish Parliament, mere withes of straw. They will agitate, agitate, until every barrier is thrown down, and then there will be bloodshed and civil war. It is a dark time; it is a crisis. Mr. Gladstone does not realize that in the government of Ireland he has to contend with a religio-political power—Catholic emancipation as to Parliamentary powers, apart from freedom of conscience as to worship, has proved itself a snare and a suicidal step. . . . Mr. Forster's death sad—a great man fallen. Was privileged to discuss with him along with others in his own house about the Education Secretaryship question. Mr. John Polson of Paisley sent me his printed sheet about George's views as to the Land question, and as to crime in Ireland. Collecting material for the visit of Lord Moncrieff on 24th inst. I was surprised at finding myself portrayed in the periodical *Fairplay* of 20th March under the heading "Clydeside Cameos." A sketchy kind of thing, and inaccurate. On 5th April invited by Joseph Somerville to take the chair at a meeting to start a Microscopical Society. Suggested Professor M'Kendrick. Very much concerned at the legislation afloat as to school fees remitted by School Boards. The danger is not obvious, but it paves the way to Free Education.

April 17.—Went to Gorbals School, where the City

Education Endowment Board had a competitive examination. Saw 160 young persons in one room, the divisions being put back so as to make three rooms into one. Very much affected with the sight. The examination hall of the Hutcheson Grammar School presented a fine appearance, filled with young people.

Mr. Menzies, Dr. Kerr, Dr. F. L. Robertson, all busy with the arrangements being satisfactorily carried out. What will be the effect of this system on the rising youth of the city when more fully developed, and more amply supplied with resources?

April 24.—Went to Kent Road School with my papers and MSS. as to the locality. Introduced to Lord Moncrieff. Spoke to him about the suppers on Sunday night at old Sir Henry Moncrieff's when N——'s mother went with her father to them. He wished to be introduced to N——, but she had left the room and had gone away to the Queen's Rooms. He told me an amusing story about Cockburn being at one of these suppers, and hearing when at prayers the click of the meat-jack and being more interested in that. Read my MSS. rapidly, and illustrated it by the oil portrait of Hopkirk and the plant from the Botanic Garden, being the first plant that flowered in it (a stone plant), the *Strelitzia Regina*. In the Queen's Rooms sat beside Lord Moncrieff. His address an extremely interesting one as to the steps which led to the measure of 1872. I think that the meeting has been a successful one. At luncheon in the Grand Hotel; Mr. Cuthbertson got over the whole proceedings very well. On Tuesday, 20th, at High School Committee. At Tract and Book Society of Scotland in Christian Institute on Thursday, 22nd. Had Mr. Graham from School Board Office on Thursday night to take down in shorthand what I had to say about Kent Road School. At the Board in committee on that day gave . . . a wipe that may likely lead to coolness, but what I said may do good. Helped by A. M'Donald, Mr. Ballan, David Murray, Mr. Weir of the Trades' House, J. Guthrie Smith, Sir D. Hooker, W. H. Hill, in preparing my paper for the Kent Road School.

"This is young Glasgow" [I thought], as we stood in the play-ground of Crookston School, and saw row upon row of boys, apparently well shod and clothed, the children of artizans, marching into school. What a blessing this Act has been.

April 28.— . . . Sent Sir Joseph Hooker to-day Hopkirk's Memoir.

May 1.— . . . How the spirit of party and personal attachment to Gladstone leads many astray in this tremendous step, unconstitutionally gone about in keeping the secret to himself and launching it on the country without an appeal to the country. We are made the sport of party. The position for Ireland is a solemn one—there may yet be bloodshed. The transference of a Protestant minority to the domination of a R.C. majority cannot be effected peaceably; it can never be anything else than confusion and insubordination.

May 6.— . . . Before going to the School Board met Mr. William Clark at the House of Refuge. Pleased with the general aspect of the Institution. There must be some way of dealing with lads advancing to maturity other than by throwing them together into a reformatory. It is all very well from twelve to sixteen; beyond that age amendment of life is beset with temptation to insubordination. Visited Stirling's Library officially. . . . Did not get to Edinburgh to the opening of the Exhibition by Prince Albert Victor, though a grand card of invitation was sent me. . . . Went to James Whyte, photographer, 37 Jamaica Street, who has enlarged a photograph of me and coloured it. It is not unlike, but the expression is distressed. I suggested the softening of a muscle of the cheek.

May 13.— . . . At Mr. Renwick's, after consulting Mr. J. Guthrie Smith, about printing Stirling Records, and decided to go on with it, though guarantee scarcely complete. Made an exchange for the "Spout" of the 143 volumes of the *Critical Review* for 26 works of a more readable character representing 49 volumes, the *Review* having been sold in mistake to me years ago, in Mr. Blair's time. Wrote Sir Joseph Hooker about Dr. Walker Arnott.

May 20.—Thursday. Grieved to find the rain come on about 11 o'clock or so. It has continued all day, and I have been quite sad at the thought of the young persons thus exposed to indifferent shelter at Parkhall, with a cold east wind. I had pictured to myself how much enjoyment they would have under the freshly bursting trees. I have prayed not to murmur; I may not distrust God's goodness to them and to myself. It is, however, a part of the discipline of this life. It may teach me a lesson of submission, to find all preparations cast to the winds. I hope that none may suffer by it. . . . Dr. R. Scott Orr's death very sudden. It took place on Saturday on his return home from seeing his patients in the forenoon.

May 22 *(Saturday).*—Attended Dr. Logan's funeral to-day—service in St. James' Church. Very much impressed. Looked at the seat once occupied by my uncle. . . .

May 27.— Met Professor Ramsay about lectures on Geography during the winter, by Meiklejohn of St. Andrews. Dined on the invitation of the Lord Provost in the Council Chambers, to meet the Marquis Tseng. The dinner a very grand affair. Amongst other dishes there were Bird's Nest Soup and Fricassée of Frogs—the frogs tasted like chicken; I just tasted the dish—nothing more. The company very demonstrative of good-will towards the strangers. Sir James Watson and Sir William Collins spoke. The Marquis Tseng a shrewd-looking man, but nothing noble in his appearance. He said a few words, and left the speaking to his secretary, who expressed himself very well in English. They may carry away with them some fresh ideas as to material progress. Is it likely that they will realize the true foundation of our greatness as a Christian country? If they shut out the light they never will. Sat next the son of Sir Peter Coats from Paisley; talked about Gladstone. As a Liberal he spoke as if he had stolen a march upon them. Evidently the Liberal party is broken up, whatever efforts may be made to heal the wound. Dr. Burns of the High Kirk on my right hand. "Auld Langsyne" at the close. On Tuesday afternoon went into Edinburgh with N——. Went to the breakfast given by the Moderator (Rev. Dr. A. N. Somerville). N—— taken in by the Moderator, and I took the Moderator's lady for the day, Mrs. J. C. White. Dr. Cairns and Dr. White of Free St. George's said a few words, and the time was completely up (10.10) when Mr. J. C. White finished speaking. Mrs. Knight from Aberdeen on my left. We then went to the Exhibition in the Meadows. The slopes from the Castle down to Princes Street were bright under the sunshine—the outline very fine. The picture gallery most attractive; wandered up and down the whole length, and through some of the side rooms. "Old Edinburgh" very good, and the quaint appearance of the old guard gave life to the narrow street and weird-looking houses. Saw the Commissioner make his State visit to the Exhibition. The Seaforth Highlanders lined the road—an imposing spectacle.

June 3.— . . . Met Professor Grant; he appeared much depressed by the aspect of the times and about Gladstone's personal influence involving such great social changes. As I said, he is sowing dragons' teeth.

June 8.—Thankful that Gladstone has received a check in his mad career. There will be a great deal of trouble arising out of this yet; men cannot commit themselves to a policy without braving out their defeat.

June 15.—Yesterday came in from the country laden with blossoms, etc. . . . . In the evening at Mr. Ballantine's musical demonstration in Wellington Palace. A very fine meeting—eight hundred children. Full account in the *North British Daily Mail* to-day by Lamont, School Board teacher.

June 17.— . . . Replied to Lord Brabazon's note about the Metropolitan Public Gardens Association. . . .

The political turmoil raised by *that man* agitating society to its very depths. The political demonstrations of to-night and further on painfully distressing. A leap in the dark under personal influence most selfishly exercised.

June 21.—Came in from the country with Mr. and Mrs. Wilson. They have had beautiful weather; the country rich in its robes of green. On Friday, 18th, at the distribution of prizes of the Springburn Public School. Had a sketch of the monument proposed to be erected to Alexander III. in my pocket, and was pleased with the answer of a little boy as to the state of Scotland at his death.

June 25.—At the Delinquency Board at 12. Sent Rev. Dr. Wallace Moncrieff's address. . . . Lord Hartington in town to-night; offered by John Muir a platform ticket, but declined. Yesterday at the distribution of prizes of the High School in the Waterloo Rooms. Said a few words about a stone in the new building commemorative of the jubilee of the reign of the Queen, when proposing a vote of thanks to the Lord Provost and Magistrates as patrons. The flowers from Parkhall gave some style to the lunch. . . . Got five stones from the old gateway of the College, and sent them out to Parkhall. . . . My life may be near an end, and yet there are many things I would like to finish up.

July 2.—Went to Bute Hall, to be present at the nomination of Dr. J. A. Campbell as Member for the Universities of Glasgow and Aberdeen. There being no contest, the meeting very small. Principal Caird presided. Dr. M'Kendrick moved, and Dr. Fergus seconded, the nomination. Dr. Campbell's speech was in the confident tone of one who had secured his seat. It was good sense, but it was without any claim to eloquence. Thought of him as the pushing, steady-going youth in the Logic Class in 1841.

July 5 (*Monday*).— . . . Voted for Baird in the Central District; the present a momentous time.

July 13.— . . . Went out by afternoon train to Parkhall. After dinner met William Buchanan, dyke-builder, as to placing the old stones of the gateway of the College over the bridge at the Bog Burn. This morning drove to the Balfron School, thence to vote; voted for Mr. Noel.

July 19.—Came in from the country to-day. Received photographs of Rev. john Russell's tomb from Provost Yellowlees. Sent one of them to Miss Sheriff, with an account of the last moments of Mr. Russell, written by his son, J. Russell of Muthill, in my mother's handwriting. Mr. Thomson, Dollar, sent back the letters relating to my father's tomb at Obia. He may yet, through his Indian friends, be able to identify it. . . . Pleased with the position of the stones at the Bog Burn; one stone gilded is a capital, taken from one of the pillars of the City Bank.

July 20.—Opened my mother's box; no one now to tell me the mementoes of the little treasures she had in it—ornaments, etc. I had not the heart to open it since her death.

July 27.—Received a note from Sir J. Hooker with drawing of Hopkirk's Cottage at Helensburgh, originally sketched by W. D. Hooker. Distributed twenty copies of Rev. P. Muirhead's sketch of Ure of Shirgarton and his times. Sent copies to the tenants at Arngomery. Considered with Wilson scheme of the commissioners of the Logan and Johnstone Bequest. . . . Sabbath day calm, but overcast and threatening. Monday morning the outline of the hills magnificent, the colour blue, almost indigo. An account, not strictly accurate, in *Stirlingshire Advertiser* about Mr. Russell's tomb restored. It brings me too much into prominence, and confuses Mr. Russell's relation to Mr. Grant. Committed myself to Bailie Dunlop to put in a window in St. David's to the Leckies of Broich.

August 2.—Went to the opening of Alexander's School under the School Board. A very unpleasant meeting. The people in the district not prepared for free education being done away with, and apparently taken by surprise. It shows the effect of training a community in dependence—the whole thing has been a school of unthrift—a charity school in the worst sense. On 30th at a Finance meeting of School Board.

August 9.— . . . Heard by letter from H. G. Henderson that William Wright had passed away on Friday night at 10.45. . . . He was unconscious from about five o'clock, but no particular suffering marked his end. The funeral to be on Wednesday. A paragraph in

interests of Greenock. Went on board the "Meg Merrilees" at 2.30 or so; got on board the "Otterburn" and sailed into the dock. The whole affair very magnificent. Came back, and at the dinner sat between M. H. Shaw Stewart, M.P., and Mr. Finlayson, late M.P. Got a very cordial welcome on rising to speak, and got through what I had to say; some expressed themselves pleased with what I said, and the newspapers took notice of it.

August 17.— . . . Looking forward to going to Edinburgh to-morrow. Surprised that I am one of the twenty guarantors selected to go and dine with the Executive Committee.

August 20.—Went into Edinburgh by train on Wednesday, 18th, leaving at 11.30. . . Introduced to Sir William Muir (in a robe with stars) by Rev. Dr. M'Gregor; introduced myself to Dr. Cameron Lees. . The Archers took up the line of view and obscured the procession. . . . Saw Lord Aberdeen in a green coat, Sir Henry Ponsonby and Lord Cross—yesterday Sir Richard Cross. The whole affair over in twenty minutes, after waiting till 4.20. Walked round the Exhibition with Dr. M'Gregor. Wyllie Guild in full court dress, and looked well. Met Mrs. Cooper, Ballindalloch, and examined some old lace. At dinner sat beside Mr. Glen and Bailie Coulstoun. . . . Talked about the Browns of Ashley. Left before dinner toasts finished. . . . Got home very wearied by 12 o'clock. . . . Heard John Morison address pupil teacher candidates with much interest on Thursday at 1 o'clock.

August 23.—Came into town to-day with Sir Charles Stirling, Glorat. Got tickets for him and his son for the Colonial and Indian visitors meeting on Thursday and Friday.

August 27.—Came home to-night after a most enjoyable day in accompanying the Colonial and Indian visitors in a sail in the "Iona"; the weather was all that could be desired,—dull, yet with occasional gleams of sunshine; sea smooth, and a refreshing gentle breeze. The boys of the "Cumberland" manned the yards—a fine sight. The mountain peaks very clear all round; Arran particularly

so. The flush of the heather on the l
the Kyles of Bute so beautiful,
moment Gairdner's (the banker) att
cussing the silver question with J
others.

September 10.—Drove with N
very creditable affair. Mr. Sneddon
it as performers. The time and mel
good. Mrs. Wilson, Auchineck, M
representation of the neighbours,
Duncan, Mr. Blackburn, etc. Did
fully. Said a few words, to which I
Brown.

September 14.—The house in Pitt
. . . I have half committed my
purchase of it. I think it may com
it is a landmark of the family—with
no visibility in Stirling.

September 21.—Wrote Mrs. Blackbu
her for having printed my speech at th
tion. Wrote Miss Buchanan about
in Balfron, and sent her Mrs. Buch
1861, asking me to be a trustee;
amissing. Had to tell the Permissive
a bit of my mind—I said that carried
consequences it involved a species o
that the intemperate advocacy of
made me wriggle. They may not be
an opinion that may check indiscretic

September 22.—Went to Kinross
N—— Reminded of the time lon
I was under Mr. Browning, when
Saw other well-known places. Reach
received a welcome from Mrs. Wi
Mrs. Beveridge. Pleased with the con

September 27.—Read about the
Loch Fyne side, in the blast at the
last. . . . On Thursday evenin

[1] This house belonged to Sir Michael's mat
Wright of Broom.

telegram an invitation from the Lord Provost to meet Count Saigo and the Japanese gentleman accompanying him, induced Mr. Nicol (Chamberlain) to invite Mr. Dyer, who was professor of engineering at Tokio, in Japan, to the dinner. . . It turned out that he knew Count Saigo, and his speech in reply to his health being drunk was the most interesting there. Rather favourably impressed with the young men. Mr. Andrew Cunningham's death took place on Friday—Depute Town Clerk. There dies with him a great deal of information connected with the city records which he did not jot down for those who were to come after him.

October 4 (*Monday*).—Came in from the country; the trees in the pony's field golden yellow. Brought flowers into town, and sent a package of heather to London. . . . Old John Graham of Skelmorlie died suddenly to-day at ninety years of age.

October 7.—Returned from Larbert at 6.20 or so. Travelled with Lord Egerton of Tatton. So far as I could make out, there accompanied him Mr. Black, secretary; Mr. Edmund Johnson, Dr. Armitage, Mr. Akkers, and two clergymen interested in deaf and dumb children. Lord Egerton of Tatton a fine, frank, handsome man of forty-eight years of age or so, apparently pleased with the Institution. Much interested in the conversation of Dr. Armitage. We talked of houses for the poorer classes, about lodging houses, evening classes, the London Polytechnic, about total abstinence societies, about the societies for the distribution of charity amongst the out-door blind in London, and how Poor Law Boards withdrew support, and then had to renew it when they found the voluntary distributions ceased. No difficulty in checking the distribution tickets; out of two thousand, at a given time of examination, only two or three tickets wanting. He appears to have a seat somewhere in Ireland. He is so blind as to use an instrument with which he punctures a sheet of paper and raises characters on it, thus taking notes. Mr. Edmund Johnson was brought up a medical man, and was tutor to a blind Lord Salisbury; he was at Hatfield when the present Lord Salisbury was eleven years old. He said the Premier was a man of very powerful mind. . A great deal of the crops out—a source of regret in the absence of seasonable weather. . . . Saw aunt to-day. Mrs. Burnley Campbell and her little boy with her. Aunt gave me my uncle's eye-glass; she said she thought I would value it.

October 18.—A busy day; wrote out a few remarks for the meeting of the poor children's dinner-table, at which I had to preside at 2. A fair meeting, principally of ladies. Referred to the Queen of Greece being amongst the outcasts of Paris, and to Dr. Chalmers (22nd September, 1840) about the management of the poor in the parish of St. John's. . . . At the thanksgiving service to-night in the church. Mr. Hall referred to breaking the alabaster box of ointment in the lifetime of our friends. . . .

October 30.— . On Tuesday went most reluctantly to the Young Men's Guild meeting—Lord Balfour in the chair. Heard A. Orr Ewing, Dr. Marshall Lang, and Dr. Charteris. . . D. Bryce, bookseller, gave me the opportunity to glance at the MS. of his new book, *Quaint Bits still existing in Glasgow.*

November 6.— . . . Rather annoyed than flattered at the notice taken of me in Mr. Marshall's pamphlet on *Secondary Education.*

November 22.—On Friday, 19th, at Academical Club dinner in the Academy—Mr. John A. Spens in the chair; had a difficult part to play in my reply to a toast. They all feel very sore about the High School competition and the School Board of Govan movement. . . Had a call from ——; he has got himself into a wrong position. But there is no use arguing with a Highlander; they are impulsive, subtle, and violent.

November 27.— . . . Went, though most reluctantly, from want of sleep all Thursday and Friday, to Sir Charles Warren's lecture in Queen's Rooms; was introduced to him.

December 15.— . . . At a Finance meeting at 1.30, and at 3 at the opening of the Seaman's Institute at 200 Broomielaw. The meeting an earnest one; I felt warms. I am struck with the value to the community of someone making such an institution a hobby; it is beyond the power of one man to work at everything. Apparently I am more than ever settling down to two or three things.

December 18 (*Saturday*).— . . . I did not attend any of the meetings of the Protestant Convention, but I told Mr. W. C. Maughan on Thursday that he was taking a bombshell into his hand in having had to do with it.

December 25.— . . . Received from W. Connal, Jun., a photograph from the picture, in his possession, of my grandmother, Marion Connal.[1] It recalls a great many things—the old house off the Broad Street—her patient sitting in her chair in the dining-room—the jam and cream—the old servants, Janet and Mary—my mother's visits to her—the bedroom, with its windows overlooking the Forth and the Ochils. . . . On Monday, 20th, dined with the Judges, Lords Young and Craighill, at 8 o'clock in George Hotel. Lord Craighill sent me a kind note apart from the official one. Burns Kidston there; J. Millar and he went to Tillicoultry fifty-six years ago. I was there in 1827.

[1] Marion Glas married Michael Connal, 1775.

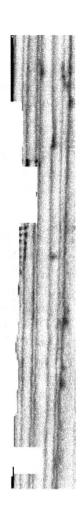

1887

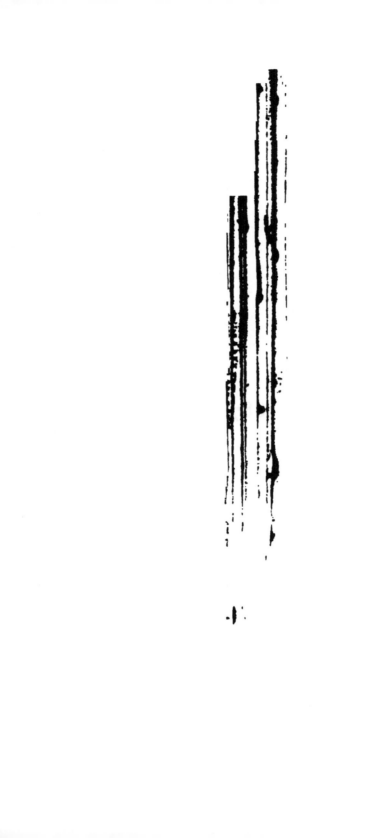

January 1.— . . At a meeting of Finance General Endowment Board on Thursday at 2.30. Dr. Robertson appears to have remarkable aptitude for business.

January 8.— . . . Met yesterday morning, out of courtesy, Mr. Stewart Parker, M.P., Mr. Cochrane-Patrick, Mr. Finlay, Dr. Craik, in the School Board rooms before they examined witnesses as to the Normal Schools. . On Wednesday evening, 5th instant, took R. L. Ewing to the Cathedral to see it lighted up with gas. Dr. A. L. Peace and a choir conducted the recital of organ and sacred music. The old pile, in the dark winter night, in its solitary grandeur, was for the time being a music hall. The carvings and proportions of the buildings beautifully brought out.

While the soft gentle tones of the instrument were followed by swelling volumes of sound that seemed to shake the venerable building, I thought of those lying outside near and dear to me. . The thought of the eternal world lifted me above the surroundings.

January 13.— . . . Much solemnized by Lord Iddesleigh's sudden death yesterday, when calling on Lord Salisbury. Taken away at the very time when moderate counsels needed. Oh! the madness of political partizanship. . . . Bought James Robertson's life (of Newington). It carried me back fifty-nine years.

January 18.—Returned the scrap book about Stirling, lent me by J. C. Gibson; very interesting. . . . Yesterday at the Stirlingshire Dinner in the Grand Hotel—Ex-Provost M'Onie in the chair; about seventy present.

Produced the *Stirling Borough Records*, the first spec
volume. All apparently interested. . . . Sent
evergreens to the poor cripple, Margaret Fergus, in
Poorhouse.

January 22.— . . . In *Harper's Weekly*, Jan
8th, found a woodcut of Right Rev. Horatio Potter,
late bishop of New York. He died on 2nd Jan
last, aged eighty-four. I think I can detect the
ments of his countenance. I remember his visi
us in 1838, in Dixon Street. . . . Sent little G
L. Ewing a great many stamps (foreign). . . . Pl
that J. B. Slimon shows his interest in the librar
presenting to the "Spout" Sir W. Scott's Works.

January 29.— . . . Endeavouring to get the Bor
Records of Stirling out and distributed. Sent Mr. Mu
the copy No. 1. . . . Spoke to Mr. Grant t
about a peripatetic museum to illustrate geography. .
On Wednesday night, 26th, at the lecture by Sir F
De Winton on "The Congo, Past and Present." The
map most interesting; a good lecture.

February 12.— . . . Very much gratified by
fessor Roberton's invitation to be a guest of the Fa
of Procurators at the banquet to Lord Coleridge on
24th inst.

February 19.— . . . Went with N—— last
to the lecture by Consul Underwood, U.S., on "Longfe
Lowell, and Holmes," in the Queen's Rooms. Felt
I had no time to read, and yet how I might have appreci
their works. I am more a man of action, and yet
insensible to the portraiture of nature in their creat
. . . . In the morning saw the picture, by Noel Pa
of *In Die Malo*—the Christian putting on the shiel
faith. Very fine in conception.

February 24.—Went to the Fine Arts Exhibition to-
Struck most with the landscape (568) "Sunshine
Shadow," by Thomas Hunt, Arran; and then by (114) "
Lord of the Mists," by J. A. Aitken—an eagle sailing am
the mist that shrouds a mountain. Went to the mee
about the Jubilee subscription lists; very few present;
have aimed too high, in my judgment.

February 26.— . . . . At Professor Meiklejohn's lecture this morning on "The Ocean." . . . Attended meeting of Ladies' Jubilee Offering—Lord Provost in the chair; Sir W. Thomson, Dr. D. M'Leod. I think that the meeting looked interested, and I hope it may be successful. In some measure relieved by Dr. M'Laren's report; while avoiding over-fatigue, prepared to go forward with cheerful hopefulness to work. Rev. Dr. M'Leod spoke to me at the ladies' meeting that I should take a note, with a view to publication, of the out-of-the-way materials that I sometimes bring forward. I think that others over-estimate their interest. Still I may some day get time to collate something worth preservation. Impressed with the thought that my days are swifter than a weaver's shuttle. Read over the notes I have taken from 1st January to 1st May. They enable me to recall what otherwise would have been forgotten.

February 28.— Received a letter from P. F. Connal-Rowan, from Algiers—hopeful . At the meeting in Merchants' Hall at 2—Professor Drummond in the chair. Rev. R. P. Ashe, from Uganda, gave some information about the causes more or less intimately connected with the murder of Bishop Hannington.

March 5.— . . . Mrs. Erskine Murray and her family provided the instrumental music at the flower show.

March 12.— . . . Examined in Corporation Galleries the design for Exhibition building. Thought a good deal of Bishop's Palace motto.

March 24.— . . . Accepted the invitation of Provost Yellowlees and Magistrates, etc., to the unveiling of the Connal window on the 31st March.[1] It is unexpected, this conferring of the freedom of the borough on William Connal of Solsgirth. If conducted modestly the community may embrace an opportunity to recall the names of old citizens for the good of those rising up around us. It is not seemly to forget those who have passed away.

[1] Window put in West Church, Stirling, by William Connal of Solsgirth, in memory of his father, Patrick Connal, and grandfather, Michael Connal.

March 26.—Thankful to get home.
Court yesterday, Mr. Gray put into my
of the town of Stirling to Robert Colt,
1678. A fine large seal;—traced som
from Fountainhall's notes, and Rogers
Coutts family. . . . So knocked up
able to speak. The Botanic Garden
whelming problem. Met Robert Macfie
street to-day—as youthful as ever.

March 29.—Two days of constant em
At Mr. Renwick's at 10.30 about Sir R.
the Burgh of Stirling. . . . Missed C
Glasgow at the public auction—very sca

March 31.—Went to Stirling. Fou
Mary's Wynd—went up to grandmother's
not get admission. Wandered up the
good many people assembled at the ch
and his daughters; William Connal's t
The ceremony attending the unveiling t
well managed. A large body of people
Mr. Underwood, U.S. Consul, there. Bef
the Guild Hall, Provost Yellowlees s
Russell's tombstone. Guild Hall ancient-l
in his robes, W. Connai on his right an
Apparently the ceremony was appreciat
130 poor folks at dinner enjoying th
W. Connal. . . . The lunch rather pr
an early hour of the day. Rather sad t
Connal's] five sons were absent—scattered

April 6.—On Monday at St. James'
the morning. The little things running l
hill. . . .

April 9.—Wrote Andrew Stewart of th
as to a show of wild flowers.

April 12.—Presided at three at Stirling
ing. Mr. Underwood, U.S. Consul, there
elevated speech in tone and manner. Dr
College said a few words. . . . On
went with N—— in the afternoon to St.
Hoisted on to the platform. Dr. Donald M

to the Smith Institute. . . . Had my photograph taken in the crowd of the Stirlingshire Charitable and Sons of the Rock Society. . . . W. Connal expressed solicitude about his son, Connal-Rowan, now at Genoa. . . . Drove to Wallace Monument; a most delightful day. The dinner a very successful affair in the Golden Lion; sat directly opposite the spot in the Ochils where, above the hamlet of Logie, in 1834 or 1835, I climbed the mountain, and in its silent solitude lifted up my heart to God. Have we not all had such solemn moments? Presided at the lecture by ex-Lord Provost Ure on "A Month's Excursion amongst the South Sea Islands, Fiji, Samoa, etc."

May 14.— . . . Saw Messrs. Scott and Craig, and gathered a few facts about the general features of Pollokshields. Got a most interesting statistical account from Mr. Aiton, clerk of the police burgh of Pollokshields, East; scarcely able to bring my ideas into shape. Drove over with N—— to Stockwell Free Church at 3.15. Received by Mr. John Macgregor, minister, and others. Laid the foundation stone—a massive block—the jar being deposited in the cavity; said a few words after presentation of trowel. Mr. Macgregor and Bailie Dickson painfully complimentary. Happy that it was all over as I drove away. . . . Had a letter to-day from Bailie Kinross [Stirling] about the Provost's chair of 1812.[1] Surprised by Provost Yellowlees intrusting to me the honour of laying the foundation stone of the addition to the High School, Stirling. Lord Balfour detained in London. Suggested the young baronet, Stirling Maxwell.

May 17 (*Tuesday*).—At dinner in Central Hotel to entertain Dr. J. Collingwood Bruce—Mr. Lindsay in the chair. Sat beside Dr. A. B. M'Grigor, J. Wyllie Guild, Professor Ferguson, etc. His lecture most interesting on "The Wall of Hadrian," but I had to tear myself away to show face at the meeting in St. Matthew's Free Church to welcome Rev. James Stalker. Mr. Ross Taylor and

as patroness, of the Kilbirnie Bazaar and Exhibition. Declined an invitation addressed to us to breakfast with Moderator of Free Church on Friday next.

May 28.—After some things were got over, went out to James Webster's, 131 Barrack Street, and gave his wife a beautiful book published by the Tract Society on "The Queen." I thought that, as the family were about to emigrate to Queensland, it might conserve their loyalty. Went to the laying of the foundation stone of the Collins Institute; saw Mr. Westlands, and was struck with his likeness to Sir Richard Cross. Told me he had been taken for him in London. . . . Yesterday met Lord and Lady Balfour at the Edinburgh train, and spent the whole day at Hutchesons' Schools and at Merchants' Hall. Presided after Mr. Ure as chairman of the General Endowment Board. Arranged with Mr. Dickson as to distribution of circulars about Dr. Somerville's portrait for presentation on Tuesday. On Wednesday heard Lord Chief Justice [Coleridge] deliver his lecture. . . Think the lecture injudicious in unsettling ideas as to property. It will bear poisonous fruit. The dinner on 26th inst. a grand affair; sat beside Mr. Underwood, U.S. Consul, and Professor Gairdner . . . Industrial School Bill a mischievous thing, and the thin end of the wedge as to concurrent endowment. . . .

June 2.—Wm. M'Ewan showed me some of the entries in the books of the Old Man's Asylum and of the Merchants' House. Very much struck with some persons on these funds. . . . What changes in the world. . . . On Tuesday, 31st May, went in to Edinburgh. . . . Sir Wm. Collins presented the portrait (Dr. Somerville). . Dr. Somerville's reply about Job drawing his own portrait, overstrained. I am glad that the business has been gone through creditably and that it is over. . . . Received an invitation to the banquet and reception, 16th June, Queen's Jubilee. . . . Went to the meeting at 2 about the Udston Colliery accident, in the Council Chambers. The expression of sympathy was given, but there was no enthusiasm in subscribing. There are "too many things just now," as

Sheriff Berry said to me on leaving the meeting. Still it is to be hoped that sufficient money may be raised to meet the calamity. There may be a feeling as if there had been gross carelessness as to light. The conference with the School Board raises the question of a national system of Education. The Government are cramping the development of the Scotch Act of 1872. A good many things to depress me, yet great mercy. Most solicitous about the scheme of Income and Expenditure for 1887-1888—School Board.

June 9.—To-day (Thursday) a painfully anxious day about the School rate. It was most painful to have to face those who would destroy the whole aim of the School Board. Mr. M'Ginn's speech carefully prepared. Cripple the resources of the Board and destroy all the buoyancy of the policy to raise and maintain the standard of Education. . Parkhall bright with rhododendrons, laburnums, and hawthorns. . . . I want the buoyancy I once had, and although the place is full of sweet associations to me, somehow I look upon it as if I had it not; I thought the possession of it at one time such an object. This must indicate a change going on in my mind. . . . Met W. Connal yesterday, apparently affected about his son—wished he could get him home—confined to bed at Genoa from pleurisy, very sad. Met Timothy Bost, one of the owners of the Udston Colliery; very much affected by the bravery of the rescuing party.

June 10.—Depressed at the unaccountable conduct of the young man —— shunning me. . . .

June 13.—The old cow-shed going fast to ruin, the arch very unsafe.

July 22.—I write this at Parkhall. I was at the laying of the memorial stone of the Barony Church. Met in the old Barony Church—old George Burns there (ninety-two). Spoke to him; he made a speech which took every one

knighted. On 18th, opening up the springs on Grotto Walk; the sky was overcast and yet the barometer at fair. Very thankful that the "Spout" lads have enjoyed such good weather at Callander. Heard of Connal-Rowan; no hope.

July 23.—I have had solemn thoughts in the warnings and advice of the medical men that I must, at my time of life, take it more easily and be more careful. I have been very much gratified by the sympathy shown me. . Heard from R. L. Ewing about the inquiries made as to my father's grave, and thanked Mrs. Thomson for the map pointing out the situation of Obia or Ubya. There is no inducement, from the spot being now jungle, to prosecute inquiries any further. . . .

July 29.—Opened the Wild Flower Show at 12 in the Waterloo Rooms—a very successful meeting. Sir James Watson, Mr. Andrew Macgeorge, and Sir J. N. Cuthbertson there. Probably a full report may appear in the *People's Friend*.

July 30.—Went this morning to Gargunnock. What a fine day; what splendid mountain outlines. Arrived at Meiklewood about 11. The little boy, George Francis Connal-Rowan playing in the avenue attended by his nurse. Struck by the style of the place. Dr. John M'Leod, Govan, there. . . . Saw Frank asleep, . . but on the point of leaving about 2.15 p.m. saw him when awake. Shook hands twice. His mind appears to have been prepared for a change. I said, "Look to Christ, the Lamb of God that taketh away the sins of the world." Dr. M'Leod and I exchanged thoughts as we drove off together; how sad, how unexpected. I said, "We are here to learn lessons for Eternity." I have felt it my duty to make out this visit.

July 31 *(Sabbath morning)*.—N—— called my attention to the old pony, Fanny; not able to stand on its feet when raised up. A relic of the past when my mother was here. How sad, everything passing away. . . .

August 1.— . . . On Thursday, Wm. Mitchell sent Scotch thistles, grasses, and heather to the Wild Flower Show. . . . Mr. Mason met me in the tramcar, and, as a naturalist, was favourable to it. . . . Buried (Fanny)

at Arngomery. Walked through the garden and glen, and then drove to the farm (Fairfield). . . . Made for the graveyard where Mr. Leckie Ewing and his family lie; went to the church where the window is (the memorial window), and then to the Flower Show, which was very creditable. Met Mr. Stewart. Called on Mr. Muirhead and his sister, left my card at the Manse (Mr. Moodie's); came home.

August 31.— . . . At the laying of the foundation stone of the working men's houses, Saltmarket, at 3. Unusually heavy rain, and continuously for an hour or so. (Note added in 1888.) Unprecedented during twenty years in so short a time—see Professor Grant, *Glasgow Herald*, 21st January, 1888.

September 5.—Colonel John M'Farlan and Mrs. M'F. with us from Saturday afternoon. Spent a quiet Sabbath Went out on Friday afternoon, watched the cutting of the corn ; a remarkable golden colour in the grain of the sheep field when seen in contrast with the green foliage of the trees.

September 7.—Yesterday went to the Presbytery House at 12. . . . I said I was the oldest member of session, whereas forty years ago I was the youngest.

September 12.—Took a short walk up to the High Wood. The twenty-six acres a blaze of colour with the heather in full bloom.

September 13.— Sent an apology to Mr. and Mrs. Burns, Castle Wemyss, for absence from the fête to receive Vice-Admiral Hewitt and Rear-Admiral Rowley of the Channel Squadron.

September 14.— . . . Returned from meeting in Free St. James' Hall; said a few things about nine Troys in America. The Troy on the Hudson apparently the original Troy. Saw Mr. Underwood, U.S. Consul, about it; he said it was obviously named so by a classical man, as there was also a Mount Ida. Then I turned my thoughts to ancient Troy, and then to Troas, and the 20th chapter of the Acts. The address well got up.

September 23.— . . . I should have only one object to serve—the good of the cause of Education.

Distributed our last flowers for the season. On Wednesday, 5th October, went to Kinross. Mrs. Williamson ninety-five years of age next month. . Took an affectionate farewell. Got a glimpse of the loch, and in passing looked down into the gorge at the Rumbling Bridge. Recalled associations sixty years past, in sweeping along by Dollar and Tillicoultry, by the foot of the Ochils. Spent the night at 3 Pitt Terrace (Stirling). Next day, ... at 11, took the oath as a J.P. before Sheriff Buntine—Mr. Bolton, Jun., and Captain Burn-Murdoch, Royal Dragoons, Aldershot, subscribed the parchment. . . . . At the dinner in the hotel (St. Enoch's) on Friday, 30th September, High School Club—Mr. Gourlay, Bank of Scotland, in the chair. On the right Dr. Dickson, and I on the left; Mr. Vary Campbell and Dr. Marshall Lang next me. Gave the toast of the Lord Provost and Magistrates. Have seen about thirty Lord Provosts. A successful meeting. Met Lord Balfour at the High School, Elmbank Street. At 11.30 lunched at Sir J. N. Cuthbertson's, and then sat on the platform next Dr. Marshall Lang, to hear Lord Balfour's address, in the Waterloo Rooms. . The jubilee of the Night Asylum for the Houseless at 3. Exhibited the parchment of Rolland Blacadyr's foundation—a night asylum long ago.

October 15.—Went to Stirling yesterday by 9.20 train; went to county meeting. So far interested in seeing men whose names are household words; shook hands with old Sir William Edmonstone. Took lunch with F——; walked with Dr. M'Laren up to High School; met Mr. Moodie of Kippen; shook hands with Lord and Lady Balfour, Henry Campbell-Bannerman, Gilbert Beith, etc. Took part in the ceremony of laying the foundation stone of the High School. At the dinner sat next Provost Yellowlees and John Ramsay; had to propose Lord Balfour's health. Not very sure if I was successful; referred to the supporter of his coat-of-arms being an otter. Came home very wearied. The outlines of the hills magnificent—clear, but cold. . . . I would seek grace to confess Thee; I would seek to consecrate myself to Thy service.

October 25.— . . . Went out on Friday night, cold

November 26.—Sent 100 copies of Lord Balfour's address on "Secondary Education" to Mr. Robert M'Luckie, Stirling, for distribution, agreeably to my promise when at the memorial stone ceremony of the High School at Stirling. . It is singular that in the *Stirling Journal* of 25th November our family name crops up twice—the name of Patrick Connal as a banker, helping ex-Bailie Watt in his business contracts, under trying circumstances; and my own name as a subscriber to the fountain.

December 3.— . . . On Sabbath, 27th ult., between sermons, surprised at the views of P—— and T—— W—— as to pensions or allowances for length of service. It is a great advantage to have a mixture of various conditions of life in a church court. The little boy, Donald M'Laren, lost on 27th June, found on 28th November, high on the hills sloping down into Glen Douglas, fully two miles south-east of Arrochar (Loch Long).

December 10.—At Shepherds' Annual Festival in City Hall—too short an interval for dinner before going down—Henry Campbell-Bannerman in the chair. Escaped after his speech and went to the opening of Dr. F. L. Robertson's church house behind St. Andrew's Square (Murdoch's School). He aims at a good many objects, all helpful to church life. His address very good. Mr. Millar (St. John's) and Mr. Paton (St. Paul's) there, and James M'Ewan. . . . This afternoon at the Weaving School, Kennedy Street, at 4.30. Fifty-seven present; most interesting. Fell, from the icy smoothness on the playground, and did not remain long. . . . Very much pleased with the extracts in *Stirling Journal* from the *Burgh Records* by Mrs. Hogg, being a paper read by her at the Archæological Society of Stirling.

December 16.— . . . Men running about and seeking money for halls, mauses, and missions are overdoing it. Saw Mr. Kennedy to-day about commercial education to meet Mr. Guthrie's inquiries. No training in speaking either French or German. Our system too bookish. . . . Yesterday at Lord Provost's at dinner, and sat beside Principal Caird and Sheriff Spens, Sir George M'Leod

1888

January 2.—The whole aspect of land-owning in this country a very serious thing. It is silently creating a great social revolution.

January 7.—Interested in finding in the *Weekly Herald* an answer to my explanation about the Walk (James Watt's Walk) in the Green, from Murdoch M'Kenzie, Reynolds, County Missouri, 12th December, 1887,—thirty-three years in Missouri. I extracted the information from Robert Hart of Cessnock, who had it from Watt's own life.

January 13.—Came home very much fatigued; a busy day; met Colin Brown about to-morrow's meeting, and got out of the library (Stirling's) *Burke on the Sublime and Beautiful*, and Schlegel's *Æsthetic Works*, to prepare myself for his lecture. . . . Handed over to John M'Gregor the minute on parchment to be presented to Provost Yellowlees, the ancient seal of Stirling put on it in sepia by Mr. James Campbell, drawing master, High School, and the narrative of the minute by Mr. John Dalziel M'Lean, writing master, *in Rundschrift*.

January 14.—Went most reluctantly to-night to Colin Brown's lecture on "Æsthetics in Music" in the Christian Institute,—presided. In connection with the Tonic Sol-fa College (West of Scotland Branch). I took with me *Burke on the Sublime and Beautiful*. Gathered from Schlegel that the word was derived from αἰσθάνομαι, 'to perceive by the senses'; and as Burke brings out in section 7, part 3, that God has endowed us with powers that prevent the understanding and even the will, which seizing upon the senses and imagination captivate the soul before the understanding is ready either to join with them or to oppose them. Met Mr. David Hartosh (a Dutchman by descent) at the meeting, and had a talk about Amsterdam. . . .

January 17.— . . . Yesterday (Monday, Auld Hansel Monday) at Stirlingshire and Sons of the Rock Dinner—A. G. Barns-Grahame of Craigallian in the chair. On the whole a success, but felt weary. Sat next Provost Yellowlees and talked about a scheme to utilize the tower of the High School [Stirling] for astronomical observations. Suggested to him to ascertain how the Paisley Observatory was doing, and to consult Professor Grant. . Met John Ramsay, late M.P. for Falkirk, on my way home in the dark. Said he was not well—getting old—going to Cannes on Monday.

January 21.—Found that I had overslept myself this morning. . . . The Chief Constable of Lanarkshire under a long examination. He appears to be bitterly opposed to any annexation. The interests of men, their pride, their prejudices interfere with a fair view of the case. The city has been hemmed in by little burghs, and they stickle for their rights as if the greater question should succumb to the smaller. At the Boundaries Committee Inquiry; the Lord Advocate M'Donald presided, supported by Lord Elgin, etc. . . . Yesterday evening at the social meeting of the affairs of the compulsory department of the School Board in St. Andrew's Halls, about School Board officials. A very good meeting, but too prolonged. Mr. Gray's death very striking (James Finlay & Co.); found dead in his chair in his bedroom with an unopened letter from his wife in his hand. . . . Went down to the Boundary Committee Inquiry yesterday. Struck with the searching character of a cross-examination. Mr. Graham-Murray very clear at it. On Thursday met Prof. Caird, Mr. Miller, Mr. James Graham (Auldhouse), Mr. Younger, etc., about the blind children in the asylum.

of Scotland." . . . The details of Arngomery and Parkhall take up time, but it is not without interest to attend to them.

January 28.—Watched the eclipse of the moon; about 11 o'clock the period of greatest obscuration; at 12.15 the moon recovering its brightness. "What is man that Thou art mindful of him?" . . . Astronomers say that this will not occur again till 1895.

January 30.— . . . Met Professor Grant in Miller Street, and had a talk about the eclipse of the moon.

February 4.— . . . Put into the printer's hands materials for interesting people about the *Stirling Burgh Records*. . . . In the evening presided at the opening lecture on "Political Economy," by Mr. John Adams. The course is to consist of twelve lectures in the new premises of the Athenæum.

February 6.— . At 4 o'clock at the Delinquency Board. Arranged to see lads along with others who, though able to earn good wages, idle and indolent after all that had been done for them. Crime is a sad thing, it propagates itself. It is almost ineradicable.

February 10.— . . . Tried yesterday to get information as to Navvies' Recreation Rooms from Mr. R. H. Hunter and Rev. J. Renfrew, to please Mrs. Hunter of Hunter (Cochran-Patrick's mother-in-law), who was to place any information before Sir A. Campbell, Succoth, who was anxious to start something of the kind.

February 13.— . . . At the Provost's invitation induced to second the motion by Sir W. Collins at the public meeting as to the destitute condition of the people in the Lewis. Most reluctant to take a prominent part. .

February 18.— . . . Declined to be one of the committee on the restoration of Dunblane Cathedral. .
In the evening went to the lecture by Sheriff Berry in St. Andrew's Halls at 8 o'clock. Came home very wearied. I wished to show respect to him, as well as to the invitation of the Juridical Society.

February 23.—Went by 10.35 train to Campsie Glen Station with Archibald Robertson. Spent about an hour in the old parlour overlooking the garden—great beauty in

the prospect; and called on Col. and Mrs. M'Farlan to
the deceased
yard—the coffin on a bier, with the Union Jack under it.
Most picturesque
building covered
hundred, all standi
form; afterwards, at the grave, Episcopalian. Spoke to
several neighbours
out by 10.35 train to New Killearn. D. Brown drove me
first of all to the lodge. Drove with Archie Robertson and
his son-in-law, Jameson, to Duntreath Castle. . . . Sir
John and Mrs. M'Farlane—apparently very composed, but
an awful trial. Their dear little handsome boy Willie was
killed in the stable at Parkhall, falling off the ladder
leading to the loft. Felt very much for them. . . .
Mr. Fiddes, Mr. Slessor, and Mr. Dick at the funeral.
The old place looked very sweet, but bare.

February 28.—Passed into the Dovehill School for a minute or so; a wholesome sight; 800 children, though the roll is 1100. Presided at the South Endrick Re-union in the Waterloo Rooms. J. Guthrie Smith's MSS. helped me. On Saturday at the Kyrle Society Show of Hyacinths in the National Halls. Seven schools represented. *Stirling's and Glasgow Public Library Catalogue* dedicated to me. Saw the picture by Noel Paton, "The Choice." . . . A. Forbes has received already subscriptions for the *Stirling Record* volume; amongst the rest, from the Lord-President. . .

March 9.— . . . . Sir Archibald Campbell welcomed back. Evidently not yet in full health.

March 10.— . . . . The death of the old Emperor of Germany yesterday morning has excited widespread interest. . . . Wrote the Lord Provost a note in answer to one addressed to him by Lord Iddesleigh's son-in-law, Reginald Macleod, about how to deal with the Lewis. A good deal of pressure in prospect. Felt more buoyant to-day.

March 31.—Came home very wearied. Thankful that the School Board contest is over. . . . Had some talk

[1] Sir William Edmonstone.

with Mr. John Renwick, 49 Jamaica Street, about Hennedy memorial bust. Suggested the Technical College as the custodians.

April 4.— . . . Yesterday at Chief-Constable M'Call's funeral. . .

April 7.—Busy with Parkhall matters. Yesterday at the Grand Hotel at the inaugural dinner of the Glasgow University Club. Some very good speaking.

April 12.—Felt wearied. Dr. Brown with us. At the first meeting of the new School Board. Occupied the chair for a few minutes, and proposed the re-election of Sir J. N. Cuthbertson. .

April 25.—On Monday, 23rd, left for Aberdeen. A very pleasant journey. . . . Met Dr. Brown on our arrival. . . . All pleased. Very wearied in getting home. Saw the glorious ocean for a good part of the way. . . .

April 28.— . . . Sent Mr. Gray, teacher, Aboyne, a copy of White's *Natural History of Selborne.*

May 3.—Received intimation of first meeting of Marshall's Trust as a representative of Commissioners of Supply of Stirlingshire. . . . John Steel promises me a bit of oak from the hull of the "Industry," the steam vessel built in 1814. .

May 8.— On Sabbath morning visited the grave of those near and dear to me. The impetuous current which has set in from the birth of Time is bearing everything onward to an interminable ocean. Their memory is sweet, and it influences me for good. Went with N—— to Exhibition, by Gray Street entrance, and took our seat near the Dais; shook hands with Sir James Gibson Maitland, Lord Craighill (looking very ill), Provost Clark, Lord Balfour, Principal Donaldson, and a good many Glasgow men. The Prince spoke like an English gentleman; the Princess quiet, not radiant. The whole ceremony passed off well, and every one appeared pleased. The situation of the Exhibition very beautiful. I look forward to examining the contents with great interest. There was something very thrilling in the welcome given, and in all the evidences of loyalty to the representative of

Murdoch lectured to them on Friday night at Professor Balfour's suggestion. . . .

July 11.—Visited panorama of Battle of Bannockburn; very good.

July 23.—Had a note from Miss Johnstone of Alva about a friendly society for domestic servants. Andrew Stewart (of the *People's Friend*, Dundee) called on Saturday about dedicating a story to me called "One False Step."

July 25.—Went to the Cattle Show yesterday; splendid Clydesdale horses, their necks clothed with thunder. The binding machine, the cream apparatus, the ventilating machine—I am sure that these shows stimulate invention and promote agricultural enterprise. The number of men, apparently country gentlemen, interesting.

July 30.—The sun shining through the trees like a furnace at 4.30. . . . Rose at 6.30. Lord Craighill is dangerously ill at Arngomery. Unable to show Mr. W. M. Campbell the attention I expected. . . . Had the honour of a call from Sir G. B. Bruce on Friday, accompanied by Dr. Boyd.

August 9.—Induced the School Board to call the school to be erected on the site purchased in North Woodside Road "Napiershall School"; very wearied.

August 13.—Presided at a meeting of the executive of the Library Association of the U.K. Committee to make final arrangements. Invited, at Mr. Barrett's suggestion, two of the English members to be my guests on 3rd September onwards, namely, the Rev. John Clare Haddow, Thornton Vicarage, Horncastle, and Mr. Charles W. Sutton, Free Library, Manchester. Wrote Lord Craighill expressing concern at his illness; wrote Sir Arthur Mitchell asking him to be my guest on 27th August. On Saturday, 11th, tried to realize it was my birthday, and that I bad now entered on my 72nd year; rather depressed.

August 15.—The legislation of Gladstone's government will ensure the extinction of ground game. . . . Declined Sir W. Collins' invitation to spend a day yachting off Helensburgh with Canon Barker and others. . . .

August 23.—Went with N——, M——, and Mrs.

Hunter Campbell to the Exhibition to see the Queen. . . . Scarcely got time to realize that in her was centred so much influence for good.

August 30.—Sir Arthur Mitchell came to me on Tuesday night, and dined at the Lord Provost's. Marquis of Bute there; sat next Sheriff Berry and Archbishop Eyre. Afterwards went to inaugural address by the Marquis; Mr. Spofforth introduced to Lord Provost. Cochran-Patrick away to London; unable to be my guest; had kind note. Have been unable to go to the excursion, but heard a few words from John Honeyman at the Cathedral. This was on Monday, the 27th. In the evening of that day at the dinner of the Archæological Society; yesterday evening the papers read were interesting. . . . "The Great Seals of Scotland," by Allan Wynn, interesting, but went to the section where Dr. Collingwood Bruce read his paper on "The Wall of Antoninus"; affected, as I reflected on it, by the wonderful power of that people. At 3.45 at Dovehill Flower Show; said a few words to the children. Mr. Fisher, teacher, said that his old Bible had a writing on it to imply that it belonged to the Dauphin of France—Philip, the first husband of Queen Mary. . . . It is difficult to recall the things that interested me since I last wrote in this book. . . .

September 11.—On Tuesday, 4th, at conversazione in the evening. Marquis and Marchioness of Bute there; some good music. On Wednesday went to University; saw the gem of the [Hunterian] library—the edition of *Plato* in vellum; saw one of twenty volumes given by George Buchanan. Went in the evening to the Exhibition; remained in the fine art section. On the 6th went to Ayr. Visited Burns' Cottage, the Monument, and Alloway Kirk; saw the Brig o' Doon; walked over the Auld Brig. . . .

September 14.— . . . . In the morning went out to the Exhibition, and devoted my attention to the contents of the Bishop's Palace; some of the relics carry one back for one thousand years. Very wearied at night; I feel a great failure of strength.

September 19.—At 3 presided at the meeting of the Orphan Homes as to the adoption of a site to build a new home. Fixed on an acre of ground at Whiteinch immediately to the west of the Partick Park—that part where the fossil trees were discovered. . . . . A knotty problem how to meet the request of the Jews as to a class for Hebrew. . . . Fixed for Hennedy's bust being presented to the Governors of Technical College.

September 21.— . . . Met a boy in Dr. F. L. Robertson's office who had won a bursary, and who would not go to City Public School; thrawn and spoiled, but clever.

September 25.— . . . In coming in from the country yesterday, saw in the newspapers Lord Craighill's death. Going to the funeral to-morrow. Very appreciative articles in *Scotsman* and *Glasgow Herald*. . . . Drove out to Blanefield on Saturday, 22nd, and called at Duntreath on the young baronet, Sir A. Edmonstone.

September 26.—Went to Edinburgh by 11 o'clock train, and returned by 4 o'clock train. Before going to Lord Craighill's funeral, sauntered slowly on to 3 Ainslie Place and looked in at the museum of antiquities. . Received by John Millar's son. The Lord Justice General, Lord Moncrieff, and Lord Fraser at it, and I understood Balfour, late Lord Advocate, there. Sir James King came back from Grange Cemetery in same carriage with J. B. Kidston and me; my mind reverted to John Millar sitting with me at the foot of my bed reading *Cicero* when Mr. Browning supposed every one to be in bed; the light of the candle concealed by a box. I must have been twelve years old then. Then I remember his patient, persistent attendance on the Greek class; when I was careless, he was always prepared.

October 4.— Stars of Saturday night magnificent, and the sunset very fine. . Accepted position of Extraordinary Director of Athenæum, and of Honorary Vice-President in Y.M.C.A.

October 9.— . . . Poor Sellars, architect, dead; very sad. . . . On the 5th presented Roger Hennedy's bust to the Governors of the Technical College—Mr. Russell in the chair. . . . Mr. George S. Venables died at his residence in London on 6th October.

appear to have been well received, in seconding the motion of thanks. . . . Appointed chairman of the General Endowments Board for another year, on 14th inst. I was not concerned about it. . . . The moon very brilliant to-night and the sky without a cloud.

November 27.— . . . At School Board to-day; finally arranged about Hebrew class for Jewish children. . . . Spoke to Mr. Swanson about my father having known Morrison of China, and he promised to try and trace my father's being intrusted by him to bring to this country the first copy of the Chinese Bible. On Tuesday, 20th, at the lecture by Mr. Jolly (opening lecture of the Ruskin Society). Thought the lecture vague, but with some good points in it. . . .

December 1.— . . . At Dr. Bonar's jubilee on Thursday, 29th. Waited for two hours to hear addresses.

December 8.— . . . Saw Mr. Aitken of Blythswood estate as to anything interesting about Grove Street district, St. George's Road, called at one time Rosehall Street. Got the loan of papers from Mr. R. Boyd about Grove Street Institute. Found in them, in the publication called *Self-Help* (printed, 1864; page 56), reference to the Spoutmouth Bible Institute. . . . Gave £10 10s. to Bearsden Free Church Manse, from my uncle's long connection with the country-side. . . . 10th inst., went by train to Stirling to attend funeral of Mrs. James Wright (Isabella Murray); service in Episcopal Church very interesting, but did not like the decorations on the Communion table. . . . Asked to be an Honorary Director of Band of Mercy Union on 13th inst. . . .

1889

January 1.—12.15. Another year has passed away. O Lord give me in Thy mercy a through-bearing, if I be spared throughout it. Prepare me for whatever Thou hast prepared for me.

January 5.— . . . Went to Logan and Johnston Institute and Buchanan Institute as usual.

January 16.— . . . At the Stirlingshire Dinner on Monday—Robert Binnie presiding. Said something about Binning who took Linlithgow Castle by stratagem. Binnie claims descent from him. A very agreeable meeting. . . . It was on 5th May, 1839, that I began work in the "Spout." . . . On Tuesday, at 12, talked over Lord Rosebery's visit with Mr. Henderson. . . . Received a very polite note from Dr. Underwood, U.S. Consul, to be present at his lecture in Merchants' Hall. . . .

January 19.— Arranged with Mr. Renwick as to the publication of a second volume of *Stirling Burgh Records and Guildry Minutes.* I enter upon this with solicitude; but I am shut up to it, or it never will be done. Last night at Merchants' Hall; Dr. Underwood lectured—some beautiful passages—Mr. J. G. A. Baird in the chair. Said a few words, more particularly referring to the pictures in the hall and the sculpture in the ante-room. Walked home with Mr. Templeton, who told me about the steps being taken to retain him in the consulship. Mr. Phelps, the ambassador, the intermediary.

January 22.— . . . In the evening at the meeting of the Boys' Brigade in the Queen's Rooms—Lord Aberdeen in the chair. J. Carfrae Alston did very well. Some good speaking.

January 28.— . . . . At Seamen's Institute, and seconded the resolution proposed by Rev. Dr. D. M'Leod. Tried to make use of the passage in Herschell's discourse on "Natural Philosophy," about Captain Basil Hall's making Rio de Janeiro; also Lord Aberdeen's (sixth earl) passionate love of the sea. . . . At the Festival of the Ancient Shepherds in the City Hall on Friday night; remained for an hour; Lord-Advocate in the chair.

February 6.— . . . Dined at Sir J. N. Cuthbertson's yesterday; Principal Caird, Dr. Ogilvy, Sheriff Guthrie, Dr. Blackie, and others.

February 14.— . . . Last night at 10 o'clock at John Muir's house to meet Mr. and Mrs. Joseph Chamberlain; a great crowd of people of all kinds of politics; pleased to meet Mr. Arrol of the Forth Bridge. . . . Came away about 11. In the forenoon (Wednesday) with Lady Trevelyan and Sir J. N. Cuthbertson, showing her John Street (Bridgeton) School, Townhead, and Garnethill. Very much impressed with the work going on.

February 16 (*Sabbath*).—Sad and unexpected news yesterday of the death of Robert Nutter Campbell Connal at Redcar, near Middlesborough. . . . In the evening (Friday) at the thirty-third annual re-union of the Deaf and Dumb—Sir C. Tennant in the chair; Lady Rosebery, in the absence of Lord Rosebery, at his right hand; the illustrations of the oral system very interesting. I am afraid I affronted Mr. ——, but he did not realize my hurry. . . . Had a letter from Commander Cameron, R.N., about the Slave Trade in Africa.

February 20.—Was at the meeting of five Bands of Mercy in the Crown Halls; a most interesting meeting. Was presented with the badge, which I wore during the evening. . . . Rather sad at the result of the Perthshire election. . . . Dr. Anderson Kirkwood died at Stirling (I think on the 16th). On Monday at the funeral of R. N. Campbell Connal; very sad.

February 21.—Met along with Sir J. N. Cuthbertson, Mitchell, Kerr, and Russell, Colonel Brine of the Science

February 23.—Heard to-day of William Kidston's death at Ferniegair. It took place this morning early. It is a solemn thing that one with whom I have been so much associated has passed away. I wrote his sister. . Had some conversation with Mr. Renwick as to the printing of the *Stirling Burgh Records* this morning, and as to the preparation of a Map of Stirling.

February 27.—The spring is advancing. . . . Presided at the Regality Club in Mr. C. D. Donald's office. A large and influential gathering at William Kidston's funeral; Principal Douglas's prayer very comprehensive, and embracing features of his character that were outstanding. He was buried in the Necropolis. Went with Colin Brown to see the Lord Provost about the China famine. He had already declined the Lord Mayor's (London) invitation to make it a public thing. H. M. Matheson expects me to take some interest in the movement. . . . Exchanged words to-day with Dr. M. Lang about the prosecution of the Bishop of Lincoln for Ritualistic practices and Romish tenets.

March 2.—Took A. C. and N—— to the lecture by Joseph Thomson, African traveller, in Queen's Rooms. . . . Gave Thomas Jamieson, who came for a line for baptism, copy of *Pilgrim's Progress*. . . . Bailie Kinross indicated that he wished me to consider being on the Stirling Endowment Trust in the room of Dr. Anderson Kirkwood, who was appointed by the Glasgow University Court.

March 7.— . . . Yesterday pleased with the prospect of Sir Thomas Wade coming to the China meeting. . . . On Monday had the meeting of those to whom notices were sent.

March 16.— . The articles in the *Glasgow Herald* very good about the China Famine Relief Fund. I sent circulars for a meeting of committee on Tuesday. The meeting yesterday creditable—Alex. Allan presided. Sir T. Wade and Bishop Scott . . . their pressure and appeals did good. . . .

March 23.— . . . Busy all the week with circulars as to China famine. . . . On Wednesday at defaulters'

meeting in Grove Street. Dr. F. L.
to give a toast, "Past and Present,"
on Tuesday next; declined, and sug
. . . The likeness of Sir James
Graphic, 23rd March), as vicar gen
sided over by the Archbishop of C
of the Bishop of Lincoln, very gooc
crossing over to Portsmouth 1st A
never likely to meet again.

March 28.—Came home from N
train; rather dull, but, on the wh
Visited school. Very much please
. . . Promised the children
encouraged to give the children a h
the Manse, and after that opened th
Town Hall. . . . I was sorely
but the minister said it was the ki
Lady Menteith of Closeburn came
was leaving. Drove with Mr. Scott
. . . up the road to Galloway al
Afton. Saw in the distance Black C
the level of Nith. . . . Saw a f
had been for 500 years,—since Bruc
Castle of Black Craig, the seat of
occupied the site where the Free Ch
was pretty entire in 1784. Dunb
kings of England. Lived in David
James Paterson's *History of the*
Wigtown, 1863). The castle said
sheltered Sir William Wallace. Bar
nock. Met the schoolmaster, Mr. St
David Rowan, who was born in the
singular coincidence my suggesting M
bazaar. . . . On Monday, 25t
fund. Had a meeting at 2. . . .
to Mr. Hedley in St. Enoch's H
Powell and Professor Jebb and Si
Provost very good, and J. O. Mitchell
Mr. Hedley's reply modest and appr

[1] H. A. Hedley, Manager of Glasgo

Bright dead. Lord Fraser, one of the chief mourners, dead,—found seated in his arm-chair in the country.

March 30.—Rather too many things on my mind. The China distress has awakened sympathy in many quarters beyond Glasgow.

April 6.—John Bright laid in the grave within the last few days. On Wednesday morning at Wolseley Street School. Dr. Hunter's (M.P.) movement about the Probate Duty being made use of to secure Free Education—a snare. Had a tiff with Mr. Beith about it before Argyll Bazaar opened.

April 7.— Wrote a reply to the note sent by Mr. Howatt, chairman of Sabbath School Society of Free St. James', and signed by George Steele, as secretary, wishing me well on the completion of fifty years' connection with that kind of work, dated 24th March, 1889. Began to teach 5th May, 1839, in Spoutmouth, in Mrs. M'Nicol's (Jean Murray), many of Mr. W. Leckie Graham's boys and girls remaining with me.

April 13.—Answered several notes; one being to Rev. G. Y. about the apparatus needed for the Observatory to be erected in Stirling. People think that I am made of money. . . . When driving home last night spoke of the articles in the *Nineteenth Century* and *Contemporary Reviews* on Monte Carlo and the Turf—their iniquity. . . . At annual meeting of Stirling's Library. Professor Ferguson very good, and Dr. Murdoch. Dr. Murdoch not unlike Carlyle. Re-appointed vice-president.
China fund a success—some touching evidences of sympathy; £1,900 remitted to London Mansion House .
The sugar cane sent on Wednesday by Mr. Hunter to New Cumnock Public School.

April 17.—Though very much fatigued went to Dr. Underwood's meeting in connection with the Longfellow Memorial in Queen's Rooms. On the whole a success—great good taste.

April 24.—Busy preparing for the China Famine Fund meeting, when the Lord Provost called with a very gratifying letter from the Lord Mayor. Just in time to be at the meeting of the Hospital for Skin Diseases—Sir A.

Orr Ewing in the chair—at 12 o'clock; said a few words suggested by Hebrews x. 22. . . . On Tuesday, at 11, in the Lord Provost's room about applications for assistance arising from disaster to boats and nets.

April 27.—Went to the opening of Barony Church. The dedication of the church to the service of God very solemn, but with more formality than usual in Presbyterian occasions of a similar kind. The desire to have the occasion a public one may have drawn Dr. M. Lang and his office-bearers into it. The Moderator of the General Assembly, Dr. Gray, animated—very sound in his short sermon. . . . Came to Glasgow with Mr. J. Wilson of Bantaskine,—talked about orchids.

May 3.—Norman and Nora M'Donald from London lunched with N—— to-day and T—— from Hayston. On Thursday, 2nd, at J. C. White's office, at the invitation of Sir J. N. Cuthbertson, to meet Lord Balfour at 11.30 about Nyassaland. Pleased to see James Stevenson, whom I have not seen for a long time. . . . A very remarkable meeting. . . . Dr. Blackie appears to-day as the Principal of the movement called St. Mungo's College. Twitted him about it. . . .

May 4.— . . . Sent fresh flowers to poor woman in Poorhouse. . . .

May 9.— . . . On Tuesday, 7th, at 12, in W. Mitchell's office to deal with fifteen cases under Marshall's Trust. . . At 12.30, at meeting in J. Gibson Fleming's office about L. C. garden; at 1, in Christian Institute, Religious Tract and Book Society meeting; at 2, School Board discussion about Government proposals as to the £171,000 of probate duty; at 3.30, at Stirling's Library, and at 7, at Buchanan Institution. On Monday met China Famine Relief Committee to bring matters to a point. Mr. A. Allan put an article in the newspapers bringing my relationship to it too prominently before the public.

May 11.—At Whiteinch annual meeting of Orphanage. The hedges bright green. Blundered out a few words.

May 18.— Wrote Mr. Yuille (Stirling) about astronomical instruments at Paisley, with a note from Sheriff

Cowan. The Stirling Observatory to be furnished with instruments by Mr. Pullar.

May 25.— . . . Pleased that old George Burns and William M'Kinnon have had titles conferred on them.

May 26.— Read more of Mr. Paton's trials and sufferings in Tanna.

June 5.— . . . The country most beautiful; the Campsie Fells green to the very top.

June 13.—On Sabbath night suffered acute pain, quite knocked up, could not fulfil my duty to prepare the Board for the imposition of the rate. . . . Have been in the house since Tuesday. . . . I have read with much interest in this enforced withdrawal from business *Lord Cockburn's Journal*, Vol. I.

June 17.— . . . Asked to John Innes Wright's funeral to-morrow. I remember him in 1827. What an unlooked-for career; how different from the methodical, correct, steady attention to business. Amiable, upright at bottom, but turned upside down by men who had overridden his conscience and who bore him along with themselves to ruin.

June 24.— . Read lives of John Knox and Wm. Wilberforce. Very much interested in them.

July 2.— . . On Saturday drove to Auchentroig and to Buchlyvie and Gartmore Show. Thankful to be better of the drive.

July 11.— . . . Replied to an invitation to meet the Shah of Persia at luncheon, on Thursday, 18th, in Corporation Galleries. Got my dear uncle's bust repaired. . . . Very much weaned from resting in anything here. My poor father's place smiling in summer beauty, but it cannot satisfy the immortal soul.

July 15.— . . . It is very pleasant to see the corn and turnips and potatoes springing up. The trees majestic in their summer garb. . . . The young man who preached yesterday told me this morning at the station that he was as yet in the Arts classes, having been in business; not yet at the Divinity Hall; that he had heard that Principal Caird had said, and it had created some sensation, that the longer he lived the more was he inclined to follow the religious views of his mother.

July 18.— . . . Luncheon at the Corporation Galleries, where the Shah of Persia was to be received. The entertainment very fine. It must be a trial to the Duke and Duchess of Montrose receiving him and his suite. We all hope his very cordial reception may do good to his own country and to our relations with him. . . . Arranged with Sir Andrew (M'Lean) to send his friend, A. F. Wilson, Balfron, *Mrs. Fletcher's Autobiography*, that he may see about the country-side in 1814-1818. Stood near the Shah when the several consuls were presented to him. . . . Sent a polite declinature to an invitation from the Mayor and Lady Mayoress of Lincoln to luncheon on the 29th inst., on opening of British Archæological Association Congress. Yesterday presided at General Endowment Board. Dr. F. L. Robertson off to London this morning about the Bill as to Education. It will bear, I fear, bitter fruit yet. It is entirely a political move to take the legs from Free Educationists and Radicals.

August 13.— . The 11th my birthday. I have now entered my 73rd year. What a solemn thing the march of time. Struck with the death of Sir J. Roberton suddenly at Grantown; this is the funeral day. Everybody regrets his removal. Sir James Watson died this morning, in his 89th year. These are solemn events.

August 19.— . Came in from the country with Sheriff Laurie—now a judge in Ceylon. . . . Felt it my duty to come into town on Saturday to attend Sir James Watson's funeral. Impressed with the event. Sir James Bain told me that he had come from Cumberland to attend it. Hozier of Newlands was in the same carriage with Alexander Mitchell and me.

August 28.— . . . Moncrieff Mitchell died at New Jersey on the 10th inst.; born 1816; an old Tillicoultry schoolfellow. I remember how he inadvertently squirted some liquorice juice on a new atlas which I had got sixty-one years ago. How he used to describe his father's and mother's domestic comfort and happiness in their mansion (where India Street now is).

September 2.— . On Friday night, after getting out of town, went to the concert in Killearn, on behalf of the home for poor children at Balmaha. . . . N—— accompanied me. The Duchess of Montrose and her friends sang. Our garden robbed of apples and plums on Friday night. Measured the footprints, 11⅛ inches in length. The policeman says that the carters hired for the season are likely to be the culprits. Two got 10 days last year for robbing Balfunning garden. The robber will not stop there. He will go on, until he is caught in some more serious crime.

September 5.— At 12.30, in committee, carried my point to have nineteen schools instead of fifteen fee paying. When the Board in committee met, Russell of Ascog, Sir W. Collins, and Dr. M. Lang helped prominently to reverse the decision, and in the face of serious contingencies and a certain deficit in revenue from the materials put before us, committed themselves to a step, in making only fourteen schools fee paying, that must hamper for the future, and may involve an increase of the rate. I consider, in the face of the statements of the teachers who were willing to exact fees, that there was a gratuitous throwing away of money, and under fear of criticism from the press. I owe the community an obligation to do my best, under strong provocation to resign Convenership of the Finance Committee, to work out the problem. . . . —— can never impose fees where he has declared the school free. I look up to Him who is my Master. I am in the work to please Him and not myself. In the afternoon at 3.30 at Stirling's Library. Wm. Stirling of Cordale dead,—his ancestor founded it.

September 10.— . . . The reapers at work in the field opposite Little Boquhan. What a joyous thing!

September 18.—Heard this afternoon that Dr. A. N. Somerville was dead. A good man, and though not a profound preacher, a remarkable man of the evangelistic type.

September 19.—Got to-day from A. & P. Stewart, masons and contractors, three stones from Athenæum, now being taken down, and a medallion from the principal apartment or front hall,—the old ball-room. . . . Had a call to-day from Mr. Muir Wood, wanting to get parties to whom to give tickets to the concert of the Bavarian Band in Hengler's Circus. Suggested various parties—Old Men's and Women's Asylum, Out-door Blind, Seamen's Institute, etc. . . .

September 20.—Messrs. A. & P. Stewart's notes to me very interesting and kind. . . . How bright and how innumerable the stars were on the nights I spent at Parkhall.

October 4.— . . . . In the evening of 1st October dined at New Club with the remaining members of Mr. Rowlatt's class of the old Grammar School—J. A. Campbell in the chair. Sir J. N. Cuthbertson, Andrew and John Oswald Mitchell, Alex. L. Mitchell, Mr. John Kidston, writer, Mr. Ferguson, banker, Mr. Henry and William Mitchell. A splendid dinner; very pleasant intercourse. J. A. Campbell spoke of some of the disadvantages of parliamentary life: the want of leisure, etc., etc. On 29th September sat for a while on the seat commanding the view of the hills; a lovely autumnal day. On the 28th marked with red paint some trees in grotto to be taken down,—a quiet day.

October 8.—John Davidson's[1] funeral; it is thirty-three years since I had to bring him to the point of leaving aunt's [Mrs. William Connal] service—a faithful servant, but a peculiar temper. . . . Went to the opening of the Municipal Buildings—six to seven thousand people there. Struck with the magnificence of the staircases and apartments. Great detention in getting to the place by some friends. . . . Sunday night wild and stormy; glass fell very much.

October 9.—Ordered copy of *Mark Lane Express*—interesting article on peat moss. . . . Made inquiry of Mr. Fraser as to Naismith's[2] heads (Tontine Faces). . . . I read Mr. Lawson's report as to his help to discharged prisoners. A very bold and noble effort.

October 14 (*Monday*).—Came in to town to-day. . . . Country beautiful in the autumnal glory of the woods.

[1] For many years porter in Royal Bank.

[2] Mungo Naismith, carver.

Sad at heart. (Mr. M'Lellan of West End Park considers the gean's crimson is the most beautiful tint.) Called on Professor Drummond and got him to consent to address the "Spout" on 8th November.

October 19.— . . . Asked to be a Vice-President of the Agricultural Association for discussion of questions.

October 20 (*Communion Sabbath*).— One or two illustrations very good. The lesser and lower lights had gone out in a lighthouse while the loftier lights were in good order (on American lake), and the vessel was wrecked. The quiet influence of Christian life at home and in humble surroundings commending the gospel. . . . It crossed my mind that He who created me could not, as a merciful God, create me to destroy me—but what must sin be to cost Christ such suffering?

October 26.—The leaves falling rapidly, but the aspect of the country still very beautiful. . . . At the Discharged Prisoners' Aid Society. Mr. Lawson's report read and generally acceptable as encouraging the incorporation of his branch of the work with the older Society. A difficult and trying work, only likely to be successful under the care of an enthusiast. . . . Had some intercourse with Mr. Renwick about the *Burgh Records of Stirling*; the map is likely to be an interesting one. On the 23rd drove to hear Dr. W. G. Blackie's address at the opening of St. Mungo's College. It embraced a very interesting historical sketch of the educational history of Scotland from remote times. . . . The University is to blame for the attitude of St. Mungo's College. In the evening at the banquet on the invitation of the Lord Provost, in the new Municipal Buildings—a grand affair. Sat next Mr. Crum, Thornliebank, and Mr. Young, the architect of the building. On the whole it passed off well, but acoustics bad. Met on Tuesday, at 1, the memorialists from Dennistoun about the action of the School Board.

October 30.—Went to the University General Council with Rev. Mure Smith of Stirling; appointed one of the Business Committee. Met in the Bute Hall—Professor Edward Caird in the chair; interested in the proceedings.

When sitting in the Council the boom of the great bell in the University tower overhead, striking 12 o'clock, very fine.

November 5.—Met Colin Dunlop of Tollcross near Western Club—he had dissolved his connection with it as he knew nobody now in it. He had outlived his old friends. At the meeting of the citizens, called by the Lord Provost, in the new Council Chamber, about the disaster in the East End in the fall of Templeton's mill.

November 14 (*Thursday*).—Went with Mr. Clapperton and John Guthrie Smith to Lord Provost Muir about Stirling's Library—got promise of £50 if two other subscriptions of same amount got. Called afterwards on J. Campbell White and he gave £50. Under some anxiety of mind agreed to give £50. At School Board at 1.30, and then to Café Chantant [University Bazaar].

November 16.—R. L. Ewing's son Robert has had a fall from a tree at Dollar—48 feet—his life nearly knocked out of him.

November 27.—Rose a little after 6—later than usual. Gave the Athenæum the medallion regained from the ruins of the old Athenæum.

December 7.—This morning to Discharged Prisoners' Aid Society. Interested in a boy who would not go home to his father—he is to go to sea on Monday. Yesterday at the funeral of H. Ewing at Cardross. The country beautiful even in the sleep of winter.

December 14.—Dreadful earache—got wages and accounts paid. On Wednesday at the banquet given to Professors Jebb, Nichol, and James Thomson—sat between Professors Bradley and Barr; good speaking.

December 18.—At University Bazaar with Henry L. Ewing; a very gay affair. Last night in Queen's Rooms, Lord Herschell's address on "The rights and duties of an advocate." Sad, sad revelations of domestic misery in the French-Brewster case. John Burns disappointed me as to Stirlingshire Society. He has no good reason. Went to the dentist's on Thursday morning with fear and trembling.

December 28.—Glad that James Grahame, C.A., has accepted Presidentship of Stirlingshire Society. Disappointed at Donald Graham not accepting; I have felt how little influence I have. Got a present of *Sir Joseph Napier's Life* from aunt on 24th instant. J. A. Campbell, M.P., sent me a treatise on *The Lord's Coming Again*.

1890

January.—Went at 9.30 to the Prisoners' Aid Society breakfast; eighty men there. On the 2nd inst. fell violently forward on the pavement, tripped by coil of wire near Wellington statue. I would seek to be guided aright in the purchase of the ground for sale next week in Great Dovehill. I think it may be turned to good account. Got copy of the Black bond (Stirling) from Mr. Bremner.

January 16.—At Stirlingshire dinner at 5.30 till 10 or so; sat next Dr. Story and Charles King—Mr. James Grahame in the chair. On the whole pleasant meeting. Declined invitation to dinner for to-day at Mr. John Mitchell's, 24 George Square, to meet Mr. J. Oswald Mitchell and Mr. Dalrymple Duncan, and others of Archæological Society; no strength. Declined invitations to other meetings—Arts and Crafts Exhibition, Teachers' Guild, Scottish Clerks' Association, Day Industrial School, Rose Street, opening of new Institute, Stirling, on 20th, Y.M.C.A.

January 18.—In the morning at the distribution of prizes to the pupil teachers (lads) in King's School, and to the pupil teachers (girls) in City Girls' School. Fine physique of both groups; what bright youthful faces, full of intelligence! Said a few words; what appliances to secure Education for the masses. James Chrystal, of Stirling, died 17th January. I am struck with the variety of character I come in contact with—youth, hopefulness, middle age, trial, misery, peculiarity of temper, disappointment, advanced years of usefulness and peace; how soon to be forgotten.

January 25.—Got through Dr. W. H. Hill the loan of M'Kenzie on *Diseases of the Eye.* On Tuesday presided at annual meeting, at 12, in the Chamber of Commerce, of Eye Infirmary; saw Dr. Reid, oculist, on Tuesday morning about 10, as to the "Eye" and M'Kenzie's book—still a standard work. Sang the hymn at family worship, "O for a closer walk with God."

January 27.—Interested in the movement for the promotion of decorative art, brought under my notice by Mr. Jolly, H.M. Inspector of Schools. At the funeral of John Roxburgh, my next-door neighbour. Heard to-day of Colin Campbell's death; distressed with these sudden calls. Important meeting at the School Board as to memorializing the Government postponed. At meeting of Governors, General Endowment Board, at 3; heard from Mr. Mundella, acknowledging copy of *Burgh Records.*

February 15.—At 4 o'clock presided at the exhibition of plants, under Kyrle Society, in Annfield Public School. Pleased with the children's singing and the attendance of the parents. In the evening dined at the Lord Provost's to meet Duke of Argyle. . . . Formally accepted the position of Convener of the Committee on Foreign Affairs at the monthly meeting of Chamber [of Commerce]. 3.30 on Tuesday gave the library a copy of *Burgh Records.* Could not go to Larbert as to extension of building; had Finance meeting—a large balance at the credit of the Board. Wednesday at defaulters' meeting in Kennedy Street School. Thursday a very painful day at the Board. Outvoted by eight to five as to the leaving the school arrangements as they are. Sir J. N. Cuthbertson took me quite by surprise in voting as he did. The finding of the Board, I am told, is to shut my mouth. I believe that the step to be taken cannot be recalled; prospectively, with a diminished probate grant, the Board will be on the rocks in 1891-92.

February 22.— —— persistent and impatient unless he has his own way. I broke away from him yesterday; quite annoyed with his unreasonableness. Met on Tuesday, 18th, at the Dean of Faculty's (Law), James Grahame and William M'Onie, who told me that his tenant had been pressing hay in quantity for Barnum's menagerie. Sir G. B. M'Leod there.

March 1.—Got a note from Mr. Craig Roberton; jubilant at the decision in the House of Lords as to the rights of the Buchanan Institute in £4100. . . . Our little pet dog very breathless. I fear he must soon pass away.

March 8 (*Saturday*).—I was so ill from weak action of the heart on Sabbath morning last that I had to send for Dr. M'Laren; it was a state of painful unrest for two or three hours. On Monday I had to lie in my bed until he came. The brittle thread of life might be snapped without much warning. It is evident that I may not undertake more work, and that I must limit myself. The business at the School Board very trying.

March 15.—Went to the School Board. Mr. —— aired his views and carried his point. I was left with no supporters in keeping things as they are, except the three Roman Catholics. I don't understand the policy of the rest. Already J. A. Campbell, M.P., has written Kennedy that he does not understand their reducing fees. Their policy will bring them more trouble than they anticipated. I had to go home on Monday immediately after the vote was taken about probate grant. On Tuesday re-elected by the Merchants' House to the Buchanan Institution under the new scheme.

March 30.—I am refusing all engagements for morning and evening. . . I may not undergo prolonged or fatiguing labour. The vanity of things here has been brought home to my mind.

April 5.—O Lord undertake for me; I have no strength to serve Thee.

April 10.—Heard to-day from Sir Arthur Mitchell and Mr. Sutten (Manchester Library), thanking me for copies of *Stirling Records*, Vol. III. Had a call yesterday from Mr. John Speir, farmer, thanking me for loan of books on "Agriculture," 1649-1652-1775-1811. He had found them more interesting than he had anticipated. The writers appeared to be 100 years before their time.

April 12.—Wrote John Oswald Mitchell, thanking him

for the copy of *Crossraguel Abbey*. Have been reading Neil Douglas' sermons preached in Anderston, 1793. . . .

April 16.—Tried to-night to get my mind into a right state by reading Owen; he is very powerful in describing the subtlety of sin and the violence of temptation.

April 21.—Went out by 1.40 train to Lenzie to the funeral of Miss M'Farlan. A very good turn-out of relatives—General M'Farlan and John, his brother; Mr. Menzies and his wife (Miss M'Farlan, Muiravonside); Robert Pringle, R. Leckie Ewing, Norman M'Donald, Graham Watson.

April 23.—In darkness and inward trouble; cried to God. Went to the Business Committee of the University Council at 10.30. Then sat during fatiguing speeches in the Bute Hall from 11 to 1.15. Some men want good sense in drawling out their views—a waste of time. . Had a very interesting letter from Dr. Rankine, who went out to Port Elizabeth; gave the loan of it to John Wilson for the "Spout."

April 26.—William M'Farlan died on Thursday night at 9. Sent Robert Ewing to tell N—— and M——

April 30.—Yesterday at W. L. M'Farlan's funeral.

May 24.—This afternoon at 5 o'clock our little dog died on the rug in the dining-room; poor little fellow, a little companion for fifteen years. I buried him in the back green, close to the wall, between two ferns. . . . Last evening at the opening of Washington Street School; was helped much by J. O. Mitchell. Fleming's map of 1807 very interesting. Was pleased to find that what I said was interesting. A beautiful school. Saw J. M. Hill about "Wadset," and young Mr. Colin Donald. Got a nice note of introduction to Professor Robertson (Oriental languages) from Principal Douglas, with a view to deciphering the Indian characters on the blade of the sword "Salim the Faithful." He could not make it out. Left it with John Morison's son, the Sanscrit scholar.

June 1.—Sabbath morning, rose at 3 a.m. and looked out—almost daylight; everything beautiful; the trees in their glory. Thought of God's many mercies to me and how ungrateful—that I should be at Parkhall with all its associations! The rhododendrons in bloom, the horse chestnut, the hawthorn in profusion, throwing sheets of white blossom over the hedges, the laburnum and lilac.

June 4.—Sir George Burns dead (an old landmark in the city) and G. W. Clark; notices of both in the *Herald* yesterday. The stream of the Endrick running very fast. . . . How I should cultivate tenderness of spirit!

June 14.—I am happy to see others happy. On Wednesday night at the banquet to Stanley. Sir W. M'Kinnon kindly introduced me to Stanley. Sat beside Dr. Burns; Cuthbertson very good—short and out of the beaten track. . . . On Thursday at the luncheon in the Municipal Buildings. Sat beside Archbishop Eyre and Lady Marwick.' In the evening at the lecture in the City Hall; a first-rate lecture. Exchanged a few words with the Duke of Montrose. . . . Got an idea to be followed up . . . as to inscription on scimitar so long in our possession.

June 28.—Yesterday at the opening of H. A. Long's hall in Ingram Street; declared the hall open. Declined to have medallion of myself in new school at Calton. A lovely night, the moon shining through the trees, it is scarcely dark; I think I could write a letter without a candle. Archibald Robertson has retired from the Royal Bank.

July 5.—A beautiful day with some showers; the road resplendent from Balfron side with the dog rose.

July 16.—At 7.30 at Archibald Robertson's public dinner on his retiring from the Royal Bank. Sat next David Richardson, who talked about Stanley and the poisoned arrows (cobra). . . . Paid with some reluctance £5 for an oil painting of Parkhall House, no idealism about it. On Monday, 14th, detained in the tunnel and much too late for the meeting of the Chamber of Commerce at 12. Discussion on an ocean penny postage.

July 17 (*Thursday*).—How glorious the prospect from the hayfield where the men and boys were working in getting the crop into coils. Looked down on the valley where Fintry lies, with the "Muckle Bin" in the background. . . . I am happy to find that the "Spout" lads have, by the arrangements of Mr. Grant, at Galashiels, every prospect of a pleasing and profitable visit to the borderland. Read with interest Dr. Kennedy's visit to Naples, etc. The bringing out the classical associations in a graphic style very successful and very instructive.

July 25 (*Friday*).—Robert Aitken's death taken notice of in the *Herald*. His remains interred in Sighthill Cemetery on Wednesday; one of the oldest stockbrokers in Glasgow. His death recalls the Bank of Scotland's premises where the Western Bank was in Miller Street as far back as 1826 or so. I remember his father and his sister, Miss Margaret, when my uncle lived in Miller Street. Walked out this morning by the new avenue; fine fresh air. Duncan at the turnips.

August 4.— . . . On Friday afternoon drove H. Geo. Hunter to station for train, 7.28 p.m., taking the Gartness "pot" on our way; saw the salmon attempting to leap up the rush of water into the "pot." 2nd August: Sir A. Orr Ewing and Lady Orr Ewing called. He seemed to want repose by his look. . . . Rev. Dr. F. S. Hamlin, Washington, chaplain to the President U.S., called with a letter of introduction from Mr. John Burdon. Missed his call, being at Parkhall.

August 9.— . . Went yesterday to the show at Killearn. Some beautiful animals. Proposed "The Judges" at the lunch—Mr. D. Wilson, jun., Carbeth, in the chair. . . .

August 13.—This morning, at 8 o'clock, the hills rose in majesty in the distance; clear outline.

September 4.—Made up bundles and boxes of heather for friends. . . . Drove with Mrs. M'Farlan and Frances to the "pot" of Gartness; the boiling waters in their tremendous rush into the "pot" very interesting, and the salmon trying to leap up the stream. Yesterday very wet; to-day fair; the drive very fine; the air soft and delicious.

September 10.—Superintending the transformation of the old barn into a gardener's house, and the cutting of a field of corn. The rabbits have destroyed a large part of it.

Duncan Gunn says that there are only five stooks where there should be twenty.

September 12.—Harvest progressing slowly. The rabbits have done great mischief to me in the field above the Fintry Road.

September 17.—The harvest field very pleasing; the corn tall and the stooks large. Mused in the dull but dry day on the bounty of God. How beautiful the trees, the hedges, the swelling landscape. The mountains covered with mist, and a pall or screen thrown over the distant prospect. . . . Mr. J. G. A. Baird, M.P., sent me two brace of grouse. I could not find the map of the Ganges about my father's grave, but I shall write Mr. Anderson about it. Fell in to-night with a notice of Peter Borthwick in the *Mail* of 15th September. I remember well his being in Glasgow in 1831-2. . . How I admired him. . There is another state of being where the inheritance will be ever blooming, and regenerated man will not be out of harmony with its purity and beauty.

September 20.—Left home by 9.23 train for Larbert. Met R. L. Ewing at the station; drove with Bobby Pringle; pleased with the aspect of the mansion houses of Larbert and Dunipace. Leslie Park an old-fashioned house; fine trees; and though not exceeding six acres or so, a most picturesque spot from the rise and fall of the ground. Mrs. M'Farlan's funeral service presided over by Dr. M'Laren; the brother at the funeral. Captain Christie—a tall man. . . . The interment took place at Denny—the family burying-ground of the Moreheads, once of Herbertshire Castle. Drove back with the colonel, R. Pringle, and Wallace of Clonquaird, Ayr; beautiful country. . . . On Thursday, when in town at School Board, called at the office of Kidstons, the writers; found it was the funeral day of J. B. Kidston. Saw his sons on Friday, and tendered them my sympathy. J. B. K. an old schoolfellow at Tillicoultry; affecting and solemn message to me.

September 24.—In the afternoon with the reapers at the high field; the machine at work—a cheerful sight. . . . The mountains grander than seen from the house. The elevation of say 50 feet or so makes all the difference.

September 27.—Wrote Mrs. M'Farlan about the library of 2400-3000 volumes left to her disposal.

October 4.—Sent Mr. Thomas Stedman a book he had never seen, *The Trees and Shrubs of Fife and Kinross*. . . . . On Wednesday went to Kinross—a short journey (1½ hours) over the upper Forth Bridge. Found Mrs. Williamson much the same, everything comfortable about her. . . . She is said to be 98 in November. Saw at the Alloa Station the Earl of Zetland, Lord Lieutenant of Ireland—a swarthy little man with spectacles, but with an air of distinction.

October 9.—Dr. F. L. Robertson can manage men.

October 11.—Went into town. The Duchess of Montrose introduced herself at the station; she spoke about her institution. . . . Dr. Donald M'Leod, who is to open the German Church in Woodlands Road for Mr. Geyer, told me that the Germans as a body were very indifferent about religion. . . . J. N. C. asked me to dinner to meet Lord Kinnaird, but I had to decline. . . .

October 21.—Gave Mr. Sinclair, for Peter Mackay, a modest young man of 25, who had saved a fellow workman's life at the risk of his own, Dr. Stoughton's *Great Light of the World* and *The Life of Livingstone*.

October 22.—Drove to Auchinleck—saw Mr. Wilson and his daughter; then to Killearn House, and then to Carbeth. The avenues to these sweet country places very fine. Mrs. Blackburn better, but none of the young ladies at home. . Mr. Wilson of Carbeth gave me a lithograph of the range of hills seen from Killearn. The lake apparently better seen than usual.

October 24.— . . . I got the present of a knife from Mr. Davie, of the Hammermen, with his trade mark, "Sanct Mungo."

October 30.—The earlier part of the day very fine. The lime tree in front of the house still green, but the large chestnut is naked. Walked quietly to John Buchanan's funeral at 1 o'clock, Mr. King accompanying me. The funeral service in the church. Struck with the beauty of the church. The graveyard, with the old ruin and the surrounding scenery, very picturesque and peaceful; beautifully kept. Sad that the resting place of the Napiers is all cleared away, and no stone or memorials. On Saturday, the 25th, called on Sir A. Orr Ewing; found him at home, Lady Ewing gone out; very friendly. . . . The full moon a glorious object, seen over Fintry. The hills covered with snow. Looked at the Jubilee pictures. . Went to Stirling. Introduced by Colonel Stirling to Erskine of Cardross; afterwards invited by Erskine to be introduced to Mr. Noel. Declined; did not wish to commit myself to what might have led to being involved in party feeling. . . . How humble I should be, how thankful. I pray that in leaving the country for the season, and going back to town, I may be more useful.

November 1.—The little black cat set free, after putting him in a basket to go into town. . . . Planted a fern this morning over Princie's grave in the back green. . . . How thankful I should be that I am now quietly at home for the winter; the weather mild and wet. The country will soon be losing its attractions. The glories of the departing year—in the tints on the trees, in the snow-covered mountains, in the rush of the streamlets, in the clear expanse at night, with its freshness, linger on my memory; but one thing alone can make me happy. May I accept the discipline of the holy providence of God. May I have grace to walk so as to please Thee.

November 6.—Read *Salsette and Elephanta*, by John Ruskin of Christ Church; a prize poem, recited in the Theatre, Oxford, June 12th, 1839. A great many beautiful lines, but not such a poem as to convey any very graphic idea of the subject. I am interested in it, as on 18th March, 1839, at the suggestion of Little, I finished five stanzas in Spenserian measure,[1] on the same subject, and sent them to Oxford. Sent John Morison my MSS. At the meeting about Day Nurseries—presided over by Dr. Donald M'Leod. Then at School Board; a long sederunt there. Sky very red this morning. . . . Archibald Robertson critically ill. On Tuesday at the dinner in Windsor Hotel, St. Vincent Street, given to J. Dalrymple Duncan; sat beside the chairman (left hand); surprised

[1] See page 27.

that I should be taken notice of. Replied to a toast proposed by Dr. Story, recalling the first members of Council; it was in December, 1856. Mr. Honeyman and myself are the only survivors.

November 10.—To-day a crowd of engagements. Had a letter from Mr. Burdon, N.Y., Troy, thanking me for the heather sent him. Part of it formed a wreath on the coffin of a medical man, Fairlie; believed to be from Killearn. At Chamber of Commerce at 12 o'clock. French Treaty—Silver Law of U.S.—at 1.30; at Property and Finance Committee at 2.30—fixing salaries of officials; at 3 at Irish Mission meeting; at 3.30 at Stirlingshire Society to determine about bursary and as to next president; have done rather too much.

November 15.—The Lord Advocate Robertson's visit over, in connection with opening of Calton Street School. Everything went off well; said something about the Calton which appeared to please. Produced the old parchment about the letting of houses. Very wearied, having had no sleep.

November 18.—Parnell's fall significant of the tendency of all violent political opinion.

November 20.—Went to the meeting on behalf of the navvies. Sir James King's speech good.

November 22.—Went to Dr. Adam's funeral—wet and windy weather; service in Mr. Orrock Johnston's church. A large number present—many with grey and white heads. . . . Went to Mr. Ravenstein's lecture on "Ancient Maps of Africa and the Nile." Almost incredible the amount of knowledge possessed four hundred years ago. . . . Met the representatives of the University, etc.; recommended for country districts a peripatetic system for the higher or secondary education.

November 29.—Telegraphed to T. M. Fielding, "Archibald Robertson died last night at 9 o'clock."
Spoke very decidedly to —— about F. L. R.'s policy regarding Logan and Johnston School. That man controls the minds of others too much.

December 4.—Yesterday at Campsie at A. Robertson's funeral; met at the house, where Principal Caird had service. John Macdonald, from London, and young M'Farlan, of 42nd, there. Large funeral service in the church.

December 8.—Went to the Presbytery meeting. Asked to say a few words; said what was on my mind as to Dr. Chalmers' plan for meeting the misery and destitution of cities. Can scarcely tell if what I said was taken kindly, and was acceptable as a contribution to the problem. Too much made of General Booth; he ignores what has been done for sixty years and more.

December 11.—Find that I have got a great number of book's at Keith's sale—some belonging to the family [M'Farlan] as far back as 1761 or earlier.

December 25.—On Monday at Committee on Sunken Masses; spoke decidedly about Dr. Chalmers' scheme as the best. . . . At the opening of East-End Exhibition on Tuesday at 2.

December 31.—Mrs. Williamson died on the 30th instant, in her 99th year. . . . Have had some pleasant correspondence with T. D. Findlay about Christopher North, his father's old friend. It is now drawing near the close of the year 1890. Another hour and, if spared, I shall enter upon the year 1891; how swiftly time flies!—how solemn the advance to the Eternal World!

1891

1891.

January 2.—Went for about twenty-five minutes to the meeting of the Discharged Prisoners' Aid Society, and said a few words. The Molendinar rolling past thirteen hundred years ago. A man who once met Kentigern on its banks died while writing out the verse, "They that wait on the Lord shall not want any good thing." It was Columba.

January 5.—Went to Kinross on Saturday to the funeral of Mrs. Williamson—was chief mourner: she was interred with her ancestors in the old burying ground facing Loch Leven Castle. Drove to the house in the carriage of Mr. Young of Cleish, Convener of the County.

January 12.—Mr W. Collins excited about the Railway Strike. . . . Have felt more reluctance to commit myself to a contest (School Board). I would gladly retire, but there may be something unworthy in escaping criticism for the past seventeen years of work. I am unable for fatigue now. . . . I would like to finish something before my change comes.

January 18.—My failure of strength sets me often a-thinking of putting my house in order. I would like to get something settled ere I lie down never to rise again. Most reluctant to face the School Board Election on 20th March but consenting on public grounds. This period of the year, exactly fifty years ago, my dear, sprightly sister Fanny passed away at Abbotsford Place—23rd January, 1841. Read over what I wrote on the 23rd, 24th, and 28th January, 1841.

January 27.—Trying to get my papers, etc., into order.

January 2.—Went for about twenty-five minutes to the meeting of the Discharged Prisoners' Aid Society, and said a few words. The Molendinar rolling past thirteen hundred years ago. A man who once met Kentigern on its banks died while writing out the verse, "They that wait on the Lord shall not want any good thing." It was Columba.

January 5.—Went to Kinross on Saturday, to the funeral of Mrs. Williamson—was chief mourner; she was interred with her ancestors in the old burying ground facing Loch Leven Castle. Drove to the house in the carriage of Mr. Young of Cleish, Convener of the County.

January 12.—Sir W. Collins excited about the Railway Strike. . . . Have felt some reluctance to commit myself to a contest (School Board). I would gladly retire, but there may be something unworthy in escaping criticism for the past seventeen years of work. I am unable for fatigue now. I would like to finish something before my change comes.

January 18.—My failure of strength sets me often a-thinking of putting my house in order. I would like to get something settled ere I lie down never to rise again. Most reluctant to face the School Board Election on 20th March, but consenting on public grounds. This period of the year, exactly fifty years ago, my dear, sprightly sister Fanny passed away at Abbotsford Place—23rd January, 1841. Read over what I wrote on the 22nd, 24th, and 28th January, 1841.

January 24.—Trying to get my papers, etc., into order.

January 27.—An interesting conversation about a Home for Inebriates; wrote Dr. Yellowlees and Sir Arthur Mitchell.

January 30.—At Out-door Blind meeting—Sir John Stirling Maxwell in the chair. Received friendly letters from Dr. Yellowlees and Sir A. Mitchell about inebriates; it is a serious problem to which the committee are directing their attention.

February 3.—Went with Mrs. Wright-Henderson and her daughter to the College; met Mr. Young in museum, and had my attention directed to many interesting things; then drove to Cathedral.

February 6.—The nation generally may be Protestant and Christian, but the Legislature has no fixed principles. The Church of England will some day reel under this question of concurrent endowment.

February 11.—Wrote Miss Johnstone of Alva about her scheme (domestic servants).

February 18.—Went with James R. Connal[1] to Finnieston to see the old house [Finnieston House] where his father was born. . . . All cleared away—within Messrs. Thomsons' yard.

February 24.—Read some extracts from some old pamphlets in my possession as to the treatment of inebriates. Received, to my surprise, a letter this morning from Dr. Hamlin, the chaplain to the President of the U.S.; he appears never to have got the heather I sent to Liverpool for him. Met Mr. Parker Smith for two or three minutes at School Board Offices. Recalled my visit to London in December, 1850; his father a barrister in Lincoln's Inn then.

March 9.—Meeting in Mr. Craig's office about material, shape, and colour of the academic costume and degree hoods in Glasgow and other British Universities.

March 20.—Look forward with much solicitude to the fatigue of next week. . . . Mrs. Connal, 220 St. Vincent Street, very much exhausted—apparently sinking. . . . Total strangers to me have addressed me about the election. No one can tell how it will go, but it is sad

[1] Son of John Connal, Australia.

to see the indifference of people as to the points in dispute and as to the election itself. The fatigue has been very great, and I am thankful it is at an end. Dr. A. B. M'Grigor dying in Stirling.

March 21.—Sad in coming into town. Doubtful as to the issue of the election. . . . Wilson brought me the result after I had got home. Rather disappointing, but apparently a majority for the old policy of the Board.

March 22.—When I came home from church this afternoon N—— met me at the door to say that aunt [Mrs. William Connal] had died at 1.15. . . . This will inaugurate great changes. She has survived my uncle 34½ years. I must prepare for a good deal of arrangement this week as to funeral, etc. I pray for grace to act wisely and kindly.

March 23.— . Arranged with Mrs. Spofforth as to the interment in my uncle's lair,—No. 161, new ground, High Church. Found the registrar, Ferguson, to be an old Stirling man. Funeral to be on Friday (Good Friday).

March 27 (*Friday*).— . . . Everything quiet and decorous. It is all over now. She [Mrs. Connal] was lowered into the grave about 3 o'clock. . . . Heard yesterday from W. J. Thompson, after a long silence. He has twenty-six grandchildren. Went into Edinburgh on Tuesday, 24th, to see Sir A. Mitchell and Mr. Morton. Met Sir Douglas M'Lagan at his house (Mr. Morton's), Mr. Ross Taylor, Mr. Gordon Clark, and Mr. Rankine with me, about a scheme for inebriates.

March 28.—Presided at the Marshall Trust distribution of bursaries in city schools, John Street. . . Very pleasing and a remarkably high average of attendance; a fair proportion of Glasgow, Lanarkshire, and Stirlingshire—sixty girls and boys present.

April 4.—Got my uncle's bust home and placed it in the dining-room under my mother's picture. . . . Had P. A. W. Henderson at dinner along with his son and Mr. and Mrs. J. C. Gibson on Wednesday, 1st April.

April 9.—Helped Col. Stirling, Gargunnock, to get the lad he is interested in introduced to Mr. Holmes, Y.M.C.A., London.

April 10.—Yesterday, in going over the volume of the *Glasgow Courier*, came upon the advertisement about Parkhall, 27th February, 1827.

April 16.—At School Board to-day. Look with solicitude on the policy of the Board being overturned by the united action of R. C. and Free Educationists.

April 18 (*Saturday*).—Yesterday went to Larbert by train 9.15—a beautiful morning. The Ochils with a powdering of snow. . . . To-day find that the furniture at 220 St. Vincent Street is to be sold on Friday first, and the books in three weeks or so. There may be some mementoes of my uncle and aunt Frances amongst them. Met N. Spens and Dr. Stewart of Lovedale. Dr. Stewart about to start for Africa. . . . As I left Miller Street to-day, I turned to look at the old house where I first saw the light.

April 21.—Went this morning to the grave in the new burying ground. . . . Went to the closing ceremony of the East-End Exhibition, presided over by Lord Aberdeen. Walked to George Square with James Campbell of Tullichewan.

April 23.—Sent Mrs. Fielding the name of the plant she had found, *Helleborus viridis*.

April 25.—Got home some things as mementoes of my uncle from 220 St. Vincent Street. . . . At J. M. Hill's funeral on Friday. His loss mourned by a wide circle of professional and other friends.

April 27.—Yesterday found the passage in my notebooks (January, 1843) about the "Lot." Got a copy to-day from ——'s son, the only one he has, published 1858. Talked with Dr. Bryce about republishing it.

April 28.—An invitation from the Duchess of Montrose about her Children's Home, Balmaha.

April 30.—Spoke to Dr. Charles Gairdner about his lecture on "Gold." . . .

May 2.—Returned from the opening of the Montrose Home for Poor Children, Balmaha. A beautiful day. Spoke to the Lord Provost about the Buchanan Institution and the Logan and Johnston School. T. D. Findlay died yesterday. The sail to Balmaha very enjoyable.

The great mountain mass of Ben Lomond, covered with snow, was most majestic. The Duke and Duchess very gracious.

May 7.—Administered oath as J.P. to a German lady desiring to become a citizen of this country.
Yesterday examined my uncle's books to be sold to-day. How many memories they revive!

May 8.—Very much gratified in getting so many of my uncle's books.

May 9.—Consulted Mr. Nicol as to my uncle's bust.

May 14.—This afternoon paid the bonds on Arngomery; no debt on it now.

May 20.—Heard Lord Salisbury at the presentation of the Freedom of the City. A grand sight. Drove into town with Sheriff Erskine-Murray. At the luncheon. .
On Monday, 18th, a field day at the School Board. In the evening at Stanley's lecture; most dramatic and effective, but St. Andrew's Halls only three-quarters full. Had some talk with him before any one came in.

May 25.—On Friday night, with some reluctance, went to hear Professor Vambery lecture in the Philosophical Hall. An interesting man, but sometimes too rapid and indistinct. On the same day at the Victoria Infirmary examining the method of ventilation. Very much pleased. . . . The Museum and Art Galleries Committee have accepted the marble bust of my uncle, and I hope yet to see it amongst the treasures of the Corporation of Glasgow, where he spent a useful and honourable life.

May 30.—Went out to Parkhall on Thursday. The country bright and fresh. Walked up to the field under cultivation at the high wood; walked into the high wood, and surprised to see how the trees have grown all round it. I saw and bowed to Mr. J. P. Alston of Muirburn on Monday or Tuesday last. He is dead, after four days' illness. Had a call yesterday afternoon from John D. Bryce about George Square reminiscences.

June 3.—Yesterday at Mr. David Barr's funeral. The service in St. Mary's Episcopal Church rather too long. Some features in the choristers and the Bishop kneeling before the altar rather High Church.

June 9.—Agreed to become a Guild Brother and B
of Stirling. . . . The copy of the tablet whe
father, brother, and sisters' births and deaths are re
sent me by Mr. Peter Ferguson, warden of High (
burying ground; my dear mother's birth and death
recorded on the other side.

June 12.—Home from town to-day. Wrote M
braith, Town Clerk, Stirling, about making declaration
Provost Yellowlees as to being a faithful burgess.
The children of the Band of Hope to have an ex
to Fintry; old brown horse to go with waggon, and
decorated with ribbons. . . . The Baccarat Sca
painful revelation of unbridled passion ending in
desertion, hatred.

June 18.—Country very beautiful; rhododendron
nificent. Happy to take some flowers to those wh
none.

June 22.—Rose at 6; a glorious morning.
Joseph Townsend dead. Remember sending Varta
at Nazareth) and Joseph Anton to the top of the ch
stalk before the scaffolding was taken down.
Very happy in arranging that the poor blind and p
imbecile boy has been received into the Blind Asy

June 25 (*Thursday*).—After writing a good many
about things pressing on me, went to the field
Redyett. John ploughing with brown horse; a fin
ing creature at a distance. D. Brown, boy, and girl
up potatoes. A fine breeze, soft and cooling.
Yesterday, at lunch time, Provost Yellowlees ma
appearance, and I signed the book in which Bu
and Guild Brothers are enrolled, and made the decl
Saw Lord John Russell's signature and those of E
Connal and John Connal (I think about 1780)
father's signature along with his brothers', Patri
John, in 1804. William Connal's (Solsgirth) name
as the last burgess admitted. Saw Mr. Copeland-
missionary in the Cowcaddens—father of one of th
outstanding pupils of the High School. The boy l
the Hutchinson gold medal (Latin), and has prizes in
Latin, French, and German, and in Mathematics he l

the Wellpark gold medal. What a contrast to my sinful trifling in 1826-7.

July 2.—Have felt at times very wearied. Often calling to mind the tendency to fall away altogether; my indiscretions, my temptations. "O Lord, hold Thou me up and I shall be safe."

July 8.—Rose at 6.15; dull, rainy morning. Life is a discipline, and yet how thankful I should be! There are many things to try and throw one down. I remain at Parkhall all day, having no pressing necessity to go into town.

July 11.—Had some talk about ——. I have often thought that I was too bold in speaking to that man. In the light of the Eternal World I may not have erred, but it cost me the courtesies of acquaintanceship.

July 16.—I have been too shy in my relation to others. . Learned, to my deep distress, from Sir J. N. Cuthbertson the critical state of Dr. Kennedy.

July 22.—On Monday, on coming into town, invited to meet the envoys of King Gungunbama, King of Gazaland, at luncheon in Central Hotel; Mr. Denis Doyle acting as interpreter. . . . Saw Alex. Stewart [gardener] on my way home on Monday afternoon; very weak, but with a bright eye. To-day Wm. J. Thompson holds a festival on the occasion of his golden wedding-day at St. Mary's Church, Kippington. . . . Declined the invitation to the unveiling Carlyle's bust in Wallace Monument on Saturday next.

July 23.—Happy to learn that Dr. Kennedy is progressing favourably. He is grateful for the flowers; pleased that they gratify friends. Went up to the High Church yard; pleased to find the tablets all in order, and saw Mr. Ferguson, warden. Sent him a copy of the monogram on the Mill on the Molendinar. . . . When looking at the manse of the Prebend of Provan this afternoon we spoke of constant change. I said it was part of the discipline we are under, and that it is intended we should feel it. The whole surroundings of the Cathedral greatly improved. . . . Our little hay crop being secured. Impressed with the majesty of the view from the brae where the men and boys were working. On Wednesday a fine breeze, and the fragrance of the clover and grass very sweet.

July 25.—A bright, breezy day. The haymaking carried on under the most favourable circumstances—a vast expanse of blue sky. Saw Sir A. Orr Ewing on his way to Ballikinrain. Engaged for the best part of the forenoon writing out from memoranda—my will. I hope that I may be guided aright. Saw and spoke to the Duke of Montrose yesterday morning at the station. Alex. Stewart died yesterday morning; funeral on Monday. . . . How fresh the country air as I drove along the road to Parkhall after being in town.

August 1.—Busy all day; went up in the morning to see the young men at the turnips in the high field. Elected a Governor of the Stirling Educational Trust by the University Court, Glasgow. Congratulated by Mr. Mure Smith, of the West Church. Had an early call from Lady Orr Ewing. No other interruption. Invited to meet the Lord Mayor of London on the 18th inst.; distributed illustrated and other papers. . . . Wednesday at Cattle Show, Stirling. Lunched with Provost Yellowlees; struck with the picturesque aspect of the surroundings. The outline of the castle very fine. Introduced to Mr. Noel (son of Baptist Noel) and Mr. Campbell Colquhoun of Garscadden by Alexander Crum Ewing. At the meeting of members in pavilion; heard Forbes of Culloden speak. . Pleased to get a reading of a letter from Mr. Miller, Demerara. The young men have got a fair start; surely the "Spout" has done good even so far away.

August 7.—Went up to the Cattle Show at Killearn. Beautiful amphitheatre of country, fine animals. A fine feature of agricultural life in thus bringing farmers and landowners together; had to say something at lunch time about the judges, and tried to interest those present about agricultural education. . . . Affected by the sight of the flowers to-day; what richness and variety of colour! What must heaven be? what beauty has God shed on a fallen world!

August 17 (*Monday*).—Spent Saturday quietly picking

up leaves and flowers for Monday morning. Duncan [gardener] in the garden after his illness; he has got a shake.

August 20.—Interested in getting the extract from a letter addressed to Mr. Wilson of Auchineck by Mr. Anderson, about Obia Factory and my father's tomb. The place covered with jungle and scarcely known; tomb said to be twenty feet high. Restored James Campbell of Tullichewan's coat to him, taken by me yesterday (19th) when at Buchanan Castle. The Duke and Duchess very gracious—a princely domain; some fine trees and specially a *Picea nobilis* twenty-six years old. . Banquet to the Lord Mayor and Sheriffs of London on Tuesday night, 18th. A magnificent affair; sat beside Dr. Stalker and Mr. Caldwell, Clerk to the County of Renfrew.

August 24.—Received a note from the Duke of Montrose, thanking me for the information as to the pine that grows on the Carpathian Mountains.

August 26.—Did not go into town to-day; engrossed in cutting down a large tree. Afraid to leave the men; they are so foolhardy. As the day progressed, cut down trees and branches near the garden—a necessary thing, but it interfered with work I had chalked out for myself. . . The little book, *Games of Chance Unlawful*, now issued.

August 29.—Beautiful day: impressed with the beauty of the sky, the heather-empurpled hills, the stream, the cutting of corn, the sheep in the pastures. Went over to Balfron Flower Show; what beautiful colours and designs! Affected to think what heaven is, when there is so much beauty on earth.

September 1.—Barometer very much down.

September 5.—Disappointing day; instead of clearing up it was wild and gusty, with sometimes heavy rain; sad at the postponement of reaping the little crop of corn. The weather is part of our discipline in this life.

September 11 (*Friday*).—On Tuesday went to the conversazione and reception by the Lord Provost and Mrs. Muir of the members and delegates of the Young Men's Christian Association. . . . Introduced to Mr. [George

W.] Williams, who is said to be the founder in London of the Y.M.C.A.

September 12.—I notice in the newspapers the death of Mr. Carrs, of Cambridge—a man I met at Rossie Castle, and whose name recalls Little and old times—the successor of [Charles] Simeon.

September 16.—Came out this afternoon with Sir A. Orr Ewing, who was asking about R. L. Ewing's family. Expected to have met Lord Balfour of Burleigh, but Mr. J. Ferguson, secretary, met him and *September* with him to preside at the Centenary of Stirling's Library. . . . J. Wilson put into my hands to-night at 5.30 a letter from Calcutta about my father's tomb—at last identified; but the bricks taken by a native, within the last two or three years, to build his house. What a solemn thing; everything swept away. . . . Thought of the omniscience and omnipresence of God. "Thou God seest me."

September 22.—Duncan Gunn [gardener] reported to have been very ill during the night. I fear his end is near.

September 23.—Saw Duncan Gunn this morning and afternoon. I think him rather better. . The meeting with Principal Caird to take place to-morrow. J. Guthrie Smith agreed to go if J. O. Mitchell declined—as to inviting him to take part in the Centenary of Stirling's and Glasgow Public Library, at which Lord Balfour of Burleigh is to preside. . . . Have had the burgess ticket (Stirling) of William Leckie of Broich photographed.

September 25.—At the marriage yesterday of John Wilson's daughter. Archbishop Smith performed the ceremony. . . . A great gathering of friends and neighbours. Left immediately after the bride and bridegroom had left. A magnificent rainbow stretching from Dungoyne across the strath towards Ben Ledi. The hills seen from the road leading to Finnich Toll very fine in their abrupt elevation above the strath.

September 26.—Yesterday at the unveiling of the portrait of Sir James King.

October 10.—When gathering evergreens in the avenue—a fine, fresh morning, but unsettled as to weather—heard that Duncan Gunn was dead. John's little girl came and told me. Went and saw his sister. A faithful servant gone. A rainbow, perfect but faint, spanned the heavens over the cottage. . . . Engaged for about three and a half hours with these flowers. Mary Ewing and Maggie Connal helped me to put them up. Constant occupation and weariness have prevented my writing in this book since 26th September. . . . Drove to meeting of Agricultural Discussion Society in Christian Institute—Duke of Montrose presiding—rather late, but managed to show face. . . . On Wednesday, 7th, went to the re-opening of the Mitchell Library in Miller Street, by the Marquis of Bute. His remarks original and above the ordinary level of thought. Too late for the presentation of the freedom of the city.

October 14.—Duncan Gunn's funeral to-day; his memory much respected. . . . Wrote all the people in my district about my being unable to call with Communion tickets.

October 22.—A rainbow spanned the heavens over Loch Lomond. . . . Yesterday attended the Prisoners' Aid Society in the Chamberlain's room. It proved, as Sir James King, who presided, said to me in the train, a pleasant meeting.

October 24.—Called to-day on Sir A. Orr Ewing and Honourable Mrs. Charles at Old Ballikinrain, but missed them. A most beautiful day—the hills clear, the tints of autumn very beautiful; cleared the garden of blossoms.

October 28.—Rose at 6.20, and went out to gather blossoms and evergreens, etc., for —— in the City Poorhouse; I believe that they do good in brightening the lives of those in her ward.

November 3.—Lifted my heart to the great Burden Bearer. . . . The country very beautiful.

November 17.—Very much surprised and gratified at Dr. Dougall (stranger) sending me a copy of John Young's paper on the Campsie district.

November 21.—Affected to recall, in reading the book on *The Ochils, etc.*, a period of sixty-three or sixty-four years ago.

November 28.—On Thursday, 26th, drove to the College; a weary wait for an hour from 11 to 12; students boisterous and noisy. . . . The Earl of Stair made his appearance in his robes as Chancellor; Mr. Balfour, Lord Rector, followed; then Dr. Caird in a red gown, said to be the full dress of a D.D. Not impressed with what Mr. Balfour said; it was at best a difficult task to know what to say. Lunched in the Examination Hall with the grandees; sat opposite Dr. Kerr and beside Dr. Bottomley and Dr. Cleland. Yesterday did rather too much. At the presentation of Sir W. Thomson's portrait and replica by Lord Rector. The encomiums on Sir William impressed Professor Ramsay with the idea of a funeral! Spoke afterwards to Sir William about his father, etc. His intercourse very friendly; what an immeasurable distance between that man and me!

December 3.—Sad accounts of Dr. Kennedy, not relishing or taking food; Dr. Munro has given up hope. . . . Guthrie Smith ill of congestion of the lungs. Gave Dr. W. H. Hill five old parchments and three papers lent me by the Registrar.

December 11.—Heard yesterday by a messenger from the School Board of the death of Dr. Kennedy; very sad. At the meeting of the School Board at 1 to 3.30. The event cast a shadow over all the proceedings. Lawson told me to-day that the *Prisons of the World* was useful to him. Got home my uncle's *Fall of Foyers* and my father's *Herefordshire.* Arranged to give a fir tree for Free St. James' Band of Hope.

December 14.—Snowy, ungenial day. Poor Dr. Kennedy's funeral in the Necropolis; drove to the ground with Sir J. N. C. and Dr. Munro. . . . At 1.30 at Stirling's Library with Lord Balfour, to show him the Institution. The centenary meeting passed off fairly enough; it lasted about an hour and a half.

1892

January [illegible]
made a [illegible]

January [illegible]
about [illegible]
Tribal [illegible]
the [illegible]
Ob[illegible]
to a [illegible]
parent)[illegible]

January [illegible]
delegation [illegible]
the [illegible]

January [illegible]
the departm[illegible] [illegible] land [illegible]
[illegible]
[illegible]
away and [illegible]
close to [illegible]

January [illegible]
[illegible]
received [illegible]
about [illegible]

January [illegible]
Arizona [illegible]

January [illegible]
appropr[illegible]
very [illegible]
building [illegible]
dear mom[illegible]

January 2.—I see that Sir William Thomson has been made a peer.

January 5.—Saw Mr. M——, of the Barony Board, about his article in the newspapers as to "Pauperism." Tried to arrange my books and papers; they have been thrown into great confusion by cleaning the room. . . . On coming down North Hanover Street gave some brandy to a boy who fell from a horse as I was passing; it apparently revived him.

January 6.—Went to the meeting for arranging a deputation to the Lord Provost to summon a meeting of the citizens about the Russian persecution of the Jews.

January 9.—Busy with my books all day. Went with the deputation to the Lord Provost about the Jews yesterday; spoke to —— on coming into town about the being forgotten by the rising generation. In a few weeks we pass away and the world goes on as before; he said, "Their very dust to Him is dear."

January 15.—The death of the Duke of Clarence fills everyone's mind. Very sad when so near his marriage; it occurred yesterday morning. Cardinal Manning died at 8 or about an hour earlier.

January 18.—At 4 at Stirlingshire Society meeting in Arthur Forbes' office; dinner postponed.

January 20.—At the Cathedral with N——; a very appropriate and suitable service; lit up with gas; the day very dark; one thousand people; a magnificent pile of building. Visited, before going home, the burial place where dear ones lie.

January 22.—Went to the meeting about Dr. A. B. M'Grigor's memorial at 11; decided on a window in the Bute or Randolph Hall.

January 27.—At home busy with my books and papers, trying to get them into order. . . . How humble I should be; how forbearing to the faults of others.

February 1.—Spurgeon died at Mentone yesterday; he will be much missed.

February 3.—Spoke strongly in coming out of the hall to the Early Closing Association deputation, and said that, instead of trusting to legislation, they should face the loss incurred by shutting their shops. If public opinion is so much in their favour compared with what it was, why not do it?

February 8.—On Friday, 5th inst., at Dr. M'Kendrick's about the University ordinances as to women attending University. . . . Went to the Corporation Galleries to see my uncle's bust.

February 12.— . . . —— asked me my age to-day; rather startling, but I was quite frank; men think I am old. I am nearing the Eternal World in their judgment.

February 17.—My MS. volume (Porteous Extracts) to be shown at the meeting of the Archæological on Thursday evening.

February 18.—To-day met as a Board, and appointed Mr. Alexander, of Dundee, Clerk to the School Board. . . . General David M'Farlan's wife buried to-day at Lennoxtown.

February 20.—Found in a tin box, too long left open and neglected, interesting correspondence relating to my mother and sister. I am almost inclined to think that I have retained too many papers and too cumbersome correspondence.

February 23.—The MSS. Porteous Presbytery Records much appreciated by Archæological Society. . . . At Dr. M'Kendrick's in the evening (Monday), at 7. Drove out—a cold, disagreeable night. Final meeting about the University Ordinances; two hours. I expressed my opinion, as Dr. M'Kendrick asked it, that I thought that after further experience these ordinances would be under the revision of the Commissioners within the next seven years; that we were in a state of transition, etc., etc. Dr. M'Kendrick, whom I met in Gordon Street this morning, to my surprise, expressed himself pleased with what I had said. Except the calling attention specially, at the next meeting of Council, to one or two points that might command popular attention, it was needless to approach the Privy Council or Parliament.

February 27.—Had a very kind note from John Cowan, who seemed pleased with my making my appearance in Edinburgh on Thursday, 25th. Went to Edinburgh on that day by 11 o'clock train. Went to the Exhibition of Pictures by Living Artists. Interested in two or three pictures—"Evening, Strathspey," by Denovan Adam, and "Iona Cathedral, Moonlight," by James Paterson, and "November Sunset," by Wellwood Rattray. The wonderful management of the shadow cast by the setting sun, and the glorious bright light on the bushes at the top of the hill; the weird look of the old graveyard and the tower, Iona, and the wild rush of waters in the last, impressed me. Went to the Imbecile Institute at the Bible Society at 2, and remained till the public meeting took place in the Royal Hotel. Sat between the Lord Provost and the President of the Faculty of Physicians and Surgeons (Dr. Simpson). Said a few words. Dr. Simpson referred to the dying words of Edward Forbes, the great naturalist—"dying like a stuck pig, going down a stream." I think Dr. Balfour told me this remark was made to himself.

March 1.—Yesterday took part in the proceedings of Miss M'Alpine's Training Home for Nurses at 3—Sir John Burns in the chair. Most reluctant to speak.

March 9.—Wandered into the Exhibition of Pictures.

March 12.—Went to Flower Show in Springbank School. Hyacinths very good. . . . Spoke to Ex-Bailie Simons about the distress of the Jews crowding to the frontiers.

March 18.—At a meeting of defaulting parents, Govan Street, on Wednesday, 16th. Some painful cases. One little girl of 7½ years borrowing money in pennies or so, ostensibly for her mother (4s. 6d. owing one neighbour), and spending it in sweets. . . . . Mr. Brand (Lord Hampden) dead. Miss Steven of Bellahouston dead; her will an object of much interest. . . . . Professor Ramsay apparently interested in my peripatetic idea as to Secondary Education in country districts.

March 19 (*Saturday night*).—At home all day—trying to "redd up" my books. . . . . Corrected proof of Stirling's Library centenary report. . . . Read with much interest passages in the journal of Sir Walter Scott.

April 5.—At Stirling to-day. The day dull and sky grey. How quiet the streets in the old town—yesterday the spring holiday here—the city deserted. . . . On Saturday hunted amongst books and papers to try and trace some notices of Dr. M'Leod (St. Columba) when in London, when he raised £10,000 for Highland destitution in 1835. Rev. Donald M'Leod wants to trace it.

April 7.—Tried to trace out for Mr. John Robertson, Philosophical Society librarian, the places where the society had held its meetings in the earlier period of its history. So far successful from old Glasgow directories. . . . Returned the books on the "Lot" lent me from the F.C. College Library, remarks by Thos. Gataker, B.D., 1619, and a Latin book on the same subject, 1638. I am struck with the rapid changes taking place. The faces of the population are changing—everything presses towards eternity. I sometimes think that I am putting my house in order—preparing for a change.

April 13.—Very wearied. . . . Yesterday at annual meeting of Stirling's Library—Lord Provost in the chair—and at 7 at the dinner. Sat between Dr. Muir and Mr. A. Mitchell. A remarkable company—representative, literary, scientific, and commercial. Did not leave till 11.15. . . . Mathematics to me a region impenetrable. Never introduced into the rudiments of it even fairly when at school. . . . The "Spout" in a state of transition—the future is very dark—I believe it has done good. Monday, 11th, at Chamber of Commerce at 12. Bimetalism pushed on our notice.

April 16.—Yesterday at Foreign Affairs Committee at

12 about the policy of France in the region of Western Africa overshadowing British influence and trade. . . . At the School Board . . . spoke privately to Mr. —— about his bluntness on the previous day at the Finance Committee. Rather pleased with his frankness.

April 19.—Went over with Mary Ewing old papers relative to Thos. Leckie, minister of Kilmaronock, 1702, etc. . . . At the opening of Mrs. Higginbotham's Home for Nurses, Bath Street, at 3.30. Much pleased. . . . On Monday rather pushed—Chamber of Commerce at 12, currency proposals of Mr. Goschen. . . .

April 21.—Saw Dr. Donald M'Leod, and he promised to give me back my book about the prayer of his father at the laying of the foundation of Jamaica Street Bridge.

April 23 (*Saturday*).—For the greater part of the day going over the applications for the headmastership of the mathematical department of the High School. It was a great mistake at Tillicoultry that the tuition was exclusively classical—I feel the want of mathematics now.

April 26.—Wrote C. D. Donald, resigning the position of President of Regality Club, as I thought it was expected.

April 27.—Sent Lady Burns £10 10s. for the "Empress" Training Ship. . Received by post a letter from Jerusalem—a short note from James Bell (Duncan's old partner), enclosing two olive leaves from the garden of Gethsemane, on Monday morning. Very kind and very interesting.

April 29.—Had an interesting letter this morning from Mr. Forbes Moncrieff as to Oliphant of Rossie's ancestor's relation to Walter Stirling's house in Miller Street. He was Postmaster General of Scotland, 1797. . . . Dr. Robertson full of the business of the Art Gallery. . . . Archbishop Eyre made an LL.D. to-day at the University. Talked (to a stranger, a friend of Dr. A. Bonar) about immigration of labourers from Samoa into Queensland. I went home perplexed at the changes as to the complications in educational matters. The Day Industrial School proposals before Parliament ominous for the national system of education. It is the first step to denominationalism. Yesterday at Finance meeting, then at Regality

Rhododendrons in their glory. . . . On Saturday, 4th, at a meeting of the Parochial Board; took part in the election of Dr. Roxburgh as medical man for Killearn Parish. Taylor, the smith, called the same evening with Mr. Blair about Dr. Forrester for Balfron. He gave me Miss Morrison's deed of settlement, in which my father appears prominently as a trustee—an office which he resigned on going to India. . . In the deed the Barony of Ballindalloch is referred to as having been created by a charter under the Great Seal in favour of John Cunninghame of Drumbeg, writer to the signet, dated at Whitehall, the 21st April, 1687. . The will was in favour of the British and Foreign Bible Society, Glasgow Royal Infirmary, and Chapel of Ease, Gartmore. Deeds signed 3rd Nov., 1827. . The deed was lodged in the hands of Michael Connai, Esq., of Parkhall, at the testator's particular request, as attested by Alex. Henderson, N.P., and William Meikleham, N.P., 17th Nov., 1827.

June 15.—On Saturday came into town to lay the foundation stone of Logan and Johnston School of Domestic Economy. Some rain, but on the whole all passed off well.

June 22.—Dull day, and damp. Wrote Mr. Nicol (Chamberlain) and E. Connai about Mauritius disaster. . . .

June 25.— . . . At 3, at meeting about Mauritius disaster—Lord Provost in the chair. Sir J. King, Bailie Guthrie, Mr. Martin (Scott & Co.), Ebenezer Connal. Started the movement. Doubtful if much can be done. Surprised by an invitation from Dr. Graham, Dean of Faculty, to propose J. A. Campbell as representative of the Universities of Glasgow and Aberdeen.

July 6.—Mrs. M'Farlan and Frances with us since Friday morning. . . . Voted for Mr. Baird.

July 9.—Had a delightful drive with Frances, Maggie Connal, and Ebenezer Connal's grand-daughter (Catherine), and Mrs. M'Farlan, round by Fintry. The Meikle Bin very well seen; the wild roses all along the road beautiful. The girls gathered yellow iris in a marsh, in a wild part of the road. . . .

July 15.—Sir. A. Orr Ewing called this afternoon with his two grand-daughters, the children of his son (Archibald).

July 19.—Shook hands with Mr. Ernest Noel at the station. Met last week the Duke and Duchess of Montrose at the station. The Duke was on his way to Edinburgh to preside as Lord-Clerk Registrar at the election of Scotch peers to serve in the new Parliament. The gain of the Gladstonians depressing. It appears a kind of infatuation, but the return of that man to power may be the very means to bring the country to its senses. .

July 23.—The roses in the garden in full blow. . . . Employed myself yesterday in copying out the pages of the Field Naturalists' Club that are out of print. It is interesting to note how the mind of man fastens on some pursuit, and what fascination the appearance, the varieties, the habits of the minutest forms of insect life have for him. . In the country on Tuesday, when the arm of a large tree, nearly 40 feet long, near the house, was rent away by the storm of wind from the north, disfiguring the tree. Barometer fell very much. Depression is travelling (so the *Scotsman* says) towards Switzerland.

August 3.—Wrote out some more MSS. copy of Field Naturalists' first Report, and then walked up to where M'Adam was cutting grass. Fresh bracing air—splendid panorama. . . . Thought of my mother. . . . On Monday at Chamberlain's office about a supply of meal to Lewis fishermen's families.

August 5 (*Friday*).—Drove to Cattle Show at Killearn—showery weather. Unexpectedly had to take the chair. . . . Saw Mr. D. Paterson from Drum. Visited the Flower Show—some beautiful plants. . . . Yesterday at Finance Meeting of School Board. Sent £50 to the Association for Promotion of Music and Art.

August 9.—Duchess of Montrose's invitation for 17th. Met her this morning. . . . Early this morning on the path leading to High Wood. Glowing prospect—quite clear all round. Last night bright moon. On Sabbath . . . a glorious sunset—heavens as if on fire. Georgina Gibson made an interesting statement about her work in Ludhiana. Drove out to hear her.

August 12.—Yesterday I entered upon my 76th year.

August 18 (*Thursday*).—Did not enjoy sound sleep.

September 14.—Springburn deputation claiming amalgamation with Glasgow School Board. Almost no sleep last night. This morning, sky a fiery red towards the east. . . . A kind note from Sir A. Mitchell.

September 17.—At High School yesterday, distribution of "leaving" certificates—said a few words,—a fine set of boys. . . . Spent a good part of the day making up bundles of heather, etc., for School Board clerks.

September 24.—The stream full and cheerful in the morning light. The men busy threshing corn. Distributed the newspapers that were brought by the forenoon train. At Highland Society meeting to see applicants for bursaries, and then at School Board to meet delegates about the Endowment Boards being more liberal as to books for VI. Standard.

September 30 (*Friday*).—Spent the day—which was characterized by heavy showers at intervals of half an hour or so—trying to frame some remarks for the meeting of the East Park Home on Monday, and cutting off some branches of trees that overhung the field opposite Little Boquhan.

October 6.—At 3 o'clock at East Park Home. On the whole a good meeting, but my remarks were not given in the newspapers. I thought that there was something that might have told for good. . . . On Tuesday morning went to Stirling. . . . Talked with F—— about Cawnpore massacre, awful history. . . . Called on the Gibsons. The Stirling Educational Trust meeting not important. At a meeting of the Business Committee of the University in J. B. Fleming's office; not very important.

October 8.—Yesterday in town; a dull showery day. . . Deliver us in Thy mercy from peevishness.

October 15.—Went to the laying of the memorial stone (Canal Boatmen's Institute) by Provost Muir. Leonard Gow's remarks very good. . It is wholesome but not always pleasing to visit the poor.

October 19.—At Parkhall; dull morning, but milder. Yesterday morning severe frost, ice three-eighths of an inch thick in basin outside. A glorious sunset on Monday evening. Rather solicitous in leaving town to face the cold of the country. The leaves being showered down. . . . . Declined invitation to London to Captain A. Campbell Connal's marriage to Emily Hope Bell; sent a book of photographs to her. Finished the story of Cawnpore by Captain Mowbray Thomson. At page 168 there is the passage referring to the two Hendersons on the occasion of the embarkation and the treachery and the murder, 27th June, 1857.

October 22.—Affected to think of the places in Palestine being the abode of the God man, Christ Jesus, 1900 years ago.

October 27.—Had to say something sharp to a young lady, about Baron Hirsch giving his gains in horse racing to good objects. Saw a dense crowd in Hope Street waiting the result of a race in England; a sad feature. Saw Mr. John Young when at the College and Rev. Dr. Dickson about the book printed 1535. . . . Wrote Lamont (schoolmaster) about Tennyson. His admiration of him is a little extravagant.

October 28.—The country flooded about Kirkintilloch; sheets of water like an inland lake.

November 2.—On Monday in town. Heard of the loss of two or three persons in the "Roumania," off the coast of Portugal, known indirectly to me—John Fleming's grandson, Nicol the Chamberlain's son, young Miss Dunlop of the Craigton family.

November 6.—Went to Dr. Reith's in the forenoon. Heard the newly appointed Professor of Hebrew, George A. Smith. His text John xii. 36. Some interesting remarks about the alternation of light and darkness. . . . The observation of Darwin of his indifference to poetry, music, painting, from disuse. It might have saved him this being once a week invited to read poetry, etc. He drew from this the constant living upon Christ.

November 7.—P. A. Henderson, by a letter received this morning from Oxford, has sold Broom to Mr. Morries Stirling. It is a sad blow to sentiment. My poor uncle, John Wright, was known as "Broom." These traditions are passing away. . . . I would have liked to think over the matter as to the house where my mother was born.

November 9.—I see the death of John Charles Steele, M.D., aged 71, on 6th Nov. at Guy's Hospital, Medical Superintendent. This recalls the visit of Mr. Dobree to Virginia Buildings before my uncle's death, when Dr. Steele was removed to London from the Royal Infirmary.

November 19.—At School Board, Thursday. Dr. Munro still critically ill. F. L. Robertson ill; fear something else wrong besides the dregs of influenza. At the lecture on Thursday evening by Captain Lugard. Pushed to propose vote of thanks to Sir W. Renny Watson as chairman.

November 20.— . . . F. L. Robertson is in a critical state.

November 29.—Yesterday at 12 at Chamber of Commerce. I was the oldest member there. . . . On Saturday at Bazaar on behalf of Queen Margaret College. Got away as fast as possible to Dr. Munro's funeral. Sir J. N. Cuthbertson and Mr. Blackie in same carriage with me. . . F. L. Robertson very ill.

December 3.—At the Festival in St. Andrew's Halls of Ancient Shepherds—Lord Elgin in the chair in place of Lord Aberdeen. Left early; wearied.

December 9.— . . . F. L. Robertson made aware by the doctors this morning that there was no hope. How sad. . . . A fancy ball to-night for poor musicians. When there is so much distress from want of employment, this appears out of place and incongruous.

December 12 (*Monday*).—When I was at the morning meeting yesterday, heard that Dr. F. L. Robertson was dead. No service in his church. . . Could not help reflecting on Dr. Robertson's career.

December 22.—Went to the Lord Provost's conversazione in the Municipal Buildings at 7. A great number of people from the several wards of the city. Knew very few. Left early and went to the address by Sir F. Pollock on "Archaics in Modern Law." . . . Thankful

Duke of Montrose in the chair. . The Bellahouston Bequest Trustees have made a fair beginning.

December 23.—Suggested Dr. W. H. Hill as a suitable man to be placed in the position of overlooking the business of the three endowments.

December 27.—At Stirling's Library about the Bellahouston Bequest. There appears a desire to go to the Corporation Galleries, if vacated for the new building at Kelvingrove. In my judgment matters are not ripe for looking at the position of the library. The existence of three libraries so close to each other is exercising busybodies in the Corporation and elsewhere. Lawrence Hill, C.E., dead.

December 28.—Dr. A. A. Bonar died yesterday. A man who was prepared to enter the Eternal World more than most men.

1893

January 2.—Pleased with the Logan and Johnston School of Domestic Economy.

January 4.—This morning, along with Dean of Guild, Guthrie Smith, and Mr. M'Corquodale, met Sir James King and Ex-Provost Ure about Stirling's Library's claim on Bellahouston Trust. Heavy fall of snow. At the School Board about the report on teachers and teaching. Found my way to Sighthill to mark my respect for Dr. A. A. Bonar. A large funeral, but an inclement day.

January 7.—Visited the exhibition of instruments of torture; a very painful display of human fiendishness. Visited the court-yard behind the Saracen Head Inn. Interested in a stone with the date 1761 on it. . Have had some correspondence with Mr. F. T. Barrett as to a modest beginning of district libraries.

January 11.— . . . Received to-day copy of *New York Herald* of 28th Dec., detailing the laying of memorial stone of the Cathedral of St. John by Bishop Potter. Can this be the man who was my guest in 1838 after the Queen's coronation?

January 13.—Went to the distribution of medals to Volunteers of twenty years' service by Major General Annesley. The physique of the men very fine.

January 18.—Asked by R. Balloch formally to continue Convener of Foreign Affairs Committee, Chamber of Commerce. . . .

January 23.—Lent Mr. Glashan books to assist Dr. Paton of the High School in replying to an inquiry as to the naming of Buchanan Street, and as to the meaning of the City Arms. . . . Sir Thomas M'Clure dead. . . . James Dunlop's (of Tollcross) funeral to-day.

January 25.—An interesting lecture by E. A. Maund, of King's-Langley, Mashonaland, in Chamber of Commerce. Returned thanks at the request of the President. Yesterday at first meeting of the Secondary Education Board; a difficult problem.

February 9.—Dr. W. G. Blackie pushed me by a letter to fall in with the proposal to collect memorials of the Disruption for the Jubilee in May. . On Saturday at 11 at the distribution of prizes for drawing to pupil teachers in Dr. Dymock's old class-room.

February 10.— When institutions get into the hands of public bodies, you do not know where you are. . . .

February 11.—Mr. Paton of the Corporation Galleries of Art promises help as to the Ecclesiastical Exhibition in Edinburgh. . . . I cannot tell how soon I may be called away with all my work unfinished.

February 13.—Saw Mr. Paton this morning and paved the way; afterwards wrote Mr. Taylor Innes.

February 18.—A declinature from Professor Story, as to the Carstairs relics (thumbscrew, etc.). Explained to Mr. Archibald Craig this morning more fully what I indicated on Friday, as to an element of elasticity in the salaries of Professors under the ordinances.

February 24.—Kippen Churchyard to be closed, advertisement in to-day's *Herald*. Went by tram to try and get to the Flower Show at Napiershall, Springbank. Missed my way in the dingy, populous district.
Met [G. M.] Grierson this morning. He spoke of the death of his son by cholera; a telegram being laid on their breakfast table when at Dunblane announcing it, when a letter had been received the day before written in good spirits. . . . Sad at heart [about politics]. If Gladstone's Home Rule Bill is defeated it will remain an element of bitterness, to be pushed forward again and again. It may issue in the course of years in Romish supremacy in Ireland; it may be in civil war.

March 2.—Sad at heart as to the proceedings at the

School Board. The opposition to the Bill about to be brought in (about Day Industrial Schools), by the agitation of Edinburgh people, overcome by only five voting for the opposition at the Board against eight. The Bill is fraught with mischief. It makes the Protestant and R. C. able to dip their hands in the public purse of the School Board to support denominational and truant schools, and it looks as if the measure of 1872 was fast losing the national character it originally had. Sad at heart, nothing but changes for the worse. . . . . Yesterday morning at Burgh Committee on Secondary Education. The whole scope of the measure is unsatisfactory., The men who have adopted the idea of education, free from top to bottom, will likely carry their point, but the pendulum will by-and-by swing the other way. . . . . Reluctant to go to Lafayette, photographer, but succumbed to his request. . . . . At 3.30 at Business Committee, University, till near 6. This Committee has opened up to me new ideas about the University.

March 3.—Went up to the inspection of the manual instruction class by Captain Griffiths at 12.45 in City Public School. He urged me to have more of such classes. Struck with the brightness of the boys. . . . At public meeting of the Christian Literature Society for China. Dr. Swanson spoke. . . . . His speech very good about literary distinction in China. Dr. Edkins spoke of the Emperor learning English—a little girl's primer given him. Matters settling into shape as to the Exhibition of Disruption and other relics, by a letter from A. Taylor Innes.

March 7.—Rose at 6. Feeling solicitous about the relic memorials of the Disruption movement as involving expense and responsibility. . . . . Shook hands with Cochran-Patrick when he was going into the Western Club.

March 9.—At University General Council meeting. Asked to preside, and conducted the business till 2.45.

March 10.—At the distribution of prizes at Martyrs' School. Pleased with the children. Two of them sang correctly and sweetly Mendelssohn's "Cauld Blast."

March 11.—"To do the will of Christ is rest." "Thou wilt keep him in perfect peace (margin, peace, peace),

whose mind (thought or imagination) is stayed ‹
because he trusteth in Thee" (Isaiah xxvi. 3
peace of God, which passeth all understanding, s
your hearts and minds through Christ Jesus" (P.
iv. 7). "Guard your hearts and your thoughts" (

March 12.—Day bright, but cold. Walked
church. In Argyle Street and Trongate the stree
up, and labourers working at the underground railw

March 13.—Too many things pressing on me.
Lord Provost's invitation for 27th instant.

March 16.—Had little or no sleep last night.
and lightning at 2 a.m. . . . At the Conf
Deputies about Sabbath Schools. John Wilson
calling that I was the only surviving trustee of th
in London Street; trust constituted 3rd January,

March 20.—At 6 o'clock (Monday) telegram rea
from Dr. M'Arthur, Winnipeg:—"John Leckie Ew
yesterday." Telegraphed to Dollar.

March 21.—Telegraphed Winnipeg, to do what ‹
—to secure ground for interment, etc. Wrote J
widow. .

March 24.—Yesterday evening went with some r
to meeting of Evening Classes in Albion Hall:
something about Lord Kelvin and William Li
about James Watt's walk through the Green.
School Board Property Committee, bringing in th
light into the principal rooms.

March 30.—Fell in the middle of the street
School Board Offices, having tripped when comin
curbstone. Too late to hear about the exper
Mr. Scott Moncrieff as to the Jews in Palestine.
At Chamber of Commerce on Monday at 11 abou
Mr. Goschen to speak on the currency question.
declined the invitation.

March 31.—Feel very tired; my natural streng
abated. Yet I bless God that I am spared to do so

April 1.—Interested in the family of Glas; sec
coat of arms, registered 1812; Sauchie sold in 17

April 4.—Went to meeting in Merchants' Ha
the Home Rule Bill. A most enthusiastic and

meeting—Sir W. Renny Watson in the chair. Mr. Goschen spoke for a few minutes. A. Sandeman showed me some MSS. of Mr. Glas.[1] . . . . Fine weather. John Wilson called to know the shortest way to the Whangie. Directed him to the Milngavie railway. Met Dr. M'Leod, Govan, on Monday afternoon in Hanover Street. Exchanged opinions about Gladstone and his revolutionary measures. Feel a great failure of strength.

April 10.—At Property Committee. Surrendered Little Dovehill to the School Board on the condition of £25 being annually paid for prizes for religious knowledge in connection with the Board, and that a stone be put up as a memorial of the Andersons of the Dovehill, and referring to Sir John Moore as their descendant.

April 12.—Mary M'Dougall, an old friend, died at Harrogate. Archibald Sandeman has secured for me the loan of Donald Cargill's Bible for the Exhibition.

April 15.—Wrote Joseph Bain about mill on the Molendinar. Very much cut by ——'s note about the memorial scheme. I have no time or strength to go and explain things to him. If the forty men to whom I have applied for a guarantee act in the same way, it will barely be a success. . . . . With Professor T. M. Lindsay for an hour about the memorial movement.

April 18.—Wrote Patrick Welsh about the "Broom"—a haphazard step, now or never.

April 19.—At Sailors' Orphan Society at 2.30. Said a few words, but very tired afterwards. Sent off twenty-three circulars about F.C. memorials.

April 21.—Awake since 4 a.m. this morning. Thought of many things. "What time my heart is in perplexity do Thou me lead unto the Rock that higher is than I." Had a letter from P. Welsh about the "Broom." . . . Met G. B. Young with J. H. Kerr as to the property, Little Dovehill. . . . On Thursday, 20th, resigned the chairmanship of the Regality Club. Professor Ferguson of the University appointed.

April 22.—Wrote P. Welsh. The buyer of "Broom" declines to part with it. . . . Went over in the morn-

[1] Rev. John Glas, founder of the Glassites.

would be a strange thing if Mr. Morries Stirling, agreed to surrender "Broom."

May 13.—Saw Mr. Paton, Corporation Galleries—apparently the Exhibition looks like being a success. Had a letter yesterday from A. Taylor Innes. Went for a few minutes to Townhead School. The boys and girls from all parts of Stirlingshire stood up that I might see them. Yesterday at Hutchesons' Girls' School. . . . A distinct refusal to entertain the proposal to part with "Broom."

May 19.—At the School Board, the remarks of —— and ——, as to the public meeting of the Board being a sham, shameful. The two Assemblies have met. I pray that a spirit of wisdom and of love may be given them. The Jubilee Memorial Collection is favourably noticed by the Press. What am I that I should be spared? that I should have put into my hands to do what I believe may do good?

May 20.—Got catalogue of F.C. Memorial Exhibition—some errors. Spoke to Mr. Hutton about Napoleon. Visited panorama of Waterloo on my way home.

May 24.—At 11 at Burgh Committee, then at Chamber of Commerce about the Australian Banks' suspension. Trying to get information about Queen Margaret Street School site.

May 26.—Walked down the garden at Parkhall about 7 this morning—pleased to see the urn[1] so well restored. It reminds me of the place of my birth in Miller Street. Everything beautiful—the foliage of the trees bright green and massive in its luxuriance. Left the city yesterday at 4.43. . . . Some solicitude at the School Board as to the policy of the Free Education party as to freeing more schools. This Free Education will ere long cause a revolt in the minds of parents who do not wish their children to be mixed up with those socially inferior to them.

May 31.—Sent L. Thomson £1, which I would have paid her good uncle, Alex. Stewart,[2] had he lived. Pained

[1] Urn taken from the house occupied for many years by William Connal, and where Sir Michael was born.

[2] Long gardener at Parkhall.

master in the School Board Offices on Monday last. Wrote Mr. D. M'Arthur about J. L. Ewing's headstone at Winnipeg.

June 14 (*Wednesday*).—At home all day overlooking tradesmen taking down arch over the stables. Walked up to Mrs. Paul's and saw the field under cultivation. Yesterday at Finance Committee, and saw Keppie, of John Honeyman & Keppie, as to additions to stables. Thankful to get the various articles back which had been lent for the Exhibition at Edinburgh. Monday at Teachers Committee and at 16 Lynedoch Crescent.

June 17 (*Saturday*).—Walked down to the well now in course of construction—glorious morning and the view all round very beautiful. Yesterday signed the Trust Deed of the Spoutmouth Bible Institute. . . . Wrote Mr. D. M'Arthur to put a modest headstone over the grave [of John Leckie Ewing].

Died 6th July, 1893.

A. Des

1. married George Wingate, d. s. p.

'illiam 27th uary, 90, s. p. = 1. Frances, daughter of William Wright of Broom.

2. Isabella
3. Isabella
5. Margar
8. Agnes
11. Robert

2. Margaret Turner.

10. Ebenezer, b. 17th February, 1792. = Catherine, daughter of Thomas Littlejohn, Provost of Stirling, by his wife, Christian Glassford.

1

1. Michael
2. John
3. Patrick
5. Agnes
6. Marion Gl
9. Francis W
11. Patrick

. William Wright, 26th March, 1819, 1st March, 1828.

. Frances Stevenson, 23rd Nov., 1821, 23rd Jan., 1841.

Michael, Surveyor-General, Mauritius, married Mary Aird M'Crone, with issue.

2. Christina Glassford, d. unmarried.

3. Marion Glas, d. unmarried.

3.

APPENDIX A.

SKETCH OF CONNAL FAMILY.

Michael Connal, eldest son of Patrick Connal, was born 3rd February, 1752. He was a merchant and partner in the Stirling Banking Company, of which his relative William Christie was one of the founders. He was a keen politician and took an active interest in all the affairs of the borough. He married, 4th November, 1775, Marion Glas, daughter of John Glas of Stirling, by his wife Marion Burn. For their descendants, see Table A.

Michael Connal was three times Provost of Stirling between 1803 and 1812. He died during his Provostship, 15th November, 1812. Through his mother's family he had an hereditary connection with the municipality of Stirling. His great-grandfather was James Christie (brother of the Laird of Sheriffmuirlands), who succeeded Colonel John Erskine of Carnock as Provost of Stirling in 1709. From that year till 1721 the names Erskine and Christie appear time about as holders of this office. Provost James Christie married, 4th May, 1694, Margaret, daughter of Thomas Walker of Craigs of Plean, and had, besides other children—

1. James, born 1695, married Catherine, daughter of Francis Napier, Provost of Stirling, 1696 (descended from John Napier of Merchiston, inventor of logarithms).
2. Thomas, born 1697, solicitor, Dean of Guild 1740, Town-Clerk 1743, married Mary, daughter of John Watson of Woodend, and was ancestor of the Christies of Durie.
3. William, born 1699, Provost of Stirling 1743, and subsequently. He married Margaret, daughter of William Edmonstone of Cambuswallace, Perthshire (descended from "Duntreath"), who in 1725 constructed the walk round the Castle Rock of Stirling known as the "Back Walk."
4. Christian, second daughter, married Michael Downie, and had a daughter, Isobel, born 24th May, 1721, married in 1749 to Patrick Connal of Stirling.

Patrick Connal was descended from a family which had been farmers and small landowners for several generations in the western districts of Stirlingshire. He was born in 1715, and was the son of John Connal (who had a lease of the farm of Touch, parish of St. Ninians), by his wife Agnes Wilson.

Patrick Connal was the first of the Connals who settled in Stirling, where he was admitted a burgess and guild brother, 10th June, 1749, soon after his marriage.

By his wife Isobel Downie, he had four sons and five daughters. The second daughter, Agnes, born 1754, married Alexander Peebles of the parish of Bo'ness, but had no family. The others died unmarried. The sons were—

1. Michael, of whom already (357). For descendants, see Table A.
2. John, born 1756, married Christian Arthur, by whom he had five sons, four of whom died in early life.
   Michael, the survivor, went to New Zealand, where he married, and is believed to have descendants.
3. Ebenezer, born 1760, merchant in South Carolina, died there unmarried in 1786.
4. Patrick, born 1764, was ordained minister of the Original Secession Church, Bathgate, 1787. He married Miss Roberton, daughter of Roberton of Lauchope, Lanarkshire, and had two daughters. One died in early life; the other, Janet, married the Rev. Thomas Gordon, minister of Falkirk; but had no family.

APPENDIX B.

FAMILY OF WILLIAM WRIGHT OF BROOM.

William Wright of Broom, born 13th September, 1741, was for some time in the army. He succeeded his eldest brother, John Wright of Torbrex, who died unmarried in 1792, in the lands of Torbrex, Know, etc. Wm. Wright married, in June, 1789, Frances, daughter of Captain Hugh Stevenson, descended from an old Stirling family, and died in 1812, leaving a son, John Wright of Broom and Torbrex, and two daughters, Frances, married to William Connal, and Eliza, married to Michael Connal, both sons of Provost Connal.

The Wrights were known by the name of "Pin" Wrights, from a tradition that their ancestor was the Wright who removed the pin or wedge from the bridge at the battle of Stirling in 1297. See Table B.

B. Descendants of William Wright of Broom and Frances Stevenson.

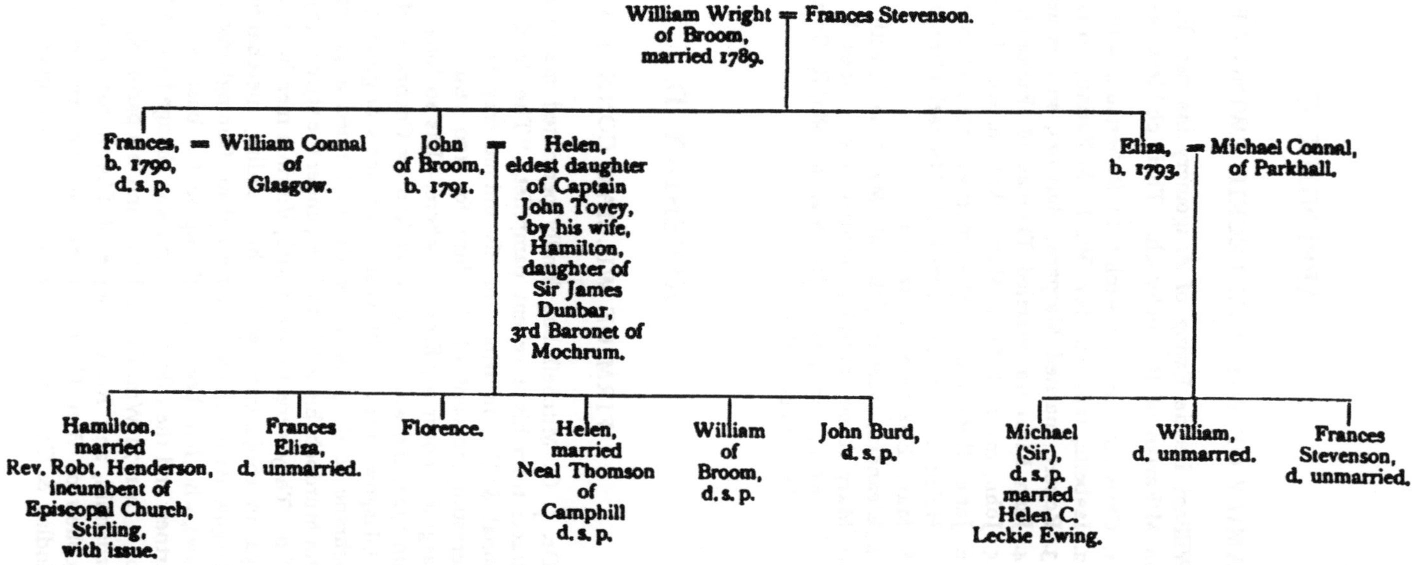

APPENDIX C.

FAMILY OF WILLIAM LECKIE EWING OF ARNGOMERY.

William Leckie Ewing of Arngomery married Eleanora, daughter of John M'Farlan of Ballindleroch. Their children were—

1. Christian, married Archibald Robertson, with issue.
2. Isabella, married Rev. W. L. M'Farlan, no family.
3. Robert, married Margaret Burrows, with issue.
4. Jean Eleanora, married Thomas M. Fielding, with issue.
5. John, married Anna Maria Watson, with issue.
6. Janet Buchanan, died unmarried, 11th October, 1873.
7. Helen Catherine, married Sir Michael Connal, no family.
8. Mary Elizabeth, unmarried.
9. Eleanora, married John M. Macdonald, with issue.
10. Mary Anne Matilda, married, first, James F. Watson, who died April, 1883; secondly, March 1886, R. Smart, M.D., who died December, 1886.

APPENDIX D.

FIRM OF WILLIAM CONNAL & CO.

Dr. J. O. Mitchell has kindly permitted me to make the following extracts from his excellent pamphlet, "The Auld Hoose" of William Connal & Co., in which in his unique way he has given a full and interesting account of the firm for 170 years. He says no firm in Glasgow,—not many firms anywhere,—has so long a pedigree. It dates from 1722, and was founded by Andrew Cochrane of Brighouse, Provost of Glasgow (1745). Provost Cochrane's original firm was (1) Andrew Cochrane & Co.; subsequently he formed a partnership with Provost John Murdoch, his wife's brother, under the style of (2) Cochrane, Murdoch & Co. They were, to begin with, Virginia merchants and shipowners. In 1750, in conjunction with other leading merchants, they founded the Glasgow Arms Bank. In 1762 Wm. Cuninghame (afterwards of Lainshaw), who had been brought up in the business, became the principal partner, and the title of the firm was changed to (3) Wm. Cuninghame & Co. In 1772 Wm. Cuninghame and his partners, Alexander Houston of Jordanhill, and Robert Bogle of Shettleston, assumed Robert Findlay (nephew of Wm. Cuninghame), and the firm became (4) Cuninghame, Findlay & Co. In 1774 the firm had great good fortune. Cuninghame was able to build himself for town house the stately Lainshaw mansion, now the front of the Royal Exchange, and to buy the Ayrshire estate of Lainshaw and other lands in other shires. Findlay bought the property of Easterhill and a house in Miller Street, then one of the best houses in Glasgow (the house in which Sir Michael Connal was born, and behind which is still the office of Wm. Connal & Co.). In 1780 Cuninghame, Houston, and Bogle retired, and the business passed into the hands of Findlay under the firm of (5) Robert Findlay & Co. In 1789 the style became (6) Findlay, Hopkirk & Co., this Hopkirk being James Hopkirk of Dalbeth. It was at this time that the firm drifted into the West India trade, and to this West India connection their successors owe their present hold of the sugar trade.

In 1802 Robert Findlay died, and the firm became (7) Findlay, Duff & Co. They now became foreign produce brokers, the largest in Glasgow. The partners of Findlay, Duff & Co. were Robert Findlay (II. of Easterhill), James Buchanan (afterwards of Blairvaddich), Richard Dennistoun of Kelvingrove, Colin M'Lauchlan, and Wm. Duff (a Banff man, afterwards sent to Liverpool to open a branch house there). In 1812 Findlay, Duff & Co. assumed William Connal, son of Michael Connal, Provost of Stirling, and in 1822 the firm became (8) Findlay, Connal & Co. In the crisis of 1826 Findlay, Connal & Co. failed, and, after some interim arrangements, was split up into four distinct firms, Robert Findlay & Son, J. & J. Wright, Wm. Angus & Co., and William Connal. The first three are extinct.

(9) William Connal. The business grew on his hands, especially in sugar and tea. The sugar was a legacy from the old West India days of Findlay, Hopkirk & Co.; the tea was Kirkman Finlay's doing. There was a time when tea came into the Clyde by cargoes, and the London mail came down crammed with buyers to Connal's sales. To facilitate the trade, William Connal built in York Street a great bonded tea warehouse, then the finest privately owned in Europe or America. William Connal was in various enterprises outside his own business. Like his partner, Robert Findlay (II.), he was an original partner in the Clyde Shipping Company, formed in 1814. In partnership with Messrs. Ross, Corbett & Co. of Greenock, he started a line of Calcutta clippers, the "Bucephalus," the "Argaum," and the "Deogaum," which made famous passages but infamous dividends. William Connal was also an original partner in the Cunard Company, holding 116 shares against 50 and 55 held by James and George Burns respectively.

William Connal carried on the business in his own name till 1845, when he assumed as partners his nephews Michael Connal (Sir Michael) and William Connal (now of Solsgirth, son of his eldest brother, Patrick Connal), and Robert Cochran. With them he formed the existing firm of (10) William Connal & Co. William Connal, senior, died in 1856. At the time of his death he was Dean of Guild for the second time. The Dean of Guildship was hereditary in his firm. Robert Findlay (I.) had been

Balloch, R., 347.
Bank, City of Glasgow (see under C.).
Bannatyne, Mark, 192.
Bannockburn, Battle of, 88.
Barony Church, 262, 292.
Barr, David, 321.
Barr, Thomas M., 186.
Barrett, F. T., 279, 347.
Beaconsfield, Lord, 149, 191.
Beatson, G. B. M., 218.
Beatton, John, 119.
Beavor, Miss, 88.
Begg, Rev. Dr. James, 336.
Beith, Rev. Dr. Alexander, 76.
Belfast, Visit to, 60, 88.
Bell, James, 335.
Bell, Sheriff, 143.
Bernard, Sir Charles, 268.
Berry, Sheriff, 262, 275, 280.
Beveridge, Dr. and Mrs., 47, 57, 227.
Binnie, Robert, 125, 287.
Blacadyr, Rolland, Institution, 266, 267.
Blackadders of Tulliallan, 151, 268.
Blackburn, John, of Killearn, 189.
Blackburn, John, of Killearn, 200.
Blackburn, Mrs., of Killearn, 248.
Blackie, Dr. W. G., 266, 278, 292, 297, 348.
Bolton, J. C., 159, 230.
Bonar, Rev. Dr. A. A., 283, 343, 347.
Booth, "General," 313.
Borrow, George, "Bible in Spain," 71.
Botanic Gardens, 39, 111, 115.
Boundaries Committee Inquiry, 274.
Boys' Brigade, 259, 287.
Bradlaugh case, 188.
Brand, Henry (Lord Hampden), 334.
Breadalbane, Marquis of, 31, 230.
Bremner, G. W. M'E., 303.
Bright, John, 202, 291.
British Archæological Association, 278.
British Association, 103.
Broom, 341, 351, 352, 353.
Brougham, Lord, 14, 15.
Brown, Colin, 239, 273, 289.
Brown, Rev. David, 54, 55, 231, 259, 277.
Brown, Hugh, 230.
Brown, J. T. T., 201.
Brown, Sir Richard, 84, 93.
Brown, Col. Robert Johnston, 161.
Browning, Rev. Archibald, 30; family of, 76.
Bruce, Dr. J. Collingwood, 260, 280.
Bruce, Sir G. B., 279.
Bryant, William Cullen, 58, 154.
Bryce, Dr. John, 33, 149.
Bryce, J. D., 114, 321.
Buchanan, Dr. Andrew, 108, 146.
Buchanan, Dugald, Diary of, 48.
Buchanan, George, 113, 280.
Buchanan Institution, 112, 118, 164, 167, 181, 230.
Buchanan, John, of Carbeth, 135, 145.
Buchanan, Dr. John, 130, 170.
Buchanan, President-elect U.S., 107.
Buchanan, Professor, 43, 54.
Buchanan, Rev. Dr. Robert, 57, 149, 158, 180.
Buchanan, Thomas, 113.
Buchanan, Walter, M.P., 107, 114, 205.
Buchanan-Kincaid, Mrs., 173, 185.
Buller, Sir Redvers, 218.
Burd, Miss, 100.
Burdon, John, 308, 312.
Burke, T. H., Murder of, 197.
Burn-Murdoch, Captain, 267, 268.
Burns, Rev. Dr. John, 80.
Burns, Lady, 335.
Burns, Robert, 140; statue, 166.
Burns, Sir George, 262, 293.
Burns, Sir John, 237, 298, 333.
Bute, Marquis of, 136, 274, 280, 327.
Bute, Marquis of (Commissioner 1842), 40.
Buxton, Sir Thomas Fowell, Life of, 75.

Cadder House, Dinner at, 113.
Caird, Principal, 166, 235, 245, 269, 293, 312.
Caird, Professor Edward, 220, 297.
Cairns, Rev. Dr., 228.
Cameron, Commander, 288.
Campbell, Archibald (Drimsynie), 106.
Campbell-Bannerman, Henry, M.P., 267, 269.
Campbell, Captain, of Boquhan, 339.

INDEX.

Abbotsford School, 185.
Abel, Professor, 201.
Aberdeen, Lord, 247, 287, 320.
Academy, 166.
Adam, Dr., 312.
Adam, Lord, 166, 203.
Agricultural Association, 297.
Aikman, Rev. Dr. Logan, 168.
Ailsa, Marquis of, 227, 228.
Aitken, Adam, 283.
Aitken, Robert, 308.
Albany, Duke of, 199, 208.
Albert, Prince, 42; Visit to Glasgow, 76; Death of, 123.
Albert Victor, Prince, 242.
Alexander, Edward, of Powis, 127.
Alexander, G. W., 332, 339.
Alexander, Sir J. E., 127, 128, 135, 159, 169, 171, 178, 220.
Alexander II. of Russia, Death of, 190.
Alexander's School, 246.
Allan, Alexander, 289.
Alison, Sir Archibald, 206.
Alston, J. Carfrae, 259, 287.
Alston, J. P., of Muirburn, 321.
Anderson, Dr. Andrew, 138.
Anderson, George, M.P., 220.
Anderson, Henry, 227.
Andrews, Professor, 163.
Annesley, Major General, 347.
Arabi Pasha, 198.
Arbuthnots of Ballikinrain, 162.
Argyll, Duke of, 218, 304.
Armitage, Dr., Glasgow, 249.
Arngomery, 129, 198, 205, 229, 265, 279, 321.
Arnold, Dr., Letters of, 57.
Arnott, Dr. Walker, 70, 73, 79, 80, 86, 242.
Arran, Visit to, 67, 82.
Arrol, Sir William, 288.
Arthur, James, of Barshaw, 223.
Ashe, Rev. R. P., 257.
Ashley, Lord (see Lord Shaftesbury), 84.
Athenæum, Opening, 274, 295, 298.
Atlantic telegraph, 107, 111.
Ayr, Visit to, 80.
D'Aubigné, Jean H. M., 57.

Babington, Professor, 55.
Baccarat scandal, 322.
Bailie, The, 173, 178.
Bain, Sir James, 237, 294.
Bain, Joseph, 351.
Baird, J. G. A., M.P., 245, 287, 309, 337.
Baird, James, Death of, 162.
Balfour, A. J., 328.
Balfour, Dr. Bayley, 55, 58, 67, 71, 98.
Balfour, Isaac B., Professor of Botany, 179, 184, 191, 220.
Balfour, Lord, of Burleigh, 203, 250, 260, 261, 266, 267, 269, 292, 326, 328.
Balfron, Opening of reading-room, library, 182.
Ball, Professor Sir R., 207.
Ballincleroch, 127, 129.
Ballindalloch, Barony of, 337.

Loch Katrine, 81; London (1850), 38, 84, 85; Interest in botany, geology, etc., 88; Visit to Belfast, 88, 89; Commissioner General Assembly, 93; Self-criticism, 95; Visit to Staffa and Iona, 95; Lecture on the antiquities of Dovehill, 103; Parkhall, 103; Stirling's Library, Director of, 104; His uncle William Connal's death, 105; Interest in discharged prisoners, 107; President Stirlingshire Society, 107; Director of N. S. Savings Bank, 109; Parkhall, Re-purchase of, 111; Visit to, 113; Marriage, 127; Justice of Peace, 127; Love of flowers, 128; Stirlingshire Charitable Society, President of, second time, 130; Director, Logan and Johnston Institution, 130; Endrickfield, 137; Visit to Dumfries, 140; Elected Member School Board, 147; Death of his mother, 158; Elected Chairman of School Board, 161; Endrickfield, Purchase of, 163; Interest in young people, 167; Family histories, 167; Failure of strength, 177; Thoughts about his father, 190; Purchase of Arngomery, 198, 199; Mr. Mundella's visit to Glasgow, 207, 208; Vice-president of Geographical and Ethnological Section, 213; Stirling Burgh Records to be printed, 217; Meeting about Free Education, 221; Knighthood, 223; Osborne, 225; Elected Member of Council of the Scottish Geographical Society, Edinburgh, 229; Member of High School Club, 236; Speech to boys of "Cumberland" Training Ship, 238; Old Edinburgh Exhibition, 244; Window to Leckies of Broich, 246; Opening of Seamen's Institute, 250; Read Cicero with John Millar (Lord Craighill), 281; Chairman of General Endowment Board, 283; China Famine Fund, 289-291; Agreed to become a Guild Brother and Burgess of Stirling, 322; Elected a Governor of the Stirling Educational Trust, 324; Father's tomb identified, 326; Agricultural Discussion Society, 327; Mathematics, 334; Lays foundation stone of Logan and Johnston School of Domestic Economy, 337; Great failure of strength, 339; Sale of Broom, 341; At festival of Ancient Shepherds, 342; Asked to continue Convener of Foreign Affairs Committee, Chamber of Commerce, 347; Sad about politics, 348; Free Church Memorial Exhibition, 348, 352, 353, 355; Offers to buy Broom, 351-353; Death of, 355.

Connal, Patrick, 98.

Connal, Patrick (1749), 142, 196.

Connal, Robert N. C., 288.

Connal-Rowan, George Francis, 263.

Connal-Rowan, P. F., 257, 260, 264.

Connal, William, 7, 82, 98; Death of, 104, 107.

Connal, William, & Co., 360, 361, 362.

Connal, William (Junior), 251, 264.

Connal, William, of Solsgirth, 87, 106, 136, 139, 144, 150, *passim*.

Connal, Lady, 135, 139, 143, 148, *passim*.

Connal, Mrs., of Solsgirth, Death of, 168.

Connal, Mrs. (Eliza Wright, mother of Sir Michael), 34, 101, 152; Death of, 158.

Connal, Mrs. Alexander, 354.

Connal, Mrs. John (Isle of Man), 138.

Connal, Mrs. William, 318, 319.

Connal, Eliza, 100.

Connal, Emily, 197.

Connal, Frances S., Illness and death of, 33, 34, 35.

Connal, Marion, 251.

Connal, Marion Glas, 99.

Connal window, Stirling, 257.

Connaught, Duke of, 226.

Constantine, Grand Duke, 67.

Cooper, James, 218.

Cooper, W. S., of Failford, 212.

Cooper, Mrs., of Ballindalloch, 247.

Cooper, Miss, of Ballindalloch, 160.

Copland, James (Register House), 213.

Cowan, John, 228, 268.

Craig, Archibald, 348.

Craig, Deacon Convener, 102.

Craighill, Lord (John Millar), 129, 152, 153, 165, 166, 177, 199, 206, 224, 281.

Craik, Henry, 172.

Crarae Quarry Disaster, 248.

Crimea, 101, 103.

Cross, Richard A. (Lord Cross), 164, 224, 225, 226.

Cruikshank, Matthew, 204.

Crum, Alexander, of Thornliebank, 297.

Cunningham, Allan, 16; Son of, 16.
Cunningham, Andrew, 249.
Cuthbertson, Sir J. N., 178, 180, 192, 195, 204, *passim*.
Cyprus, 170.

Dale, David, 211.
Dalglish, R., 114, 136, 188.
Dallinger, Principal, 196.
"Daphne" disaster, 205.
Darwin, Professor C. R., Biography, 270.
Deane, Sir James Parker, 226, 290.
Deas, Lord, 204, 205.
Dickson, Rev. Professor, D.D., 169, 192, 196, 258, 267, 341.
Dickson, Sheriff, Death of, 164.
Disestablishment, 161.
Disraeli, Benjamin (see under Lord Beaconsfield).
Disruption, The, 50.
Dods, Rev. Dr. Marcus, 179, 204.
Donald, C. D., 218, 289, 306, 335, 336.
Dougall, Dr., 327.
Douglas, Lord, 76.
Douglas, Principal, 238, 289, 306.
Dovehill church, 83.
Drummond, Professor Henry, 257, 260, 297.
Duff, Rev. Dr., 10, 79, 166.
Duke Street Reformatory, Riot in, 195.
Dumyat, 20.
Dunblane cathedral, 167, 275.
Duncan, J. Dalrymple, 303, 311.
Dunlop, Colin, 298.
Dunlop, James, 348.
Dunlop, Miss, 341.
Dunoon, Mr., 8.
Dyer, Professor, of Tokio, 249.
Dymock, Dr., 24; Pupils of, 119, 159.

Eadie, Rev. Dr., 79; Funeral of, 162, 210, 227.
Earl's Seat, 125.
East Park Home, 340.
Ecclesiastical Exhibition (Free Church) in Edinburgh, 348, 349, 352, 353, 355.
Edinburgh, 41; Queen's visit to (1842), 42, 71, 72.
Edinburgh, Duke of, 129; Marriage of, 150, 226.
Edmonstone, Sir Archibald, 281.
Edmonstone, Sir William, 157, 159, 267, 276.
Egerton, Lord, of Tatton, 249.
Elder, Mrs., 235.
Elgin, Lord, 274, 278, 342.
Emerson, Ralph Waldo, 70.
Endrickfield, 162, 163.
Established Church, 238.
Eugenie, Empress of French, 119.
Ewing, Alexander Crum, 324.
Ewing, Sir A. Orr, 182, 292, 308, 311, 326, 327.
Ewing, H., 298.
Ewing, H. E. Crum, 202.
Ewing, John Leckie, 350, 355.
Ewing, Peter, 56.
Ewing, R. Leckie, 309, 326.
Ewing, William, 110.
Ewing, William Leckie, 198, 199, 211, 265; Family of, 360.
Ewing, Mrs. Leckie, Funeral of, 186.
Ewing, Edith Orr, 168.
Ewing, Ella Orr, 169.
Ewing, Helen (Lady Connal), 124.
Ewing, Janet, 148.
Eye Infirmary, 86, 236.
Eyre, Archbishop, 280, 307, 335.

Fairplay, 239.
Faithfull, Rev. William, 84.
Faithfull, Emily, 119, 171.
Faithfull, Marion, 336.
Fenianism, 131.
Ferguson, J., 326.
Ferguson, Professor, 202, 351.
Field Naturalists' Club, 338.
Fielding, T. M., 128, 129, 222, 312.
Fielding, Mrs., 320.
Findlay, Charles B., Death of, 167.
Findlay, R., of Easterhill, 123.
Findlay, T. D., 313, 320.
Fine Arts Exhibition, 256.
Finnieston House, 168.
Fisher, John, 29.
Fleming, Dr., 56.
Fleming, J. S., 127.
Fletcher, Archibald, 150.

Fletcher of Dunans, 150.
Fletcher, Miles, of Parkhall, 150.
Fletcher, Rev. Dr., 119.
Fletcher, Mrs., Autobiography of, 294.
Forbes, Dr., Bishop of Brechin, 159.
Forbes, Edward (Naturalist), 333.
Forestry Exhibition, 210.
Forman, R. B., 98.
Forster, W. E., 200, 240.
Foulis, Dr., 94.
Franchise Bill, 213.
Fraser, Lord, 281, 291.
Fraser, Rev. Dr. Donald, 200.
Fraser, Sheriff, 166.
Free Church, 50, 238.
Free Education, 240, 353.
Frere, Sir Bartle, 149.

Gairdner, Charles, LL.D., 248, 320.
Gairdner, Professor W. T., 184, 207, 261.
Galbraith, Andrew, 118.
Galbraith, T. L. (Stirling), 322.
Galloway, H. H., Writer, 159.
Gardner, Ephraim, 210, 211.
Garnethill School, 171.
"Garonne," Loss of the, 135.
Garscadden, 81, 85, 104, 105, 106.
Gavazzi, Father, 86.
Gawne, Edward, 43, 99.
Gawne, Alice, 99.
Gawne, Marion, 57.
General Assembly (1841), 39.
Geological Society, 186.
Gibson, Dr. Charles (Stirling), 100.
Gibson, J. C., 223, 255, 319.
Gilbert, Graham, 158.
Gilbert, Mrs. Graham, 135.
Gillespie, Andrew, 228.
Gladstone, W. E., 118, 128, 129, 150, 184, 223, 240, 244.
Glas, Captain John, 142.
Glas, John, Provost of Stirling, 127, 145.
Glas, William, 70.
Glas, Catherine, 127.
Glas, Isabella, 145.
Glas, Jean (Mrs. Kirkpatrick), 142.
Glas, Marion, 251.
Glasgow, Lord, 211.
Glasgow Academy, 209.
Glasgow Benevolent Society, 87.
Glasgow Exhibition, 259, 277.
Glasgow Gaelic and English Schools Society, 38, 85.
Glasgow Riots, 70.
Glasgow University Club, 277.
Glenmurchie, 105.
Goldsmith, Oliver, 224.
Gopaul, Rev. P. Rajah, 80, 81.
Gorbals School, 240.
Gordon, Dr., 40.
Goschen, G. J., 350, 351.
Gourlay, Robert, 267.
Gow, Leonard, 340.
Graham, A. G. Barns, 274.
Grahame, James, C. A., 299, 303, 304.
Graham, John, of Skelmorlie, 249.
Graham, Rev. Dr. John, of Killearn, 114, 115.
Graham, T. Dunlop, 212.
Graham, Thomas, Master of the Mint, 107, 146.
Graham, W. L., 52.
Grammar School dinner, 296.
Grant, A. W., 222.
Grant, General, 168.
Grant, Mr., 308.
Grant, Professor, 119, 130, 163, 169, 244, 275.
Grant, Sir John P., 140.
Grant, Mrs., 202.
Gray, George, 258.
Gray, Mr., Aboyne, 277.
Gray, Rev. Dr., 292.
Greely, Lieutenant, Lecture by, 229.
Grierson, G. M., 348.
Griffin's Chemical Museum, 59.
Guild, J. Wyllie, 190, 197, 247.
Guthrie, David, 231.
Guthrie, Rev. Dr., 147, 154.

Haddow, Rev. John C., 279.
Haldane Academy, 179.
Hall, Admiral Sir W. King, K.C.B., 228.
Hamilton, Buchanan, of Leny, 178.
Hamilton, Lord George, 282.

Hamlin, Dr. F. S., 308, 318.
Hannington, Bishop, 257.
Hart, Robert, 144, 171, 179, 273.
Harte, Bret, 209.
Hartington, Lord, 245.
Haselrigg, Major, 168.
Hebrides, 201.
Hedley, H. A., 290.
Henderson, H. G., 246, 354.
Henderson, Mrs. Hamilton, 108.
Henderson, John, 108.
Henderson, John, of Park, 102.
Henderson, Rev. P. A. Wright, 341, 354.
Henderson, Rev. Robert, 8.
Henderson, Robert, 108.
Henderson, Mrs. Wright, 318.
Henderson Street School, 163.
Hennedy, Roger, 165, 277, 281.
Herald Centenary Dinner, 195.
Herschell, Lord, 298.
Higginbotham, Mrs., Home for Nurses, 335.
High Church, 206.
High School, 153; Prizes, 162, 167, 171, 245, 335, 340.
High School, Edinburgh, 166.
High School, Stirling, 260, 266.
Hill, J. M., 199, 306, 320.
Hill, Lawrence, 104, 343.
Hill, William Henry, LL.D., 128, 130, 212, 231, 259, 343.
Hirsch, Baron, 341.
Hogg, Mrs. (*Stirling Journal*), 269.
Holmes, Mr., 319.
Holms, William, M.P., 202.
Home Rule Scheme, 240, 348, 351.
Homer, Statue of, 170.
Honeyman, John, 192, 280, 312.
Hooker, Sir Joseph, 6, 130, 153, 169, 187, 238, 239, 242, 246.
Hooker, Sir W., 84, 104.
Horn, R., Advocate, 150, 154, 169.
Howatt, H. R., 291.
Hozier, William, of Newlands, 294.
Hunter, Dr., M.P., 291.
Hunter, Mrs., of Hunterston, 275.
Hunterian Museum, Frieze of, 141.
Hutchesons' Grammar School, 162.
Hutchison, A. F., 259.

Iddesleigh, Lord, 255.
Imperial, Prince, Death of, 182.
Industrial Day School, 192, 336, 349.
"Industry," Engines of, 268.
Innes, A. Taylor, 348, 349, 353.
Innes, Cosmo, 126, 152.

Jack, Professor, 201, 207.
Jamieson, Rev. Dr., Death of, 189.
Jocelyn, Lord, 100.
John Street School, Bridgeton, 203.
Johnson, Edmund, 249.
Johnstone, Miss, of Alva, 279, 318.
Jolly, William, 283.
Jowett, Professor B., 143.
Jebb, Professor, 290, 298.
Jews, Russian persecution of, 331.
Juridical Society, Glasgow, 282.

Katrine, Loch, 117.
Keddie, Professor, 67, 73, 75.
Kelvin, Lord (see under Sir William Thomson).
Kelvin, The, 60.
Kelvinside Academy, 181, 209.
Kennedy, Dr. Wm., 189, 196, 219, 239, 269, 305, 323, 328.
Kent Road School, 226, 241.
Ker, James, 235.
Kerr, Dr. John, 241, 278.
Kerr, J. H., 352.
Kew, 187.
Kidston, J. Burns, 251, 309.
Kidston, Wm., of Ferniegair, 71, 161, 167, 219.
King, C. M., 235, 303.
King, Sir James, 281, 312, 326, 327, 339, 347.
Kinross, Bailie, 289.
Kippen Churchyard, 348; Church, 150.
Kirkpatrick, John, 142.
Kirkpatrick, Professor John, 203, 223.
Kirkpatrick, Sir Thomas, 142.
Kirkpatrick, Marion, 143.
Kirkwood, Dr. Anderson, 213, 288, 289.
Knox, John, Parochial Board, 164.
Kossuth, Louis, 100.
Kyrle Society, 219, 304.

Laing, Dr., 200.
Landsborough, Mr., 73.
Lang, Rev. Dr. Marshall, 236, 237, 267, 289, 295.
Laurie, Sheriff, 294.
Lawson, John, 297, 328.
Leapp, Mr., 58.
Leckies of Broich, 246, 326.
Lecropt Church, 184.
Leighton, Archbishop, 167.
Lewis, 201, 275, 338.
Limited Liability Companies, 148.
Lincoln, Bishop of, 289.
Lincoln, Mayor of, 294.
Lincoln, President, Assassination of, 127.
Lind, Jenny, 73.
Lindsay, John, 127.
Lindsay, Rev. Professor, 219, 351.
Livingstone, Dr. David, 108, 146.
Loan Exhibition, 170.
Loch Katrine Water Works, Opening of, by the Queen, 117.
Loch Lomond, 80.
Lockhart, Dr. L., 154.
Logan, Dr., 243.
Logan & Johnston Bequest, 246; Institution, 287, 320.
London, Early Life in, 3, 224.
Long, H. A., 221, 307.
Lorne, Marquis of, 207, 226.
Love, Rev. Dr., 224.
Lowe, Robert, M.P., 146.
Lugard, Captain, 342.
Lumsden, Sir James, Funeral of, 178.
Lushington, Professor, 220.

M'Alpine's, Miss, Training Home, 333.
M Arthur D. 355.
M'Call, Chief Constable, 277.
M'Clure, James, 93.
M'Clure, John, 192.
M'Clure, Sir Thomas, 97, 162, 348.
M'Cosh, Dr., 104.
Macdonald, Canon, of Lincoln, 183.
M'Donald, Colonel, 282.
Macdonald, J. H. A., Lord Advocate, 274.
Macdonald, John M., 313.
M'Dougall, Duncan, 235.
M'Ewan, W., 231.
MacFarlan, General, 306, 332.
MacFarlan, Dr. Patrick, 235.
Macfarlane, Principal, 51, 108.
MacFarlan, Miss, 306.
MacFarlan, Helen, 161, 235.
Macfie, Robert, of Airds, 258.
Macgeorge, Andrew, 263.
M'Grigor, Dr. A. B., 230, 260, 319, 332.
M'Gregor, John, 221.
Macgregor, Dr. J., 247.
Macgregor, Rev. John, 260.
M'Kellar, Rev. Dr. (Moderator, 1840), 31.
M'Kendrick, Professor, 240, 259, 332, 333, 352.
M'Kinnon, Sir William, 197, 293, 307.
M'Lachlan, W. A., of Auchintroig, 198, 199.
M'Lagan, Sir Douglas, 319.
M'Laren, Dr., 257, 267, 305.
MacLehose, James, 212, 231.
M'Lellan, Mr., 163, 297.
Macleod, Rev. Dr. Donald, 257, 258, 288, 310, 311.
Macleod, Sir George, 269.
Macleod, Rev. Dr. John, 263.
Macleod, Rev. Dr. Norman, 143, 145.
M'Leod, Reginald, 276.
M'Luckie, Robert, 269.
M'Naught, Duncan, 199.
MacNee, Sir Daniel, 158, 162.
M'Onie, Provost, 255, 304.
M'Pherson, Cluny, Death of, 197.
M'Vail, Dr., 204.
Mainwaring, Hon. Massey, 207.
Manchester, Bishop of, 183.
Manning, Cardinal, 146, 331.
Markham, Captain, 165.
Marshall, Robert, 21
Marshall's Trust, 277, 319.
Marwick, Sir James, 192.
Marwick, Lady, 307.
Mason, Mr., 263.
Matheson, Hugh, 52.
Matheson, Hugh M., 169, 197.
Maughan, W. C., 251.
Maurice, Rev. F. D., 101, 145.

Mauritius disaster, 337.
Maxwell, Sir John Stirling, 260, 318.
Maxwell, Sir W. Stirling, 161.
Maynard, Captain, 110.
Maynooth College, Grant to, 56.
Mechanics' Institute, 180.
Meiklejohn, Professor, 257.
Melvill, Henry, 4.
Menteith, Lady, of Closeburn, 290.
Microscopical Society, 240.
Middleton, John, 189.
Miller, Hugh, 69, 72, 89, 94, 107.
Miller, Rev. Dr. Samuel, 191.
Milton School, 170.
Mirrlees, James B., 183.
Mitchell Library, 151, 168, 192, 327.
Mitchell, Alexander, 294.
Mitchell, Sir Arthur, 268, 279, 280, 305, 318.
Mitchell, James L., 354.
Mitchell, J. O., LL.D., 198, 239, 290, 303, 305, 306, 326.
Mitchell, John, 168.
Mitchell, Moncrieff, 294.
Mitchell, William, 221.
Moffat, Dr. Robert, 42.
Moncreiff, Lord, 239, 240, 241, 281.
Moncreiff, Sir Henry, 123, 196, 241.
Moncrieff, Forbes, 335.
Moncrieff, Robert Scott, 350.
Monteith, Robert, 143.
Montgomery, Robert, 7.
Montgomery, Sir Graham, 112.
Montrose, Duke of, 278, 294, 307, 321, 324.
Montrose, Duchess of, 294, 295, 320, 321.
Moore, Alexander, 190.
Moore, Sir John, 351.
Morison, John, 219, 221, 247, 311.
Morrison, Dr., 188, 283.
Muir, Dr. John, 20, 32, 52.
Muir, Sir John, Lord Provost, 288, 325, 340.
Muir, Sir W., 219.
Muirhead, Dr., 208.
Muirhead, Rev. T. P., 237, 246.
Mundella, A. J., 200, 207, 218.
Munro, Rev. Dr., 290, 328, 342.
Munro, James, Captain, R.N., 151.
Munros of Teaninich, 151.
Munro, Catherine, 151.
Murchison, Dr. Charles, 179.
Murray, A. Graham, 274.
Murray, Sheriff Erskine, 128, 206.
Murray, Mrs. Erskine, 219, 257.

Napier, Sir Joseph, 125, 153.
Napier, or Christie, Catherine, 116.
Napier, Margaret, 211.
Napiershall School, 279.
Natural History of Selborne, 277.
Natural History Society, 87; Vice-President, 125.
Neilson, Beaumont, 204.
Newberry, F. H., 236.
Nichol, Dr., 56, 76.
Nichol, Professor, 298.
Nicol, James, 229, 249, 337.
Nicolson, J. Badenach, 230.
Noel, E., 245, 311, 324.
North, Christopher, 313.
"Northampton," H.M.S., Launch of, 165.
Nurses' Training Home, 195.

Obia, India, 119, 220, 221, 246, 325.
O'Connell, Daniel, 15.
O'Connor, Captain, 136.
Oliver, Miss, 100.
"Orion," Loss of, 80.
Ormidale, 87, 106.
Orphan Homes, 231.
Orr, Dr. R. Scott, 243.
Osborne, 226.
Owen, Sir Philip Cunliffe, 184, 207.

Palmerston, Lord, 97, 124, 128.
Parker, Charles Stewart, 266.
Parker, Dr., 118.
Parkhall, 65, 66, 67, 103; Purchase of, 111, *passim*.
Paterson, Dr. Alex., 201.
Paterson, Joshua, M.D., 114, 238, 336.
Paterson, Walter, 157, 259.
Paton, Dr., Rector of High School, 196.
Paton, James, 348, 353.

Patrick, R. W. Cochran, of Ladyland, 259, 266, 280.
Patrick, Dr. W., 178.
Peace, Dr. A. L., 255.
Peddie, J. Dick, 202.
Peden, John, 352.
Peel, Sir Robert, 34, 42, 80.
Permissive Bill, 248.
Phelps, Mr., American Ambassador, 282, 287.
Philosophical Society, 74.
"Pin" Wright, 246, 336.
Plato, 280.
Playfair, Patrick, 117.
Pollock, Sir F., 342.
Polwarth, Lord, 228.
Ponsonby, Colonel, 225, 247.
Poor, Supper to the, 185.
Porteous, Rev. Dr., 137.
Porteous Presbytery Records, 332.
Potter, Dr., Bishop of New York, 187, 256.
Pringle, Robert, 306.
Prisoners' Aid Society, 107, 115, 157, 297, 303.
Pritchard, Mr., of South Seas, 114.

Queen, The, Proclaimed, 12; Coronation, 20; Visit to Edinburgh, 42; Visit to Glasgow, 76, 117, 225; Jubilee, 262.
Queen's Dock, Opening of the, 168.
Queen's College, 42.
Queen Margaret College, 217, 342, 352.
Queen Margaret Street School, 354.

Raeburn, Sir Henry (Works), 164.
Railways, 84.
Rainy, Dr., 33, 37, 147, 158, 162.
Ramsay, Sir Andrew Crombie, 68.
Ramsay, Professor George G., 188, 229, 243, 270, 278.
Ramsay, John, M.P., 189, 203, 267, 274.
Randolph, Charles, 173.
Rankine, Dr., 306.
Ravenstein, Mr., 312.
Regality Club, 222; President, 229, 289, 335, 351.
Reith, Rev. Dr. George, 341.
Renwick, R., 229, 242, 289, 297.
Richardson, Dr., 206.
Richardson, T., 146.
Roberton, Sir James, 203, 205, 220, 256, 294.
Robertson, Archibald, 135, 199, 218, 223, 275, 312.
Robertson, Rev. Dr. F. L., 241, 255, 269, 278, 281, 290, 294, 310, 335, 342, *passim.*
Robertson, Professor James, 306.
Robertson, Rev. James, of Newington, 180, 255.
Robertson, John, 334.
Robertson, J. P. B., Lord Advocate, 312.
Robertson, Rev. Dr., of Irvine, 218.
Robertson, Atta, 202, 203.
Robertson, Miss Minnie, 184.
Rollo, Lord, 206.
Rosebery, Lord, 153, 171, 287, 288.
Rosebery, Lady, 288.
Roslin, Visit to, 75.
Ross, Sir John, 89.
Rost, Dr. Reinhold, 188.
"Roumania," Loss of, 341.
Routledge, Hon. Arthur, 259.
Routledge, Miss, 259.
Roxburgh, John, 304.
Royal Infirmary, 120.
Ruskin Society, 283.
Russell, Rev. James (Yarrow), 146, 180, 336.
Russell, Lord John, 59.
Russell, Rev. John, 245.
Russell, Thomas, of Ascog, 295.
Russian Imperial Yacht, Launch of, 188.

Saigo, Count, 249.
St. Andrew's University, 204.
St. David's Burying-ground, 210.
St. James' Free Church, Laying Foundation Stone, 55.
St. James' Sabbath School Society, 291.
St. Mungo's College, 278, 292.
St. Nicholas' Hospital, 120, 123, 192, 222.
Salisbury, Lord, 222, 249, 255, 321.
Saltmarket, Workmen's Houses in, 265.
Sandeman, Archibald, 351.

Sandford, Sir Daniel, 4.
Sandford, Sir F., 186, 229, 230.
Sandford, Lady, 230.
School of Art and Design, 167, 235.
School Board, 147, 161, 209, 230, 335, *passim*.
Scott, Bishop, 289.
Scott, Dr., of St. George's, Edinburgh, 237.
Scott, John (London), 93.
Scott, Sir Walter, 143, 256; Journal of, 334.
Scott, Mrs. John, 93.
Scoular, Dr., 80, 124, 192.
Seamen's Institute, 250, 288.
Sellars, James (Architect), 259, 281.
Shaftesbury, Lord, 143, 144, 148, 183, 189.
Shah of Persia, 293, 294.
Shand, Lord, 203, 237.
Shaw-Stewart, M. H., 247.
Simons, Ex-Bailie, 333.
Simpson, Dr. P. A., 333.
Singing Saloons, 157.
Slimon, J. B., 256.
Smith, Archbishop, 326.
Smith, Professor George A., 341.
Smith, J. George, 205.
Smith, John Guthrie (Mugdock), 173, 218, 229, 242.
Smith, John Guthrie, Advocate, 177.
Smith, Rev. J. Mure, 297.
Smith, J. Parker, 318.
Smith, Rev. Dr. Walter, 149.
Social Science Congress, 153.
Somerville, Rev. Dr. A. N., 238, 239, 244, 261, 295.
Somerville, Joseph, 240.
Somerville, Mr., 227.
Spens, John A., 250.
Spens, Nathaniel, 197, 320.
Spens, Sheriff, 210, 222, 269.
Spofforth, Mr., 226; Mrs., 319.
Spoutmouth, 52, 72, 85, 94, 97, 116, 126, 138, 228, *passim*.
Spreull, Miss, 352.
Springbank School, 211.
Springburn Public School, 244.
Spurgeon, Rev. C. H., 183, 332.
Staffa and Iona, 95-97.
Stair, Earl of, 328.
Stalker, Rev. Dr. James, 260, 325.
Stanley, H. M., 307, 321.
Stark, Mr., 228.
Stedman, Mrs., 86.
Stedman, The Misses, Obelisk to, 182.
Steel, John, 277.
Steele, Dr. J. Charles, 342.
Stephen, A., Dean of Guild, 200.
Stephenson, George, 117.
Steven, Miss, of Bellahouston, 334.
Stevenson, Frances, 100, 358.
Stevenson, Captain Hugh, 100, 358.
Stewart, Andrew, 258, 279.
Stewart, Rev. Dr., of Lovedale, 320.
Stirling Burgh Records, 235, 256, 259, 289.
Stirling, 48, 58, 62, 76, 139, 157, 258, 340, *passim*.
Stirling, Sir Charles, of Glorat, 247.
Stirling, Charles, 195.
Stirling, Graham, of Craigbarnet, 206.
Stirling, James, of Cordale, 205.
Stirling, James, 239.
Stirling, Colonel John, of Gargunnock, 185, 195, 200, 311, 319.
Stirling, J. M. Morries, 341, 353.
Stirling's Library, 104, 124, 127, 145, 191, 192, 295, 334, 336.
Stirling, William, of Cordale, 295.
Stirton, Dr., 204.
Stockwell Free Church, 260.
Story, Professor, 151, 210, 303, 312, 348.
Stowe, Mrs. Beecher, 93.
Sutton, Charles W. (Manchester Library), 279.
Swanson, Mr., 283.
Sweeps' Friendly Society, 118.

Tannahill, 151.
Tay Bridge Disaster, 185.
Taylor, Isaac, 89.
Taylor, Rev. Dr. W. Ross, 260, 319.
Temple Church, 224.
Tennant, Sir Charles, 120, 183, 203, 226, 288.
Tennent, Hugh, 126.
Thomson, Dr. Andrew, 228.

Thompson family (London), 19.
Thompson, Harry (London), 12.
Thompson, James (London), 6.
Thomson, Professor James, 180, 336.
Thomson, Dr. James, 62, 74.
Thomson, James, 36.
Thomson, John, 65.
Thomson, Joseph (African traveller), 289.
Thomson, Neale, of Camphill, 34.
Thomson, Rev. Robert, 266.
Thomson, Walter (Bengal), 221.
Thomson, Sir W. (Lord Kelvin), 62, 165, 195, 196, 201, 218, 229, 235, 328, 331.
Thompson, William (London), 8, 11, 36, 49, 84, 98, 135, 190, 323, 336.
Thomson, Lady, 235.
Thompson, Esther, 11, 84.
Total abstinence, 164.
Tovey, Captain John, 34.
Townsend, Joseph, 322.
Trayner, Lord, 237.
Trevelyan, Sir G. O., 240.
Trevelyan, Lady, 288.
Tseng, Marquis, 243.
Turner, Angus, 163.
Turner, Miss, 191.

Udston Colliery Accident, 261.
Underwood, Francis H., 237, 240, 256, 258, 261, 265, 287, 291.
Union and City Banks, 108.
University Bazaar, 298.
Ure, Ex-Lord Provost, 260, 347.
Ure, James, of Shirgarton, 167, 190, 236.

Vambery, Professor, 321.
Vaughan, Rev. Dr., 224.
Veitch, Professor John, 179, 207, 239, 268.
Venables, G. S., 187, 281.
Victoria Infirmary, 321.

Wade, Sir Thomas, 289.
Wales, Prince of, 124, 144, 164; Collection, 185, 277.
Wales, Princess of, 277.
Wallace, Dr., 202.
Warrand, Major R., 106.
Warrand, T. A., 168.
Warrand, Thomas, of Warrandfield, 151.
Warren, Sir Charles, 250.
"Warrior," 125.
Washington Street School, 306.
Watson, J. Græme, 339.
Watson, James, 152.
Watson, Sir James, 144, 165, 178, 184, 226, 235, 243, 294.
Watson, Sir W. Renny, 342, 351.
Watson, Mrs., 206.
Watt, James, Dock, Opening of, 246.
Watts, G. F., 58.
Wellington, Duke of, 49.
Welsh, Patrick, 351, 352.
Welsh, Rev. Dr., Moderator, 40, 51.
Wemyss Bay, 125, 188, 213.
Western Bank, Failure of, 108.
White, J. Campbell, 227, 244, 298.
White, Mrs. J. C., 244.
Whitehouse, Dr. Wildman, 107.
Whitelaw, Alexander, 147-150, 157, 160, 182, 190.
Wigan Railway Accident, 148.
Wild Flower Show, 263.
William IV., King, Death of, 12.
Williams, Sir George, 326.
Williamson, A. (Kinross), 112.
Williamson, Mrs., 227, 248, 267, 313, 317.
Wilson, D., jun. (Carbeth), 308.
Wilson, David, of Carbeth, 310.
Wilson, John, of Auchineck, 325.
Wilson, John, 350.
Wilson, William, 191, 198, 223, 244, 246, 319.
Winton, Sir Francis de, 256.
Wiseman, Cardinal, 82, 127.
Wolseley, Sir Garnet, 151.
Wolseley Street School, 291.
Woodrow, Rev. R., 137.
Wordsworth, William, 278.
Wright family, 358.
Wright, Hamilton, or Henderson, 108.
Wright, J. Innes, 177, 293.

Wright, John, of Broom, 14, 52, 101, 227.
Wright, Warner, 153.
Wright, Captain William, 34.
Wright, William, of Broom (grandfather of Sir Michael), 100.
Wright, William, of Broom, 58, 86, 246, 248.
Wright, Mrs. James, 283.
Wright, Florence, 58.
Wright, Frances, 101.
Wright, Helen, 210.
Wylie, Dr., 109.
Wynn, Allan, 280.

Yellowlees, Dr., 318.
Yellowlees, Provost (Stirling), 245, 258, 260, 274, 322, 324.
Young, G. B., 352. - 357
Young, J., of Kelly, 189.
Young, John, 318, 327, 341.
Young, Lord, 165, 200, 206, 251.
Yuille, Rev. G., 292.

GLASGOW: PRINTED AT THE UNIVERSITY PRESS BY ROBERT MACLEHOSE AND CO.

Lightning Source UK Ltd.
Milton Keynes UK
UKOW06f2059200617
303778UK00012B/643/P

9 781332 817085